SEGA MEGA DRIVE SECRETS

Rusel DeMaria

Nintendo® Games Secrets

Sega Mega Drive® Secrets

Turbografx® and TurboExpress® Secrets

SEGA MEGA DRIVE SECRETS

Rusel DeMaria

Published by Kuma Computers Ltd in association with Prima Publishing & Communications

    Kuma Computers Ltd
    12 Horseshoe Park
    Pangbourne
    Berkshire. RG8 7JW
    Tel 0734 844335. Fax 0734 844339

Copyright © 1990 Rusel DeMaria

Printed in Great Britain

ISBN 0-7457-0037 3

This book is supplied in the belief that its contents are correct, but the author and publishers shall not liable in any circumstances whatsoever for any direct or indirect loss or damage to property incurred or suffered by the customer or any other person as a result of any fault or defect in the information contained herein.

ALL RIGHTS RESERVED

No part of this publication may be reproduced, stored in a retrieval system or transmitted in any form or by any means, electronic, mechanical, photocopying, recording or otherwise, without the prior written permission of the authors and the publisher except for the inclusion of quotations in a review.

Secrets of the Games Series Editor: Rusel DeMaria
Layouts by Doug Pointer, Rusel DeMaria and J. Douglas Arnold
Editing and Proofing: Zach Meston, Marsha Ehrman, Rusel DeMaria and Tom Anderson
Interior Design by Renee Deprey, Bookman Publications
Cover Illustration by Matthew Holmes
Cover Design by Dunlavey Studio
Special Processing, Maps and Original Drawings by Ocean Quigley
Controller Images by John Odams Design
Film Prints by MacConcepts

ACKNOWLEDGEMENTS

Thanks to Tobin Koch of Data Translations for providing a Quick Capture board to capture screen images. Thanks also to Adobe Systems for PhotoShop, Microsoft for MS Word, Quark for Quark Xpress, Aldus for Freehand, and CE Software for their indispensable utilities like Quickeys and Disktop.

I also want to acknowledge the help I received from MacConcepts, Connecting Point, and Scott Waters.

Special thanks to Al Nilsson, Bill Lewkowitz, and Jamie Wojik for all the help they offered. Also thanks to Joanna Elm at TV Guide for sharing her contacts.

Then there is Ocean whose gut wrenching puns made me stop and shed the pressures every once in a while.

On a personal note, thanks go to my publisher, Ben, for his support and faith; my agent, Bill, for keeping me together in so many ways; Diane Winter for powerful support behind the scenes, and my family—Marsha, Shan, and Max.

Finally, there were many game players who helped put this project together. Chief among them was Donn Nauert. Donn is one of those exceptional players who can master just about any game. He currently works as an assistant editor for Video Games and Computer Entertainment Magazine, but he took some time off to help me with this project. He also helped develop the chapter called DeMaria's Guide to Games. Donn is in the Guinness Book of World Records for some of his video game accomplishments, he's a former editor with Electronic Gaming Monthly, and he's a former national video game champion. And, believe it or not, he was only the third person ever inducted into the Video Game Hall of Fame. I can't thank Donn enough for coming and helping out.

Another of my player/writers is John Sauer. John is the former editor of The Sega Gamers' Magazine, and has been at the forefront of the video game industry for many years. He is still a consultant for several companies in the industry.

Other players also did a wonderful job. Chief among them was Shan Cutts, who was my main helper. In addition, I had substantial contributions from Adrian Finland, Aaron Nakahara, George Fontaine, Max Ehrman, and Zach Meston.

Finally, Zach Meston was my chief assistant writer and copy editor. His contributions can't be overstated.

CONTENTS

First Words
1   DeMaria's Guide to Games   1

The Complete Story on...
2   Air Diver   9
3   Altered Beast   17
4   Budokan   28
5   Forgotten Worlds   38
6   Ghouls'n Ghosts   53
7   Golden Axe   67
8   Insector X   86
9   Michael Jackson Moonwalker   102
10   Mystic Defender   125
11   Phantasy Star II   136
12   Populous   153
13   Rambo III   164
14   Revenge of Shinobi   178
15   Space Harrier II   196
16   Target Earth   206
17   Truxton   220
18   Whip Rush   231
19   Zany Golf   242

A Final Note...
20   More Tips   252
21   A Parents' Guide to Video Games   253

INTRODUCTION

The Sega Mega Drive is a killer machine. Its graphics are some of the best you'll see. If you already have a Mega Drive, you already know that. You already enjoy a new generation of games.

This book, Sega Mega Drive Secrets, is meant to get you farther than you've ever gotten in the games you love to play. By combining detailed descriptions with lots of graphics, this book not only tells you what to do, but often shows you, too. Like all books in the Secrets of the Games series, Sega Mega Drive Secrets goes an extra step for you. In fact, you can read this book in three ways:

1. Use this book as a guide to games you don't yet own. What kind of game is it? Does it sound like fun? Learn about the games before you buy them.

2. Use this book as a strategy guide. How can you play this game successfully? Check the General Strategies section of each chapter for the most successful techniques and ideas. Then check the level-by-level, step-by-step strategy session in which you'll learn exactly how to go from the start to the finish of each game.

3. Find the ultimate secrets for each game. Did you know you can have lots of extra lives? Or maybe you just can't figure out how to beat one of the really hard bosses. Is that puzzle just a little too mind-bending? Look in The Secrets section of each game. Whenever we can, we reveal the deepest, darkest secret tips, strategies for succeeding against all odds. We put this information in The Secrets section because we want you to have the opportunity to try it on your own. Go to The Secrets after you've really enjoyed your games and want to know more, or when you get really stuck.

Sometimes you have to press a sequence of buttons to perform a secret move. When we give you these sequences, we abbreviate throughout the book. Here's how to understand the abbreviations: U = Up, D = Down, L = Left, R = Right, A = the A Button, and B = the B Button. So U D L R A B would stand for Up, Down, Left, Right, A Button, and B Button pressed in sequence.

At the beginning of the book is a special chapter devoted to people who want to be the best game players around. Called

DeMaria's Guide to Games, this chapter looks at strategies that apply to all games. You'll learn the strategies and techniques developed over years of playing. Many of these strategies came from other expert players over the years—game counselors and game designers. In particular, I had lots of help from Donn Nauert, one-time national champion video gamer. Donn helped me put together the section on action and arcade games.

For parents, we've provided a short chapter to help them understand why we all love video games so much, and how they can enjoy, or at least live comfortably with, our mysterious obsession with these games. Any parents who are concerned about video games in their homes should read A Parents' Guide to Video Games at the end of the book.

I'd like to end with a personal statement. Video games are often violent in content. That's OK. They're games. Enjoy the games, but please remember what's important:

Respect the Earth.
Respect all Life.
—*RDM*

CHAPTER 1

DeMaria's Guide to Games

by Rusel DeMaria and Donn Nauert

Playing games is hard work. That's right. It might be lots of fun, but it's also hard work. You can spend hours, days... even weeks on some games. You'll get completely caught up in mastering the story, or in developing a character in a role playing game (RPG). Or you may want to test your reflexes in a fast-paced arcade game. Whatever kind of game you're into, you'll play best if you play smart. In this chapter, I offer some guidelines for playing smart.

A GAME BY ANY OTHER NAME

Not all games are alike. Some require the reflexes of a lightning bolt. Raw speed and joystick agility are primary skills you need in those games. You also have to recognize patterns and be able to make fast adjustments. These games are called arcade games.

Other games require a patient approach to puzzle solving. Such games are made up of a series of situations with one or more solutions. These games are called adventure games.

Another type of game features puzzle solving and character building. In them, part of the fun of the game is to watch your characters grow in strength and ability. These are role playing games or RPGs.

Still other games combine puzzle solving with fast action. Usually the action isn't quite as intense as in a pure arcade game, nor are the puzzles so perplexing. There's just enough of both to allow the joystick jockeys to have fun while the deep thinkers get to exercise their gray matter, too. Such games are called action adventure or action role-playing games.

There are some basic (and obvious) differences between arcade games and adventure or RPGs. Therefore, I've divided my game guidelines into two sections.

RPGS AND ADVENTURE GAMES.

First, you need to know the difference between an RPG and an adventure game. Adventure games are games of exploration, where you have to solve puzzles along the way. Your character, however, doesn't change much (if at all) during the game. He is more or less the same at the end as he was at the beginning. If he does change, it is as the direct result of the plot of the game. In other words, if your character changes from a mild-mannered librarian to Super Danger-Man, he did so because you solved a puzzle or a series of puzzles to get him to that point in the story. Adventure games tend to have more difficult puzzles to solve than RPGs, often involving some real twisty logic.

In contrast, role-playing games are games of exploration, puzzle solving, AND character building. It is the change in your character(s) that makes the difference. That's why they're called role-playing games. You actually become the characters you control. They always start out weak and defenseless. In time, as they gain experience and money, they become stronger and better equipped. Part of the fun of an RPG is to watch your characters grow in strength and ability until they are the mighty warriors that you always hoped they'd be. On the other hand, in most RPGs, by the time they reach that stage, their enemies are colossal beings of supernatural power—nearly indestructible. One way or the other, things keep even in RPGs. If you're good, you keep a step or two ahead of the game, that's all.

Just as the plot determines how a character changes (if at all) in an adventure game, characters

Game Guide

in RPGs develop as a direct result of their encounters with various enemies. In RPGs, characters gain experience, just like real people, and as they gain that experience they become better at what they do.

In most adventure games and RPGs, quick reflexes are secondary to planning and deep thinking. Most RPGs and adventure games take a long time to complete. So you'll want to keep notes on the clues you obtain. Also, in many such games, you'll want to create maps.

In role playing games, the keys to remember are patience and caution. Don't take chances without being able to recover from disaster.

Rule # 1: Save Often—I can't state this rule emphatically enough. Save your game—if you can, that is. Some games can't be saved. But many can, whether on a battery backup or by writing down a password. If you have such a game, always save or get a password at each new milestone. Got a new super-duper laser beam whirling sword? Or maybe your character just learned the Squish 'em spell. Don't take a chance and lose it. Save your game or your password often.

Rule #2: Be Prepared—Yes, a good role-player is like a good Boy Scout. Be sure you have what you need. Don't just barge into the next dungeon without a torch (or other light source). Don't head into a nest of dragons without some powerful weapons.

In RPGs, you'll find that an ounce of preparation is worth a pounding headache... no, it avoids a pounding. That's right. If you spend some time building and equipping your characters at the start, you'll be rewarded later. It's tedious, yes. It's time consuming, definitely. But it's worth it. Spend time in the wimpy dungeons and the easy areas, never straying far from home base. Build up experience points and head for safety whenever you get a little low. Follow Rule # 1 very attentively, or you could lose several hours work in one mighty blow from the Giant Dog Spirit you never saw before or the Orc Magi that suddenly appeared out of nowhere.

Rule # 3: Make Maps and Take Notes—You're probably really smart, so you don't really need to do this. But humor me. You'll find that something said way back at the beginning of the game suddenly makes sense a week later. But who said it? What exactly was that clue?

And don't tell me you can find your way through an eight-level maze with twists and turns and invisible doors everywhere you look. OK. So you can. Can you also remember where those poison traps and invisible pits are lurking? After you've almost made it a few times, but died just short of the entrance, you'll probably conclude that making maps is worth the effort. So get some graph paper (about a 1/4 inch grid or so) and fill in the walls, doors, traps, clues, and other points of interest.

When making maps, move slowly and cautiously. Mark each step and turn as you go. That way, even if some Evil Pegasus drops an anvil on your head, you'll be able to come back to the same spot quickly the next time. Be careful. Count your steps and be sure to keep the map oriented properly so you don't go drawing a hallway out into space.

Watch out for hidden doors, one-way doors, wrap-around mazes (which start on one side and continue on the other side of the maze), teleportation traps (which send you to another place without warning), and any other landmarks. Use spells or items that can show you where you are. Label all stairs or ladders and other special places. Write down any clues you obtain.

Finally, save your maps! You never know when you might want to relive some of the excitement, or come back to a game after several weeks, months, or even years. I save all my maps.

Rule #4: Read the Manual—OK. This one should have been earlier, but no one really wants to read the manual. You should, though. Especially in RPGs and adventure games, you'll find lots of important clues and instructions, not to mention a list of magic spells and other indispensable tidbits of essential information.

4

In addition to my basic rules for playing adventure and role playing games, here's another tip that might help:

Use It Where You Find It (but save first). When you find a new item in a game, it's often there for a reason. Try using it. If you find a magic lamp, try rubbing it. If you find a glittering golden harp, maybe it wants its strings stroked. However, the corollary to this suggestion is to save the game first. That way if the genie in the lamp is in a bad mood and decides to turn you into a two-headed chicken, you'll be able to recover. Remember, programmers and game designers love bizarre twists. Don't try anything new unless you save first. If you can't save, don't do it (or hold your breath and hope for the best).

ARCADE AND ACTION GAMES

Arcade action games usually feature a fast pace and a whole lot of shooting, punching, kicking, and/or jumping. Here are some guidelines to more successful arcade gaming.

Watch patterns. In most games, each level or screen behaves exactly the same way each time you come to it. At first it might seem completely overwhelming, but if you observe how things move, you can often find a simple way to succeed. For really difficult places in a game, have a friend watch you play. He or she might see something you didn't. Or tape record your game. Sometimes you'll miss something in the heat of battle that you'll see with a cooler eye.

Practice each level until you know everything it does. In most games, you'll have to master the early levels to get to the later ones. Just keep practicing and eventually the early part of the game, which used to be hard, will be a breeze.

Good players practice a game again and again. In time you become familiar with the patterns that occur. You'll recognize patterns quicker and react more quickly to attacks.

Don't take unnecessary chances if you're playing to win. There are those games, especially the "shooters," where you might see a chance to get a special bonus item or extra man or something, but the way to it is dangerous. Your split-second decision will often be to go for it, even though you know it is foolhardy. That's a good way to lose one of your men (ships, lives, or whatever). Use some caution when it comes to such situations and let a few of the hard-to-get items pass on by. There will be other opportunities and you'll survive to see the end of the game if you are a little careful.

Watch the whole screen. Be aware of what is happening on other parts of the screen. Most action games are busy and fast. Lots of stuff is going on all over the screen. If you get tunnel vision and concentrate only on the guy you're about to destroy, you may get caught by a bullet (fist, rocket, boulder, laser beam) in the back (side, top, or bottom). The whole screen is usually full of danger. Don't lose sight of it.

If you're playing for high scores, look for places you can get lots of easy points. Sometimes this becomes academic. If you find a place where you can tape the fire button down on Turbo and go to sleep, it's not really playing, though it may impress your friends. On the other hand, there are legitimate opportunities to gain lots of points if you figure out a clever strategy. You can build up points, but, more importantly, you can often build up extra lives if you find such places. Watch the patterns to see if you can stay in a relatively safe place and continue to destroy an endless stream of enemies.

Try different methods to defeat the hard enemies. If you come across a creature that seems to be too difficult, try getting as close as possible to him and striking. If that doesn't work, look for patterns. Shoot in various parts of him, or look for a place where he's vulnerable. Also try different weapons, because some may be more effective than others.

Some enemies can't be damaged until they open their eye, mouth, arms, or other body part. Or they may lower their shields when they strike. Watch for that moment of vulnerability and strike quickly. Usually you'll find a pattern of movement that puts you in the right position to strike quickly without being hit. You'll know you hit the enemy because he'll either die or at least he'll flash to indicate that he's been hit. Also, some sound effects in the game can tip you off. A pinging sound often means you haven't done any damage. The sounds of success vary a lot, though. You'll figure it out.

Test your character's limits. Find out how far and how high your character can jump. Walk to the edge of platforms. Does your character fall off as soon as he reaches the edge, or can he walk almost all the way off a ledge and just stand there holding on with his toes? Each game is different. Learn how this one works.

Pull backwards to stop sliding. Many characters in action adventure type games slide when you stop them. For instance, when they're running forward and you want them to stop, they keep going a little. This is especially frustrating when you're trying to jump onto a narrow platform. The character will slide right off if you can't stop him in time. The trick is to reverse direction while the character is still in the air. That way, you can control the sliding when he lands.

Face the opposite direction for tricky jumps. Some jumps are hard to make because your character tends to overshoot the mark. Sometimes, if you start out by facing in the opposite direction, then turn and jump, you'll be able to hit the jump exactly. Try it if you are going too far in a jumping situation.

Use the manual. For action games, you can often play without ever cracking open the manual, but if something doesn't make sense, check out the documentation. Often you'll have missed some super move or other detail if you don't read about it in the manual. Take a moment between battles to check it out.

Take breaks when you're tired. Sometimes your reflexes slow down. If you find yourself making a lot of dopey mistakes, and you know you're better than that, take a deep breath and go out and shoot some hoops or rest, or run a couple of miles. Anything to change your focus. Some exercise doesn't hurt. Video games only exercise your eyes and your fingers. The rest of you is important, and you'll play better if you're in shape.

Choose the controller that works best for you. If you're playing a 'shooter' you may prefer a joystick type controller. The best players prefer pads for some games and joysticks for others. Experiment if you can.

Get used to the skills needed in the game. To master many games, you'll have to have very fine control over your character. Get used to using your pad or joystick as a fine instrument. Try to learn to move your character in very small amounts. Also practice the longest and shortest jumps. If you can control your character in the air, after he jumps, practice that, too.

Practice any other moves—attacks and defense—that your character can use. Get to know how the controller works and how the character responds. If you practice your moves early, you'll find it easier later on.

Even if you get killed, don't give up. You never know. Keep on going. This may be the time you'll succeed. At least the additional practice will help you later. To master a difficult game, you'll need to know each level as well as possible.

Make a safe zone. In scrolling games, lay down a fire pattern that opens a lane of safety.

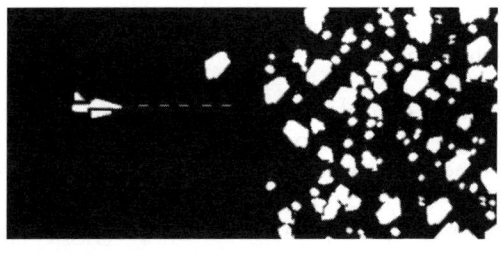

In some games, you don't have to destroy every enemy. If you can safely pass a difficult level by concentrating on one side or another, that may be the best policy.

Figure out who's important. In some games, you'll need to take care of specific enemies to help you get through. That means, identify the first priority enemies and take them out. Then you can concentrate on any stragglers. Sometimes you need to get to the most dangerous enemy first. Other times, you want to clear the screen of all nuisance enemies to make it easier to beat the more dangerous ones. Try different strategies to find out.

Save or get passwords whenever possible. Some games let you save or get a password for a level. Write down passwords or save the game as frequently as you can. You'll make it to the end much quicker that way, and with less frustration.

CHAPTER 2

Air Diver

Distributor: Seismic
Game Type: Arcade Action

WHAT'S GOING ON?

Terrorists have taken over the world! Their name is not known, but their strength is—they've crushed anyone trying to defeat them in battle. They even have the help of powerful aliens! Their pilots are murderous, evasive, and almost unstoppable. Their alien protection is... well, it's out of this world! Who can possibly hope to stop them?

WHO ARE YOU?

Maverick. Ace. Choose any good pilot name. You're the ace pilot of the F-119 Stealth Fighter. With the remaining support of the Earth's defenses, you've got to destroy the aerial forces of the terrorists! Use every trick in the book—and come up with a few new ones! You'll be flying the F-119 on the most important mission of your career!

PLAYERS

Air Diver is for one player only.

SCORING

Score points by shooting down the terrorist aircraft. Score bonus points for finishing a level; there are four bonus categories.

Time Bonus for finishing a level quickly.
Missile Bonus for having missiles left.
Fuel Bonus for having fuel left. Of course, you'll have at least some fuel left if you finish a level.
Rate of Hit Bonus for high levels of accuracy. Your accuracy is rated from 1% to 100%.

LIVES AND HOW TO LOSE THEM

Use the Option Screen to start with anywhere from three to five planes.

Your F-119 will gradually be damaged by enemy cannonfire. Each time you're hit, you may lose one of three sections of the plane. If a Cannon is disabled, you won't be able to fire it. If the Engine is disabled, you won't be able to do Vertical Loops. If the Wing is disabled, you'll burn fuel at a faster rate than normal. Run out of fuel and your plane is history.

You'll be destroyed instantly if you're hit by a missile.

Fortunately, you can't die by hitting the ground!

CONTINUES

There are eight areas of the world to clear of terrorists. If you continue the game after losing all your planes, any areas you cleared will stay cleared. You can continue endlessly.

CONTROLS

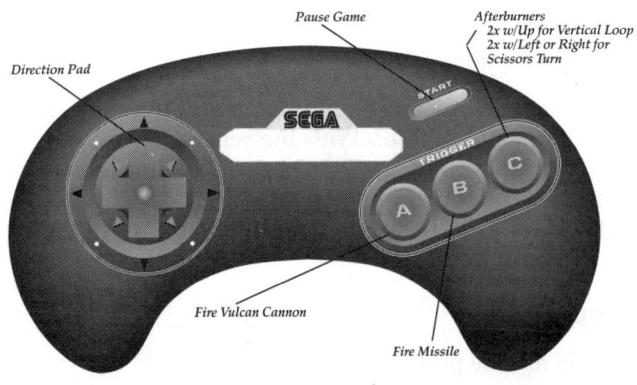

WEAPONS

The F-119 is armed with two Weapons: Sidewinder missiles and the Vulcan Cannon.

Sidewinders are heat-seeking missiles that will instantly destroy any plane unlucky enough to be hit by one. Your F-119 can hold up to 78 Sidewinders. You receive 48 Sidewinders after completing an area, so conserving them is important.
The **Vulcan Cannon** is a twin machine gun with unlimited ammunition. You can not only shoot down enemy planes, but incoming missiles as well!

SPECIAL ITEMS

After clearing out an area, you'll receive a Spare Item. There are three types of these.

The **Fuel Item** will refuel your plane if you run out of fuel during a mission.
The **Missile Item** will fully restock your Sidewinder supply to 78 Sidewinders if you run out of missiles during a mission.
The **Auto Repair Item** will repair your F-119 if you suffer three hits (which is normally fatal).

You can't hold more than two of each Spare Item.

FRIENDS

The whole world is behind you, but nobody can help!

ENEMIES

There are three waves of attackers in each area.

Fighter Planes attack in waves, firing Sidewinders and guns as they fly past. Some of them will turn after they pass you and try to get a lock on you from behind. Defeat enough Fighters and you'll be attacked by the Fighter Ace.
The **Fighter Ace** is an exceptional pilot, and his plane can take a lot of damage. He'll try to get behind you a lot. Pump enough lead into him and he'll crash, leaving you to face the Super Carrier!
The **Super Carrier** is a huge aircraft with several different points that you must attack. Your Sidewinders won't lock

on to the Carrier, so you'll have to aim very carefully! Defeat the Super Carrier and you've freed the area. Then it's time to move on to the next area...

There are four types of Super Carrier; each one has its own weak points.

Doomsday fires bullets from its middle.
Metallica is literally "heavy metal"!
Black Widow is a long ship heavily armed with cannons.
The **Fortress** is the biggest Super Carrier of all.

STRATEGY SESSION
General Strategies
The order in which you attack the areas is very important. You must conserve the fuel of your Super Transport, which takes you to each area. An excellent strategy is to attack one or two weak areas to get some Spare Items, and then attack a tough area.

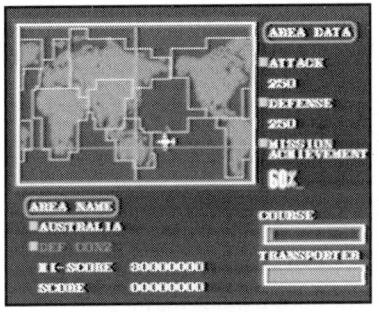
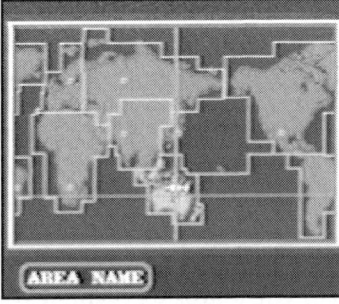

The Mission Map.   *One Area Cleared.*

The tougher an area, the more planes will attack and the more Sidewinders they'll shoot at you. However, the tactics of the planes in each area are quite similar.

Don't be afraid to use the continue feature. In fact, this game is tough enough so that you'll certainly need to use it!

Fighter Planes
The Fighters usually attack in waves from the front. They'll attack from several different altitudes; keep raising the nose slightly so that you can see them if they attack from a high altitude.

A few of the Planes will turn around when they fly past you, and then get on your tail. Sometimes, you can steer hard in

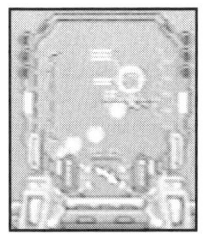

If you lock on your Sidewinders as they just appear on the horizon, you'll blow them away before they have a chance to dodge the missile or shoot at you. As they get closer, however, they'll be able to return fire of their own and do Scissors Turns to dodge your missiles. If they're within the circle on the radar, and headed in your direction, use the cannon.

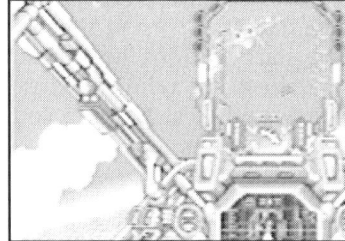
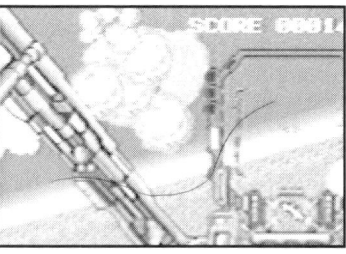

one direction to evade them, but most of the time you'll have to do a Vertical Loop, which burns precious fuel. Conclusion: shoot as many attacking planes as you can! You'll need to bag a lot of them before the Fighter Ace shows up.

Fighter Ace

Don't be tempted to waste many Sidewinders on the Ace. He's very good at dodging them, and if you only use missiles you'll need a dozen or two to shoot him down. The Vulcan Cannon should be the weapon of choice here.

Don't use your Afterburner trying to catch him, either. The Ace's plane is faster, so if he zooms off ahead of you, you'd be

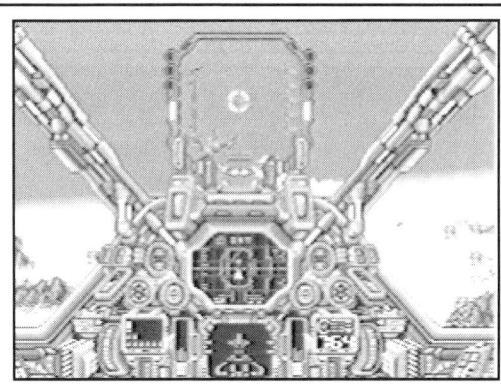
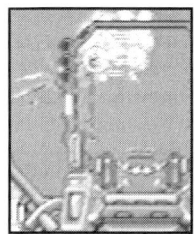

Get behind the Fighter Ace and take your best shots at him.

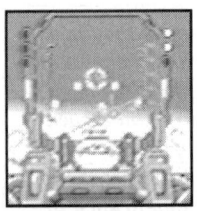

Cannon fire.

smart to wait until he comes back. There are occasions where you can use spurts of Afterburner to keep the Ace in sight, but he'll usually spin away and get behind you.

The Vertical Loop becomes even more important with Ace; attacking while in a Loop is a skill you'll have to learn. Don't use missiles; fire the Cannon in a slow rhythm as you Loop above the Ace and you'll usually get him with some flak.

When the Ace starts to burn, he's close to the end. This is the time when accurate cannonfire really pays off. Beat Ace and you'll zoom up to the Super Carrier.

Super Carrier

There are four types of Super Carrier, each with its own weak points. You'll have to blow up every one of these weak points before the Carrier goes down. The tricky part is that your Sidewinders don't lock on; you'll have to free-fire. Don't launch a flurry and hope that one will hit; launch them individually and carefully.

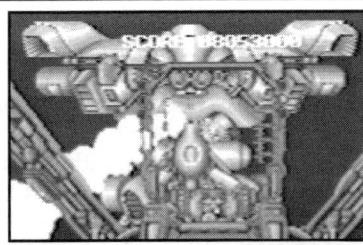
Shoot Doomsday in the center first; this will disable a powerful cannon. Then aim for the sides of the center, at the "hips" that move in and out of the Carrier. Finally, destroy the upper portion of the Carrier.

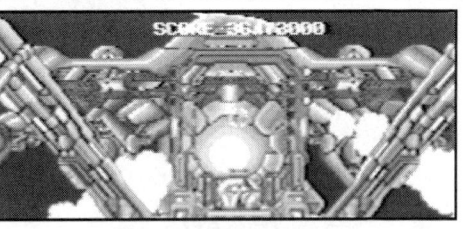
Metallica has four large claws that will shoot at you; take them out in any order, but be ready to dodge their fire. Take out the middle last.

Use the Cannon to find the weak points of each Carrier; it will flash when your Vulcan starts doing damage. Then line up with the missiles.

Air Diver

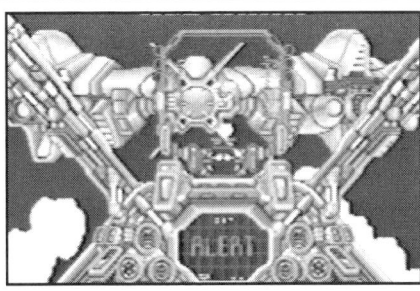

Start shooting at one end of Black Widow, and work your way down to the other end, blowing up the weak spots along the way. This way, you'll only have to dodge fire from one side of the Carrier at a time.

The Fortress is quite large, and shoots large bullets at you too! Take out one end of the Carrier at a time, and work your way down. Each pillar is a weak point.

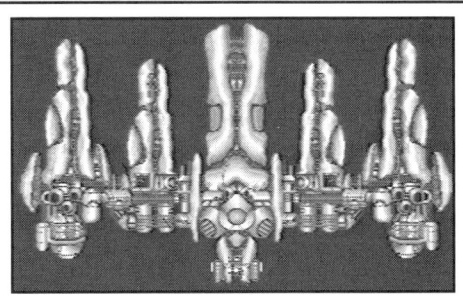

The Last Fighter

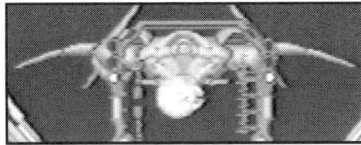

Are you ready for this guy?

If you manage to liberate all the areas, your Super Transport will be shot down by a mystery plane! You'll have to beat this plane to truly succeed in your mission.

This final opponent is really a very powerful Fighter Ace. It's also got stealth equipment, so it will blink in and out on your radar. If it gets out of your sight, it's a good bet that it's coming up behind you!

Sidewinders are basically useless against this plane. The Cannon is what you should use to attack. If the plane leaves your visual range, fly steady and be ready to do a split-second Vertical Loop, because he'll come up behind you and fire a missile incredibly quickly.

The main problem with beating the Last Fighter is Fuel.

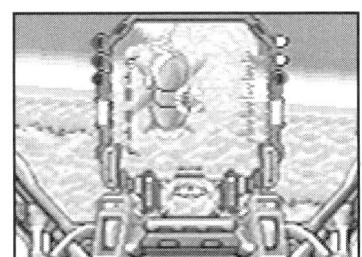

Be fast. Or else...

You'll need lots of it, because this plane will take an extraordinary amount of punishment. Try to have Fuel Spare Items when you complete the eighth area. Outgun the Last Fighter, and you've freed the world!

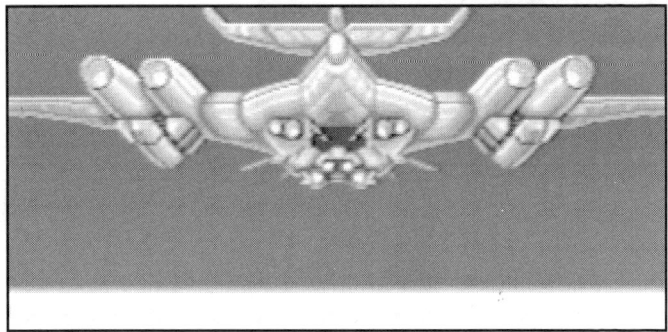

Happy landings!

SHH... THE SECRETS

Is there an invincibility mode? On the Mission Selection Screen, move the crosshair to a place on the map that's not an area. Hold down the Start button and press the buttons in this order: A, B, C, B, A, A, B, C, B, A, B. Release the Start button and you'll hear a soft ping.

Now move the crosshair to an area you wish to attack and hold down Start to be invincible, A to square off against the Fighter Ace, B to fight the Super Carrier, and C to go right to the Last Fighter! You have to hold down the button until the area begins. Note that you can hold down Start with any of the other buttons; for example, hold down Start and C to take on the Last Fighter and be indestructible!

CHAPTER 3

Altered Beast

Distributor: Sega of America
Game Type: Arcade Action

WHAT'S GOING ON?

"Rise from your grave!" These are the words spoken to you by Zeus, the God of Thunder. He has resurrected you to undertake a mission for him; a mission that means more to him than to you! His daughter Athena has been kidnaped by Neff, the evil God of the Underworld. No ordinary man could take on such a creature; but you have the power of the Altered Beast!

WHO ARE YOU?

You were once a Roman Centurion; brave, strong and alive! But with your second chance at life, Zeus has given you the ability to transform into various Werebeasts, and you'll need their powers to defeat Neff and his cohorts.

PLAYERS

One or two Altered Beasts can take part; with two players, both get to play at once.

SCORING

Collect points by wiping out Neff's brigade of bad guys. Generally, the more dangerous the bad guy the more points he's worth. The major points are to be had by beating a Boss. Neff will appear three times in a round; if you are the Altered Beast, he will change into the Boss. Beat him the first time he appears and you get 100,000 points; the second time he appears, 50,000 points; and the third, 20,000.

LIVES AND HOW TO LOSE THEM

You start the game with anywhere from one to five lives, depending on what you select on the Option Screen. Option Screen? Yes, press B and Start at the title screen for a menu of options. A power bar measures your vitality in the game. Set the length of the bar from one to five bars. The default settings are three lives and three bars on the Gauge.

As you're hit by enemies, the bars will change color and then disappear altogether. Run out of bars and you lose a life. Run out of lives and you're dead—again! There's no way to regain lost lives or bars, so you must fight skillfully.

CONTINUES

You can continue a game at the beginning of the last round you reached by holding down Button A when you press Start. If you want more tricks, see The Secrets at the end of the chapter.

Teamwork in the two-player mode.

Altered Beast

CONTROLS

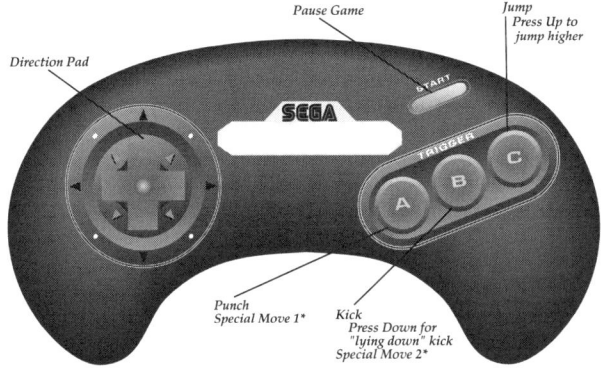

* as Altered Beast

WEAPONS

In his normal form, the Centurion's only weapons are his feet and fists. As he collects Spirit Balls, he'll grow stronger. When he's collected three Balls and mutates into Werebeast form, he gains different powers. Here's what you can do in each form.

> **Werewolf** (Round One): Button A shoots a **Fireball**. Button B causes the Wolf to jump into a **Flame Streak** that shoots across the screen, destroying anything in its path.
> **Weredragon** (Round Two): Button A shoots a **Lightning Bolt**. Button B electrifies the Dragon in a **Laser Barrier**, zapping anything close to it.
> **Werebear** (Round Three): Button A shoots the **Bear Breath**, which turns anything it touches to stone. Button B executes the **Body Spin**, which turns the bear into a spinning ball of destruction.
> **Weretiger** (Round Four): Button A shoots the **Bouncing Flame**, a wobbly fireball. Button B makes the Tiger jump into a **Pillar of Fire**, killing anything above or below him.
> **Golden Werewolf** (Round Five): Button A fires **Golden Fire** (which is similar to the Fireball). Button B activates the **Golden Arrow**. It's similar to the Flame Streak.

SPECIAL ITEMS

In order to become the Altered Beast, you must gather Spirit Balls. These are contained within the blue Three-Headed

Wolves. If you destroy a Wolf, the Ball will start to float slowly towards the top of the screen. Collect it and you will power up. The order of the power-ups is:
- **One Ball**: Giant Man.
- **Two Balls**: Super Man.
- **Three Balls**: Altered Beast.

FRIENDS

Two beasts in action.

Zeus was nice enough to bring you back to life, but that was more convenience than anything else. And Athena probably wouldn't be interested in a mere mortal— OR an Altered Beast. What's a Centurion to do?

ENEMIES

Each Round has its own enemies. Fortunately, they are few enough so that we can detail them here for you.

Round One:

Slow Feet are shuffling zombies that lose their heads when you first hit them. Hit 'em again to get rid of them.
Headless Horrors carry their heads around in their hands! Kneel and punch these guys.
Skinny Orcuses are winged creatures that love to swoop down onto you! Use the laying-down kick.
Grave Zombies have a long reach and a short temper. Kneel and punch them.
Three-Headed Wolves come in two disgusting varieties. The brown ones just try to bite you. The blue ones contain Spirit Balls.
Aggar is the Boss. He's a disgusting blob that likes to pluck off his head and throw it at you—again and again!

Round Two:

Round Leeches will try to latch onto your head and suck your life away! Kick them away. If they get on you, move left and right quickly to shake them off.
Chicken Stingers have very pointy tails. If you're powered up, kick them; if you're not, kick them anyway.
Rattle Tails make their arrival known by sticking their tails out of the walls of the cave for a few moments; then they fly from the roof to the floor or vice versa. Kick their tails

Altered Beast

before they get a chance to emerge, or punch their heads when they make the jump.
Octeyes is the Boss. He'll shoot an insane number of eyeballs at you.

Round Three:

Cave Needles look like ants, but they're a lot sharper! A punch or kick will do the trick.
Fossils are stone monsters that are created when you breathe on an enemy!
Rock Turtles move slowly, but can do a lot of damage. Kick 'em hard!
Moldy Snail is a Boss hybrid of a snail and a salamander, and loves to spit projectiles at you!

Round Four:

Hammer Demons are like Orcuses, but they've got weapons! Jump and punch them.
The **Crocodile Worm** is a floating creature Boss that shoots huge fireballs—and small Dragons—at you.

Round Five:

Saw Fishes have saws for fins! Punch or kick.
Gory Goats bounce around, looking to sneak a punch in. Kick them.
Rad Boars are armed with clubs!
The **Dark Unicorn** kicks with deadly precision. Use your kneeling punch.
Neff is the man behind all the madness!

STRATEGY SESSION
General Strategies

Altered Beast is a very easy game. In fact, here's a tip that you might find strange—turn up the difficulty on the Option Screen! Playing through the game in Normal Mode probably won't satisfy even an average game player.

Each Boss has a weakness. By trying several techniques, you'll usually find the solution quickly.

Round One—The Acropolis

Move to the right, kicking the Slow Feet. You'll be surprised when some gravestones shoot out of the ground! Destroy the

Kick the Blue Wolf, get the Spirit Ball, and watch your power grow.

first one. You'll see the blue Wolf above you; jump and punch it to get the Spirit Ball. Finish off the stones and the Feet.

Now the Headless Horrors will appear; kneel and punch or they'll catch you with their punches. Another Blue Wolf will appear; you'll be a Super-Man unless you somehow missed the first Ball.

A few Feet and Horrors will appear, and then a Skinny Orcus will fly onto the screen. Lie down and kick up to get him. If you can get the third Blue Wolf, which appears just as Neff does, you'll be able to face him now (with a potential for 100,000 bonus points). Otherwise, keep fighting until you get a third Ball.

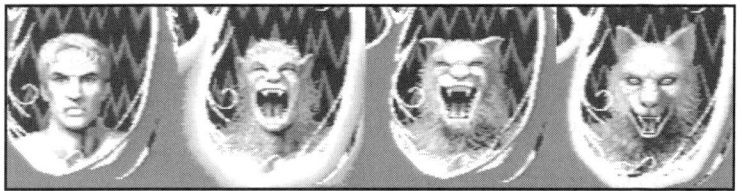

After you get the third Spirit Ball, you transform into the Altered Beast.

Use the Werewolf's Flame Streak to destroy all enemies unfortunate enough to get in the way.

22

Altered Beast

Aggar throws heads at you in sets of four. Stand at a medium distance, shooting Fireballs and dodging the heads as they come down at you.

Or use the Flame Streak, though dodging the heads is just about as easy. Eventually, Aggar is the latest dead person in the Acropolis!

Round Two—The Cave

Round Leeches and Wolves attack at the start of this level. Be sure to kick the Leeches before they can get to you. They can be very annoying if you let them. The third Wolf will be blue; get him and get the Ball! Then the Rattle Tail will make its first appearance; kick that Rattle before he jumps up!

The second Ball you grab will be between two Rattlers. Punch the right one as it comes down, and then the left one. The Chicken Stinger will appear after or during this; kick it.

Turn to your left; three Wolves will bound from that side, one of which is Blue. Get the third Ball and you're the Weredragon. Don't waste time with the Bolt; fly around and use the Laser Barrier to zap everything in sight. If you miss the Ball, use the same fighting techniques until you do get it.

Octeyes is tricky. Fly right up to him and start using the Laser Barrier. He might get you with the eyeballs, but if you hang

Use the Laser Barrier on Octeyes.

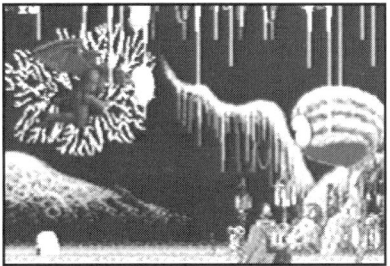

back at the left side of the screen and try to shoot from a long distance, you'll lose a lot more. Try to blast him in the eyeball (the one that's still attached), then dodge around his barrage of flying eyeballs. Move in for the kill again, using the Laser Barrier the whole time. If you're fast, he'll never touch you.

Round Three—The Cavern

Three Cave Needles will jump at you from the ledge to the right, then two from the left. Then three Wolves will bound off the right ledge. The third one will be blue.

You'll need to use the high jump (press up while pressing Button C) to get onto the ledge. If you don't, you'll be forced into a pit and an instant return to your grave. As you're crossing this first ledge, several Grave Masters will appear. Another two wolves, one blue, will jump at you from the left. Be ready. Near the end, Cave Needles will also come from the left. When you reach the other side, jump down and quickly kick the Turtle. By now, you should be the Werebear; Neff appears just about now. If you're not altered yet, keep going until you are.

Altered Beast

 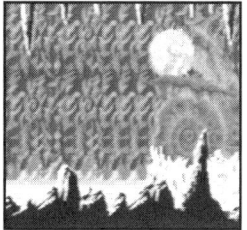 

The Moldy Snail shoots at you, but your spin move will defeat him.

Use your Body Spin and start spinning at Moldy Snail. Try to spin up and into his body. Now his spores can't hit you, and you'll be hitting him. If he knocks you back, just jump right back at him. You don't get damaged by being knocked back out of him. You'll defeat him easily this way. He'll turn red, and eventually blow up!

Round Four—The Palace Gates

 Slow Feet and Wolves (one blue) start you out. The second blue Wolf will jump from the right, along with a Hammer Demon. The third blue Wolf appears  when the statue of Neff (yep, the rhino guy) appears in the background. Neff will appear shortly after this. If you miss

 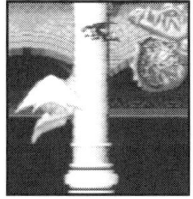 

Here's how to fight the Crocodile Worm: Stay at the left side of the screen and fire your Bouncing Flame at the Worm constantly. When he fires a Dragon at you, use the Pillar of Fire to total it when there's not a stream of fireballs headed toward you. By the way, duck the fireballs and keep shooting while you're ducking.

becoming Weretiger, there will only be one more blue Wolf before Neff's second appearance.

An alternate strategy (but a much more risky one) is to try to use the Pillar of Flame on the worm, himself. You have to hit

 him on his front edge, and you have to avoid his fireballs. If you can succeed at this strategy, you'll be wormless even sooner, but you might be missing a life or two of your own if you mess up.

Round Five—Neff's Lair

The Saw Fishes and Gory Goats are easy to dispose of; a few good kicks do it. The Rad Boars must be avoided unless you're powered up, otherwise you can't reach past their clubs. And kneel to punch the Dark Unicorn; if you're standing, it will connect every time.

Gory Goats!

Neff is pretty tough. Kneel down and use your Golden Fire; if you do it properly, he'll keep punching at the air above you while you set him ablaze.
He might kick you occasionally, but it won't hurt you too much. Another strategy is to wait until he starts to charge at you. Then use your Golden Arrow to meet him head on.

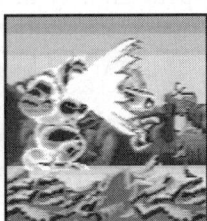

You must be fast, though, because he packs a powerful punch and an equally powerful low kick.

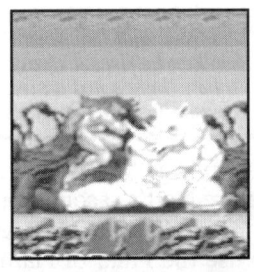

Altered Beast

SHH... THE SECRETS

What? You want secrets? O.K. There is some fun to be had here:

To continue if you die, hold down A and press Start twice.

For a sound test, hold the direction pad to the upper right diagonal and press A C and Start at the title screen.

O.K. You want the real stuff? To select any monster on any round, hold the direction pad to the lower left diagonal and press A B C and Start at the title screen.

To begin on any level, use the Round selection on the Option screen. Doesn't seem to work, does it? There's a trick. First press Start to exit the Option Screen, then press A and Start to begin the game. Whaddya know? You're on the level you chose!

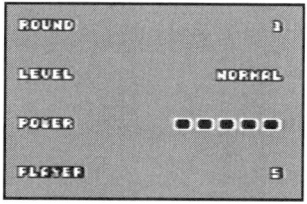

The Stages of Altered Beast.

CHAPTER 4

Budokan

Distributor: Electronic Arts
Game Type: Arcade Action

WHAT'S GOING ON?

The path of the warrior is long and difficult. It requires complete dedication of the mind and of the body. The only rewards you receive are inner strength and peace.

Which is why you're about as far away from that path as anyone's ever been. You were starting another gang fight when an old man dragged you into a doorway. He told you that he owed a debt to your father, and that you have the potential to be a warrior. You tried to slug him. Next thing you knew, you were picking yourself off the ground.

You will train at the Tokibo-Ryu dojo. With training, you can try for the ultimate goal, to succeed at the Budokan—where twelve of the greatest warriors from other dojos have gathered. You're on the path—can you avoid falling off?

WHO ARE YOU?

Once a punk, you're now an aspiring warrior. Tobiko-Sensei has given you a chance to make something of yourself.

PLAYERS

At first, the path is wide. Two players may fight on the Free Spar Mat. The path narrows later on—only one player may participate in the Budokan tournament. And only one player is allowed to practice in the various training halls.

SCORING

You're a warrior; points mean nothing. Your goal is simple, yet focused; defeat all challengers at the Budokan. In training you will see a point score to evaluate your effectiveness, but in real combat, the only point is the one at the end of a blow.

LIVES AND HOW TO LOSE THEM

You can't be killed in this game; you can be beaten badly. In each bout, you and your opponent have two bars at the top of the screen. These are the Stamina and Ki bars. Stamina is an indication of your energy. Ki shows the "inner strength" behind each move you make. Your Strength and Ki will grow as you rest, and is used as you attack. The higher your Ki when you strike an opponent, the more Stamina he will lose. The person to run out of Stamina first loses the match.

CONTINUES

There are no continues in the game. At the Budokan, you get three chances to beat each opponent. Win, and you advance to the next foe. Lose all three matches, and you are demoted to the previous opponent. Lose three matches to the first opponent and you must return to the dojo for more training.

CONTROLS

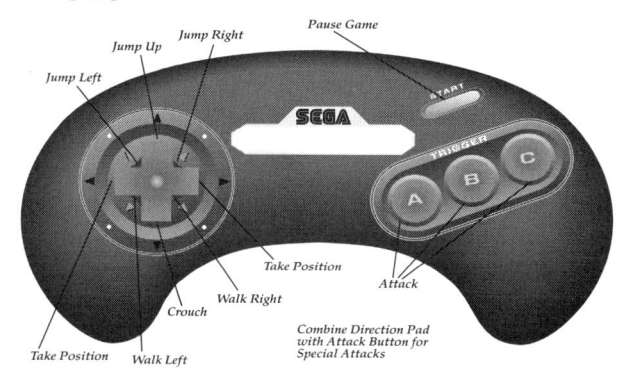

You have an incredible number of moves at your disposal. Each martial art—there are four you will train in—has anywhere from thirty to forty moves (or more). These are controlled with Button D and any of the action buttons (A, B or C). The instruction manual that accompanies your game contains charts of each move. Keep it handy during training and perfect each move. Here, we'll show you a few of these moves.

WEAPONS

Each of the martial arts uses a different weapon. One of them uses your own body as a weapon! Here are the four disciplines.

> **Karate** was developed on the island of Okinawa, where the people were not allowed to carry weapons. It was eventually brought to Japan, where it became extremely popular. Karate practitioners can attack with a variety of punches and kicks.
>
> **Kendo** is derived from the ryus (schools) where samurai trained in swordfighting. Training with actual swords was both dangerous to the students and to the weapons, so wooden swords were created. The concern for safety grew and shinai (bamboo swords) were next used. Kendo was eventually introduced into school curriculum, and became a marital art in its own right.
>
> The **Nunchaku** was not a weapon when it was first created; it was used to harvest grain! It was eventually adapted into karate, but did not become popular until recent interest in Okinawan weapons (of which the Nunchaku is one). This interest was brought on by Teruo Hayashi (a karate teacher) and Bruce Lee (the most renowned marital artist ever). The Nunchaku is comprised of two hexagonal sticks joined by a chain or cord.
>
> The **Bo** is a staff about six feet in length. It was a weapon favored by the samurai, because its length could keep opponents at a distance while the samurai struck with it. If the opponent got close, the Bo could be used to distract the enemy while karate was used by the samurai. The Bo has changed slightly in shape over the years, now being tapered on both ends.

Your opponents will be masters of different martial arts.

> The **Tonfa** is another farming tool from Okinawa. It is a long stick about twenty inches long, with a handle

protruding from it about five inches from one end. Tonfa masters can block blows with their arms, and then spin the Tonfa in their hands to strike back at an enemy.

Kusari-gama, the sickle and chain, was another farmer's tool and was used both by farmers and by samurai. The sickle was attached to a handle, which was attached to a long chain with a weighted ball on the end of it. The warrior armed with the Kusari-gama twirls the chain around with one hand while holding the sickle in the other.

The **Naginata** is a long pole, about seven feet long, with a huge curved blade at the end, about two feet in length. Fighters used this weapon to cut off the limbs of attackers' horses, and the limbs of the attackers as well (ugh). Modern-day Naginatas have bamboo blades.

The **Shuriken**, or throwing star, was the weapon-in-trade of the ninja. Ninja, unlike their high status today, were considered the lowest form of life in ancient Japan. They attacked with stealth and sold their services to whomever could pay, while samurai fought openly and for honor alone. The Shuriken can be used for deadly effect.

The **Yari** is a huge spear, similar to the Bo and Naginata. It had a variety of spearheads, which could tear an enemy apart. The Yari did not offer protection if the opponent got close, which was its main weakness.

SPECIAL ITEMS

Life is special; the true warrior will enjoy it in every way possible. (No, there are no special items.)

FRIENDS

Tokibo-Sensei is your mentor; he will always be willing to give you a small part of his near-infinite wisdom if you'll listen.

The sparring partners in the training halls will not attack like headless chickens; they will work with you to perfect your martial arts techniques, striking only when struck against.

ENEMIES

While the twelve opponents in the Budokan tournament aren't enemies, they are standing in the way of your spiritual progress. So you must fight them so that you don't need to fight them. Got that? Try to fight them using your training. If you don't succeed, you'll learn about each opponent later in this chapter.

STRATEGY SESSION
General Strategies

Tokibo-Sensei's advice is well-meant, but it has nothing to do with your techniques; he's been reading a few too many fortune cookies. Here is some humble advice from us instead.

To execute the maneuvers correctly, you must time your controller movements with your on-screen movements. Bad timing means you'll just waste Stamina and Ki while you flail away at air and leave yourself open to attack.

Don't get forced off the mat; you'll lose precious Ki. Back your opponent up instead; they won't want to back off the mat and will have to walk into your blows.

The martial arts vary in power. From strongest to weakest, they are: Bo, Nunchaku, Kendo, Karate.

In general, the more powerful moves of a martial art also eat up the most Stamina. Use them sparingly.

Karate.

You'll get your kicks from this martial art; that's because you should be using your kicking moves far more than your punches. The kicks do more damage and will keep your opponent farther away.

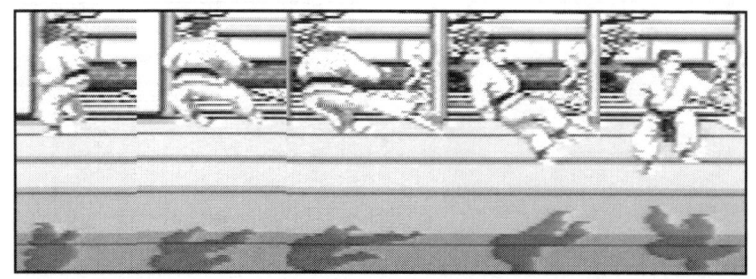

The regular kicks are easy to execute, and do a good amount of damage. The spin kicks or the jump kicks can really wear out your opponent.

The crouch sweep kick can't be defended against by your opponent; but they'll often attack with low attacks of their own, so you'll have to strike quickly.

Block the Bo Attack.

The jumping kicks do the most damage, but (of course) take the most Stamina to use. Try a spinning jump kick like the one shown on the previous pages for some real fun!

Kendo.

All of the Kendo maneuvers seem to be about the same; the jumping strikes are the finish-off blows, while the other maneuvers are soften-up blows.

For major softening up, try the two-handed strikes. Their double hits will do double damage, which doesn't double your chances, but makes them better!

The crouching hits are best used as defensive strikes, since they don't do enough damage to be used offensively, especially with your other choices.

Jumping blows can be strikes or lunges; both are effective, but the strike is more satisfying.

Nunchaku.

This weapon's repeating blows are deadly; as long as you hold down the action button, your Nunchaku will be flying.

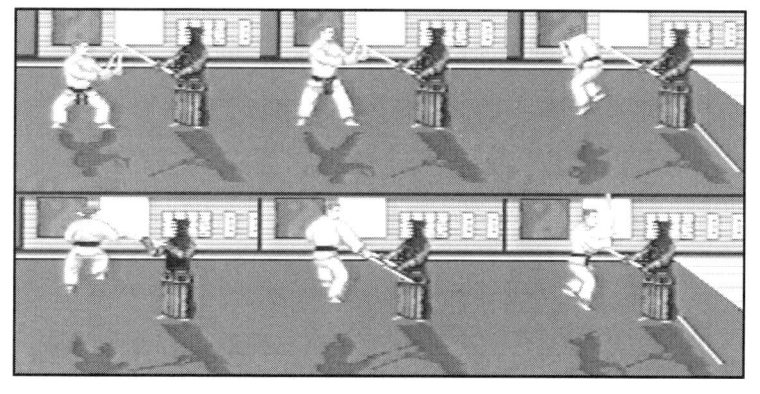

Not only does the triple strike look very impressive, but it's by far the most damaging maneuver. The underhand twirl is often for show, though it can be useful at close range.

The roundhouses and whips are your bread-and-butter blows; they'll hold off your opponent so that you can Ki up for the triple strike.

There are lots of jumping strikes, and the spinning ones are the best to use. But like any other jumping strike, they eat up Stamina, so be prudent with their use.

Bo.

The most powerful weapon, the Bo should be heavily practiced because you'll be using it against the heavies in the Budokan.

The thrusts are all right, but try using overhead strikes and spinning jump strikes. These are a lot better, even if they get you a little closer to the enemy.

The crouch spin strike, like the crouch sweep kick of Karate, can't be blocked. Use it heavily to keep your foes far away from you.

SHH... THE SECRETS

One day, you knew your training was complete. It was time to board the train and test your skills against the best. You were ready for the Budokan. Are you prepared both mentally and physically? Now is the time to study your opponents' styles and learn how to combat them. If you pay close attention, you may bring much honor to your school and your Sensei.

Use Karate to defeat Goro's Karate techniques. Adopt a blocking stance and wait until your ki is at its maximum. Then kick him with a straight kick for 1500 points and an instant knockout.

Beat Eiji Kimura by attacking with a furious barrage of jump kicks. He uses Kendo. Use your Karate skills to drive him back and stay inside his sword.

Jimi Doran uses the Tonfa. Beat him with Kendo. Just whack him over the head with powerful down strokes. Keep the pressure up and he's history. You might also use the Bo Staff against Jimi. Its superior reach will help you prevail.

Shigeo Kawahara uses the Nunchaku. Beat him with Karate. Use the upper block to block him, then kick him with full ki. For a greater challenge, use Kendo. You'll have to attack very fast to win.

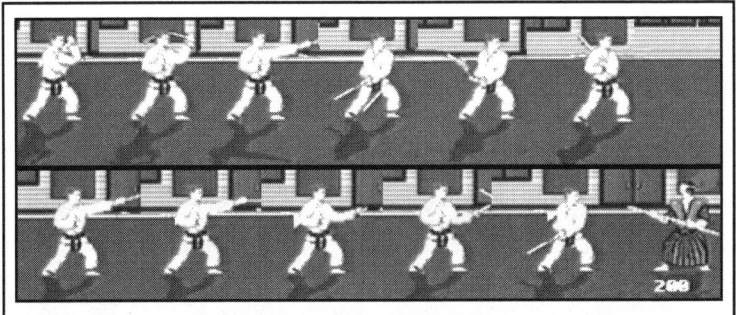

Counter Tetsuo Okabe's Bo with the Nunchaku. Use the jump strike and the triple strike. If you wish to test yourself, try using Karate against Tetsuo. You can win with jump kicks—fast and furious.

Arnie Gustavson uses Karate. Use Kendo and just whack the guy. If you try to fight using other methods, remember, his recuperative powers are great. You must attack quickly and leave him no time.

Hiroshi Shikeda uses the Kusari-Gama. You must use the Nunchaku against him. Keep up a barrage of attacks and you'll wear him out. Use triple strikes, single overhead strikes, and jump strikes. He's on the offensive all the time, so he'll come to you. The Kusari-Gama is a very dangerous weapon. Don't be careless.

36

Miyuki Hirose uses the Naginata. Use the Bo against her. After a series of spin moves, finish her off with a few forward jumping attacks. You may also succeed using the Nunchaku.

Randy Wu uses Nunchaku. We don't like to repeat ourselves. Treat Randy just like you treated Shigeo and you won't have any trouble.

Ayako Maruyama uses Ninjitsu. Use Kendo to fight Ayako. Use forward jump attacks and overhead strikes to prevail. If the ninja doesn't use too many dishonorable ninja tricks, you can do it.

Kazuo Sakata uses the Yari. He is a very formidable opponent. Use the Bo Staff to defeat him. Jump strikes and overhead strikes will succeed if you are relentless.

Tokage is the unknown fighter. He will challenge you with your own skills and weapon. If you have gotten this far, you must fight your own battle to win. It would be dishonorable for us to tell you more. Good luck.

CHAPTER 5

Forgotten Worlds

Distributor: Sega of America
Game Type: Arcade Action

WHAT'S GOING ON?

The world is enslaved, and the people are waiting for freedom. Is there a warrior powerful enough to defeat the alien masters and return the world to the humans?

WHO ARE YOU?

You are a Nameless One. You fight for the Human Beings on this Dust World—fighting against the Aliens who attacked so long ago, enslaving the planet. You were brought up in secret, and trained as a Warrior. Now you are ready for the ultimate battle. To win back the Dust World and win back its true name—Earth! You don't have a name, but you've got the muscle-power to make up for it!

PLAYERS

Forgotten Worlds can be played by one or two Named Ones.

SCORING

All of the minor Aliens are worth 200 points. The Bosses are worth more, and the ones on higher levels are worth the most. You'll also receive Bonus Points depending on how quickly you finish a level. The faster you finish, the more points you get! The points are turned into Zenny (money) as well.

LIVES AND HOW TO LOSE THEM

The Nameless One you control has a Strength Bar at the bottom of the screen. This Bar shrinks as Nameless is hit by Alien Fiends and their weaponry. If the Bar runs out, you become the Lifeless One.

You can gain Strength by flying over certain objects during battle, and by entering a Store. You can also buy Merchandise that will partially protect you from damage.

CONTINUES

In a one-player game, there are no continues; if you lose, you start from the beginning again. In a two-player game, if one player dies, he can restart provided that the other player is still alive. The player that restarts will lose his points, but will keep all the Zenny he's gained.

CONTROLS

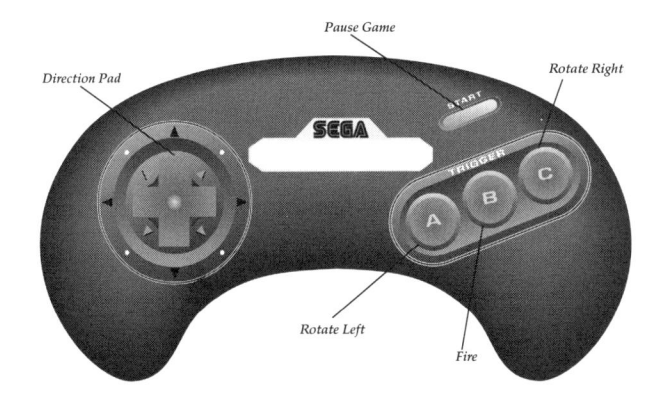

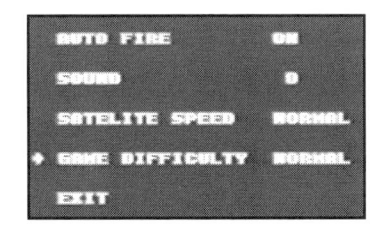

The Option Screen

WEAPONS

Buy weapons in Mirabella's Store. The Store appears at various points during the game. Pay for the Weapons by collecting Zenny dropped by the Alien Fiends.

The **All Direction Shooter** costs 3,000 Zenny. It fires in eight directions at once.
The **Balcan Cannon** costs 50,000 Zenny, but is the most powerful weapon by far.
Booster 1 goes for 10,000 Zenny. It increases your shot power.
Booster 2 is a cool 20,000 Zenny. It doubly increases your shot power.
Bound sells at 30,000 Zenny. It makes shots that hit obstacles rebound at the enemy.
The **Burner** is 20,000 Zenny. It's a hot flame-thrower.
The **Homing Laser** costs a staggering 99,900 Zenny. It will home in on the enemy.
The **Laser** is a lightbeam weapon that goes for 20,000 Zenny.
The **Missile** sells for 5,000 Zenny. It homes in on the enemy like the Homing Laser.
The **Napalm Bomb** is 5,000 Zenny. It frazzles everything in its explosion radius.
Super Booster costs 50,000 Zenny. It powers up your shots to maximum!
Wide Shot costs 50,000 Zenny. Its bullets cover a wide range.

SPECIAL ITEMS

Like the Weapons, Special Items are purchased in the Store. Here's a shopping list for you.

Armor costs 3,000 Zenny. It will absorb three enemy shots.
The **Aura Stone** is 30,000 Zenny. It doubles your current Strength.
The **Dress** costs 99,900 Zenny. It will give you 1,000,000 bonus points if you win the War and defeat the Aliens. It's available only in the Tower of Dread.
The **Flying Stone** is 100 Zenny. It increases your flying speed. There are three colors. Copper is normal speed, Silver is high speed, and Gold is the fastest speed of all.

Information costs 100 Zenny. It gives you advice about your future battles.

The **Life Pack** is 600 Zenny when you first purchase it; its cost doubles every time you buy it after that. It completely fills the Strength Bar.

The **Potion of Resurrection** costs 20,000 Zenny, and its price also doubles every purchase afterward. It will bring you back to life if you die, and you'll keep both your points and your Zenny.

Special Armor costs 5,000 Zenny. It will take five enemy hits before it's destroyed.

A **Treatment** is 300 Zenny, and doubles in price every time you buy it. It will partially restore your Strength Bar.

Zenny are what you collect to purchase all these things; they're left behind by Alien Fiends. They come in four sizes: A Tiny Coin is 100 Zenny; a Regular Coin is 500 Zenny; a Large Coin is 1,000 Zenny; and the Huge Coin is 5,000 Zenny.

FRIENDS

Mirabella is the owner of the Store, and she'll help you. Buy all your items from her, and sell your current Weapon to her at half price in order to afford a new one.

ENEMIES

The Alien Fiends look somewhat different, but are the same in value. It's the Bosses that you should be concerned about. Here they are in all their glory (or is that ugliness?).

The **Paramecium** is worth 15,000 points. He's protected by a bunch of spinning garbage!

The **Dust Dragon** gives you 30,000 points. He'll breathe fire—and Reptilian Thugs—at you!

The **Iron Warlord** is 50,000 points. He's got large arms, but poor eyesight.

The **Sphinx** is 60,000 points. It won't stay in one piece for very long.

Ymesketit is worth 70,000 points. He's got a long name and a destructive streak!

Iceman scores 80,000 points. He's made of ice, but he isn't at all cool!

The **War Tyrant** leads the Aliens. He's worth 100,000 points—and beating him wins the War!

STRATEGY SESSION
General Strategies

Controlling the Nameless Ones is the most difficult thing to learn. Spinning around wildly isn't the way to succeed in this game. You need to know which directions to face to catch the attacking waves of Fiends.

Be patient when collecting Zenny. They'll stay on the screen for several seconds after they appear, so don't go flying to grab one—and end up flying into a Fiend.

The Dust Planet

The battle starts here, in the city. You've got to destroy the Aliens here before you can take the fight to the Aliens in space. So get started!

In the early stages, fight the reptiles and get Zenny from the cannons.

Fly down to the lower left corner of the screen; that's where you should handle the first few waves of attacks. Spaceships will fly at you from the right side of the screen; rotate in their direction and fire away! The next few attackers are missile-toting Reptilian Thugs. The first time you shoot them, they'll drop their missiles, and then pounce back up at you!

A few metallic Spydro-bots will pop out of the ground; shoot their legs out from under them. Then turn to your left to take out the next wave of Reptilian Thugs. About this time, a huge pillar of garbage will form! The best place to shoot is the bottom; this will destroy the entire pillar.

The Shop will appear shortly; go inside. You want to trade in your V-Cannon for the All Direction Shooter. You should also

Forgotten Worlds

buy a Gold Flying Stone and a Treatment (if you need it, which you probably will). Once you're done, leave the Shop.

After a few waves of Reptilian Thugs, you'll be flying into a tunnel. This leads to the Machinery Room. There are lots of hazards in the room—flame jets, cannons, and lots of attackers!

Get Big Zenny from the cogs and machine parts!

Shoot at the Cogwheels to get rid of them; they'll block your way (and reduce your Strength) otherwise. Also, they'll leave some major Zenny behind. Blast your

43

way past them and two pillars will clamp together on the right side of the screen. Blast through the pillars to reach the Paramecium. Yuck!

A circle of garbage surrounds the Paramecium. Get horizontally aligned with its mouth, blast through the circle, and fire at the mouth. Don't try to get inside the circle; you'll just get nailed. Eventually, the Paramecium will turn back into the garbage he was in the first place!

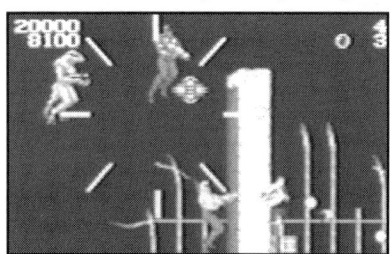

Now you're at the Doomed Harbor. Stay in the middle of the screen, because the Thugs will be attacking from both sides. Fight through them and the Shop will appear again. Thank goodness!

Your main investment should be in a Booster. You shouldn't buy a Treatment unless you have to, because doing so will double the price the next time you need it (which may not be too long).

The Thugs will be attacking from both sides now. With two players, each of you can cover one side of the screen; if you're flying solo, you'll have to rotate to catch all of them. Stay in the middle of the screen, high above the water. Because your next attacker will be a surprise.

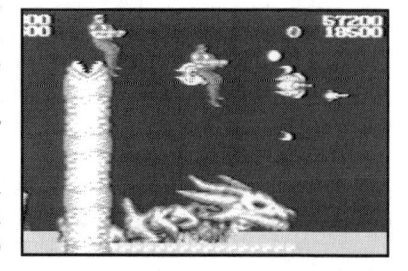

The Zipper Worm will lunge from the water, and you can't hurt him at all. So

Forgotten Worlds

dodge him! Stay pointed towards the left to handle the Thugs in between Worms.

Later on, the Thugs will pounce from the water; as long as you dole out punishment against them like the other Thugs, you won't have a problem. Until you reach the Dust Dragon!

Fly down to its chest. Fire away, stopping only to rotate and shoot the Thugs

it will spew out. The dragon's fire streams won't hurt you if you stay low. Eventually, the chest will burst open to reveal the heart. Fire at the vital organ until

it blows up! Now that you've dredged the Harbor—what's next?

The Wasteland is next. The foes will be the same old Thugs and Spydro-bots—you won't have a hard time making it to the Shop. By now, you'll have enough Zenny to consider the purchase of a Laser or Burner. You may want to save it, though; the bigger, better and more expensive weapons will be coming up.

Now you'll be flying up the Iron Fortress. Fly close to the Fortress to shoot the cannons on its surface. The Thugs will attack from the left every so often; be ready to spin and shoot.

When you level out, be prepared for the return of the pillars. They'll be making more appearances on this level. Stay close to the ground, because the cannons will still be around. When you have to blast your way through three pillars, the Iron Warlord is near.

Rotate to face upwards. The Warlord's arms will try to pound you from the sides of the screen; you can shoot them to stop their movement for a moment.

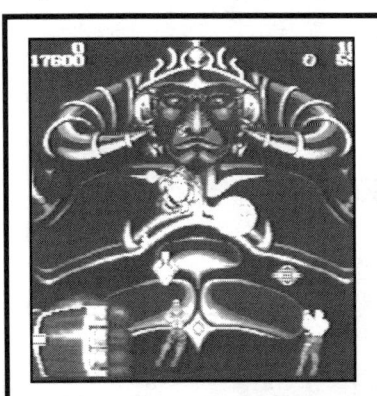

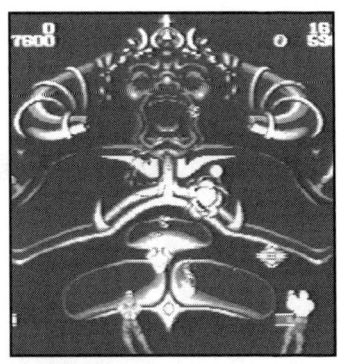

The Warlord will shoot fireballs in your direction, pausing in between each volley; dodge in either direction and fire away at his head and shoulders. You can fly up to the side of his head or stay in the middle of the screen; staying in the middle gives you more room to breathe.

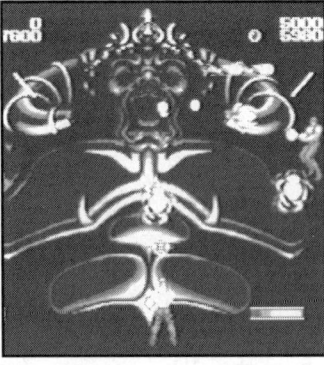

Wherever you go, keep firing until the Warlord screams in defeat!

The Pyramid of Terror

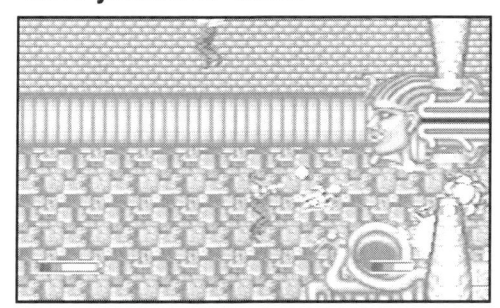

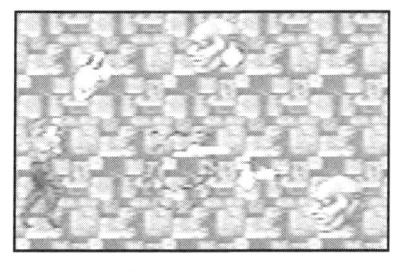

The first Fiends attack a lot like the Thugs, except that they home in on your position. Shoot away! You'll reach an Egyptian head with pillars above and below it. Shoot the bottom pillar and get ready to head down.

These Skulls fly quickly. Shoot the ones you can, but dodge the ones you can't! You'll reach the Shop when you start flying horizontally again. Get in there!

Bound is for sale, but the Balcan Cannon is what you want. You'll also want to reinvest in the Gold Flying Stone. Spend those hard-earned Zenny and get back into the fray.

The next pattern is similar to the beginning of the Pyramid; homing Thugs, the pillars (shoot the top one this time), and Skulls. You've passed them before, so pass them again. Only this time, when you level out, the Skulls will continue to attack. Rotating in all directions will be necessary if you hope to survive.

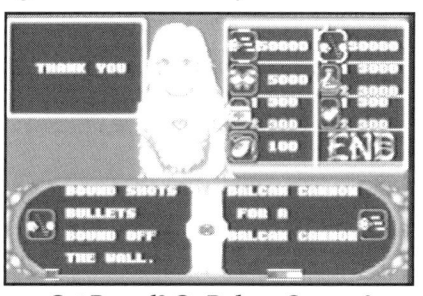

Get Bound? Or Balcan Cannon?

Stay slightly to the right side of the screen, because the objects that will drop at you seem to come more from the left. You'll fly out of the tunnel and into open space; this means the approach of the Sphinx (see next page.)

You're going to get a heavy sense of deja' vu—the next patterns are the same you've seen before. Handle them as before, and you'll soon reach the Shop.

Booster 2 is for sale—now's a good time to buy it. You should have more than enough Zenny to afford it. And grab a Treatment if you need it.

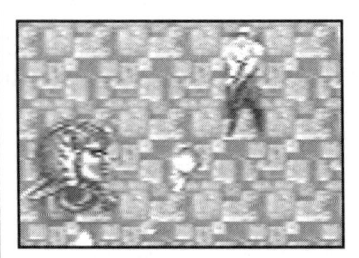

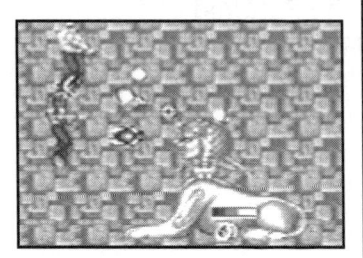

The part that thinks on this Sphinx—his head—will pop off and attack first. It shoots horizontally, so stay above or below it as you shoot it. This way it can't shoot back! Then its body will come back onto the screen and mutate into a nasty worm! The only vulnerable spot is its head/eye—shoot it while you circle around the screen, dodging it. Keep it up until a chain-reaction explosion occurs!

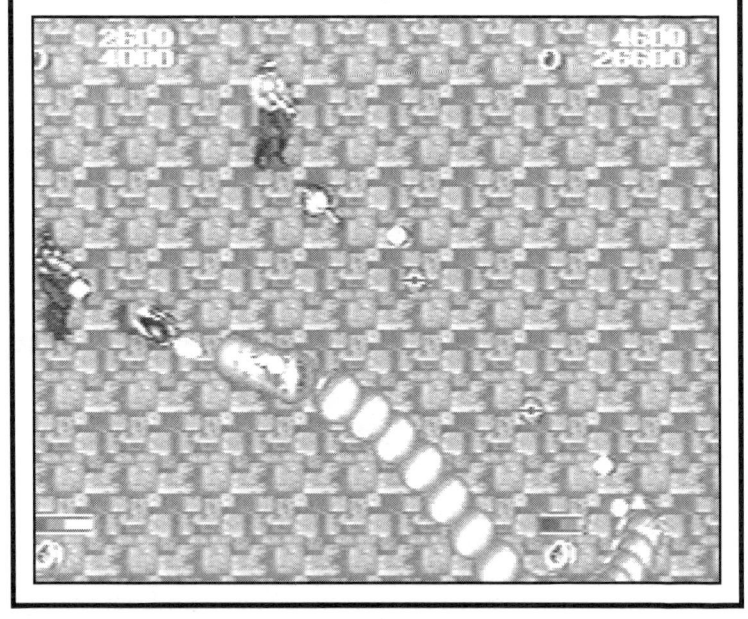

Leave the Shop and blast through the Thugs until you reach your next pillars. Blast the lower one. You'll be going down—and facing Aliens that approach you slowly, almost in a stutter-step motion. This gives you more time to shoot them—which is good, since there are so many on the screen!

When you start flying horizontally, get ready for huge Aliens that will drop in a never-ending stream from the top of the screen.

Blast at the point where they're pouring onto the screen and scoot past them.

When you come to an open space, you've reached Ymesketit. He'll fly onto the screen from the left, position himself at the right, and then start an all-out attack.

You'll first need to blast the four cannons that attack you. When they're destroyed, missiles will drop from the top of Ymesketit. Hug the pillars guarding Y and shoot at his face. It will start to twitch—which means you're doing the right thing. Keep blasting away, but prepare to shoot the four cannons again. Y will fall sooner than you'd think.

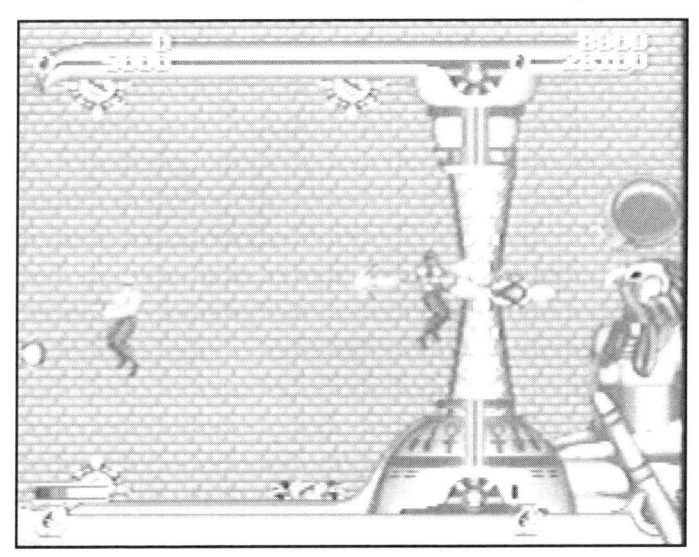

The Cosmic World

You've done well, Nameless One. Keep it up and you'll save Earth—and maybe get a name!

At the beginning is a large cloud layer known as Miasma. Stay low and you'll find a few hidden goodies within the clouds. This is also the safest place to attack, since the Aliens will appear mainly from the right. You'll reach some pillars soon.

Fight through the clouds a bit more and the Shop will appear. Inside, buy a Treatment or Life Pack; otherwise, save your Zenny for later on. Leave the shop and continue to stay low.

Aliens will start to materialize out of nowhere; blast where they're forming so they don't have time to do any damage. Keep to the lower left of the screen; this is the safest area by far.

A huge face will emerge from the clouds. This face will fire massive streams of tracking missiles; take it out as soon as you can. The other Thugs will still be coming onto the screen. To be honest, if you're by yourself, you'll need lots of luck to get through this part.

After you pass two more faces, the Iceman cometh. He'll shoot ice at you while he hides in the clouds. Fly to the top of the screen and fight from there. Shoot all the ice crystals surrounding the Iceman and then shoot his unprotected body. Boom! Watch out for his body chunks.

You've arrived at the final location: the Tower of Dread. You'll be flying up all the way, so turn in that direction and get ready to rumble!

Hug the sides of the Tower. The Aliens will attack from the sides. Most of them will fire homing

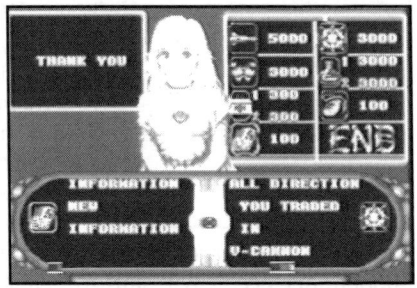

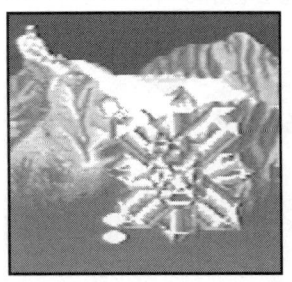

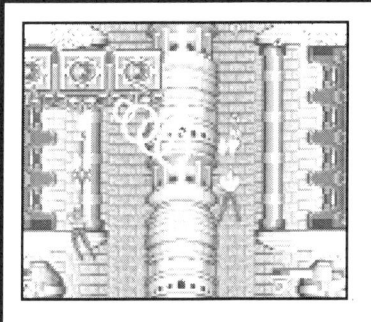

The action toward the end gets about as heavy as it can get. If you're playing a two-player game, use teamwork. Each player covers a side of the screen. Try not to get trapped behind the outcroppings. Keep firing!

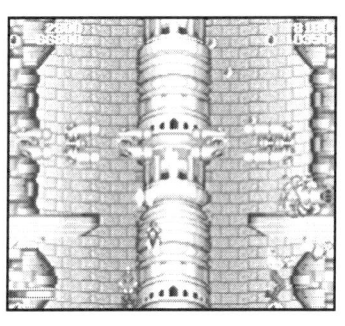

missiles, so you'll have to dodge upwards quite often. Don't get trapped behind the outcroppings that extend from the walls, or you'll lose Strength.

The Shop won't appear like it normally does; it will jut out from the left side of the screen. Fly into it. The Homing Laser is the Weapon to shoot for, but console yourself with a Super Beam if you don't have the dough.

Between here and the next Shop, the most bothersome enemy will be the Rocket Pods. These buggers pop out from the sides of the screen and fire tons of missiles at you. Stay at the opposite side of the screen from them and fire. There will also be Aliens that reach out with huge fiery arms; destroy them and scoop up the Zenny they drop.

The next Shop appears like the first one; go inside and feast your eyes on all the goodies. The Dress is here, but it may be out of your price range. Oh well, saving Earth is more important than scoring points anyway. Right?

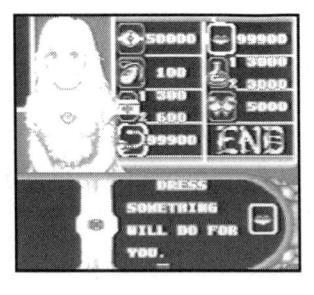

Leave the shop. A short flight later, the walls will disappear and the screen will go black for a moment. When it comes back, it's brought the War Tyrant back with it! Defeat him and you've won the War! Lose and... well, see The Secrets if you think you'll lose.

SHH... THE SECRETS

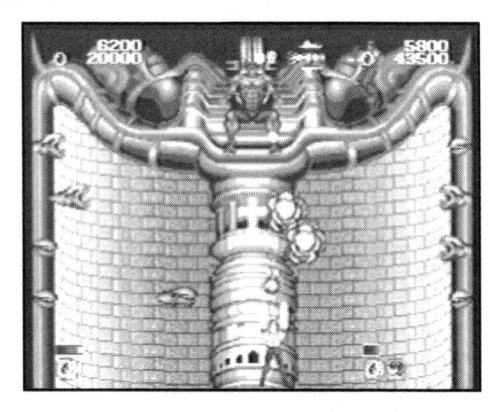

How do I defeat the War Tyrant? Don't worry about him at first; worry about the walls on either side of you. They'll fire mutant Aliens at you; shoot away! First the right wall will attack, then the left, then both at once. Make it through them and the Tyrant will fly down to destroy you. Stay as far away from him as you can while you shoot him. His wings will shoot arcing fireballs that can be shot; he will shoot long lasers that will almost always get you. Keep dodging, keep shooting and you're bound to win! You must!

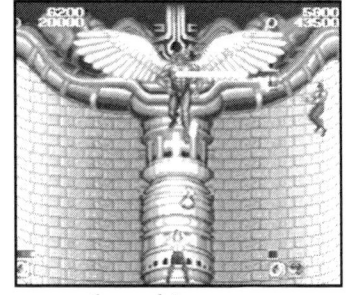

CHAPTER 6

Ghouls'n Ghosts

Distributor: Sega of America
Game Type: Arcade Action

WHAT'S GOING ON?

It seems that wherever there is a knight with a princess, there is a Prince of Darkness waiting to steal her! And once again, that's the situation. And just for kicks, the Prince of Darkness has pillaged and plundered your land.

Understandably, you're pretty peeved. In fact, you're mad enough to enter the frightening, demonic kingdom of the Dark Prince. If you don't defeat him and rescue your princess, she is going to be really irritated. And you're not sure whose wrath you prefer to face... hers or the Dark Prince's!

WHO ARE YOU?

You're Sir Arthur, the silver-suited, sword-swinging knight. Though you sometimes lose your armor... and your life... you are never without a weapon.

PLAYERS

Ghouls'n Ghosts is a one- or two-player game. Select which type of game you wish to play after the title screen. An option allows two players to play, using the same control pad, however, each player still takes turns. There is no simultaneous play mode.

SCORING

You get points for each creature you destroy and a Key bonus for completing each round.

LIVES AND HOW TO LOSE THEM

You begin Ghouls'n Ghosts with three lives. In each life you must be hit twice to die, once to lose armor and the second—when you are running about the world in your underwear—to lose your life. The point is, don't get caught in your underwear!

Ghouls'n Ghosts has five stages. Each is timed. You have 2:30 to make it through the first stage, and 3:00 for each stage thereafter. If you have not beaten the stage when the timer at the right corner of the screen reaches 0:00, you will lose a life.

CONTINUES

Ghouls'n Ghosts features unlimited continues. So in theory you can beat the game in one sitting—if you want to play over and over for sixteen hours. The problem is, each time you continue you lose whatever score you had. So you can play this game two ways; using the unlimited continues to play through or on your own skill to beat the game with the highest number of points. Your choice.

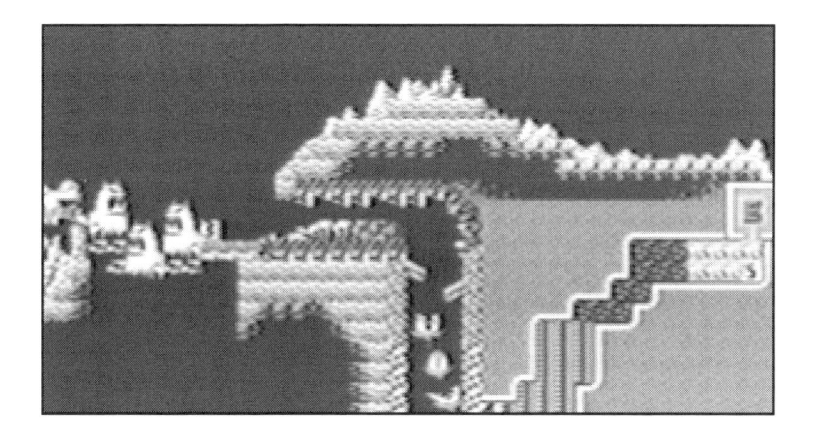

CONTROLS

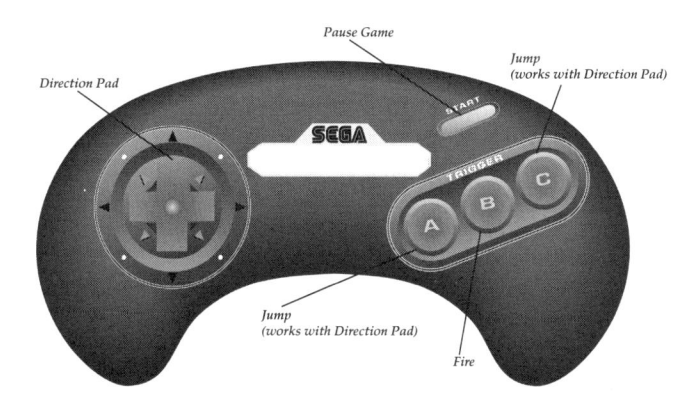

Press the Start Button on Control Pad 1 and two players can play on the same Control Pad. Press the Start Button on Control Pad 2 and two players can play using separate Control Pads.

WEAPONS

There are six weapons you can use in Ghouls'n Ghosts. Each weapon also has a special type of magic that you can only use when wearing a special type of armor. If you like the weapon you are using and do not wish to pick up a new weapon, jump over the new weapon without touching it. But be careful because some weapons are almost impossible to avoid!

The **Sword** fires left, right, down, or up and is the weapon you have at the beginning of the game. *Magic: Torpedo Magic. The sword fires lightning torpedoes up, left and right.*

The **Big Axe** is more powerful than the sword. You can even throw it through some objects. But it cannot be thrown consistently. Rapidly hitting the button results in a throw about once every three times. *Magic: Thunder Dragon Magic. Skeletal thunder dragons are released to destroy all enemies in the sky.*

Throw the **Fire Water** to release blue flames for a distance. But it can't be thrown up and it does not go very far! *Magic: Fireball Magic. This magic launches four fireballs that circle you, flaming your enemies to crispy critters.*

Throw the **Discus** left, right and up. When you kneel and throw, the Discus skims the ground, hitting all enemies there. A good all-around weapon. *Magic: Mirror Magic. This magic gives you a measure of protection, keeping your enemies away from you like a shield. It only lasts for a short period of time.*

The **Dagger** is the fastest moving weapon. You can throw five or six daggers in the length of time it takes to throw one axe. At close range you can really blast your enemies. *Magic: Double Magic. This magic releases your double, who can fight with you for a limited amount of time, doubling your firepower! Your double is invincible but will disappear if you are hit, removing your armor.*

You get the **Psycho Cannon** at the end of the first half of the game. You can't beat Loki without it. It is the most powerful weapon in the game and can easily blast all your enemies except Loki.

Using Magic

When you wear magic armor, a red meter appears at the bottom of the screen. Holding down or repeatedly pressing the fire button will cause the meter to gradually turn silver. When the meter has changed completely, the Weapon Display will change to the Magic Display. Fire now and magic will be released, hopefully to crush your enemies.

SPECIAL ITEMS

Treasure items appear in two ways; either as chests sitting on the ground or as jars carried by monsters. Shooting or hitting the chests and jars will release their secrets.

Red Armor comes from jars. Get it and you get 200 points.
Big Red Armor comes from the same places but it's worth 500 points.
When you are naked. You can usually find **Silver Armor** in a nearby chest to give you back some protection.
Magic Armor appears during play. Get it and you'll wear a cool-looking cape. Oh, and you'll be able to call forth the magic of whatever weapon you have. The Magic Armor is gold in color. It's every knight's dream armor.

The Magician

When this character appears, he throws a magic wheel at you that will turn you into an old man or a duck for a limited amount of time.

As a duck you are helpless. As an old man you can fight... barely.

Sometimes you can destroy the magician before he releases magic in your direction. That's the best plan. If you are fast, you may also be able to dodge his attack.

FRIENDS

In this game you have only two; an old wizard and the princess you are trying to rescue.

ENEMIES

Every critter in this game wants a piece of your hide. Some kingdom! Here they are, with some strengths and weaknesses.

Skeleton Murderer: These blue cloaked nasties dig up from the ground, then attack you with scythes. Easy to destroy.
Sickle Weasel: When these ugly critters fly through the air it's hard to make out their shape. When they stop moving they are vulnerable. Hit 'em then!
Poisonous Flower: Appear randomly in certain areas and spew out poisonous skulls. The skulls are indestructible. Attack the flower directly...and watch for the roots.
Pigman: Attacks with pitchforks. If they are on levels above you, Pigmen will often spit mud down on you.

Red Destroyer's King: This fast-moving demon attacks from indirect angles. Intercept them when they are moving from top to bottom or bottom to top.
Rock Turtle: Rock Turtles are indestructible when bouncing or rolling. Hit them as soon as they stop and their heads and legs come out from the shells.
Mud Armor: Dirt knights who rise from the ground. A blast of fire will return them to their muddy graves.
Bi Fang: Bi Fangs don't attack, but their bodies are covered with poisonous gas. Touch them and you will die.
Demon Dayfly: A giant antfly. Easy to destroy, but often flies at levels where you don't want them!
Fire Bat: Find them at the base of fire pillars. When born, they often launch in your direction.
Flying Goblin: These monsters lurk overhead and drop rocks. Sometimes they will come close to the ground and try to hit you when your back is turned. Typical.

Gatekeepers

Gatekeepers guard the gates to the Dark Prince's castle. You'll find one at the end of each round.

Statue of Terror: A huge, ugly beast who is more than willing to lose his head over you. Keep hitting his heads and you will beat him down.
Infernomo: A bad dog made of fire, he'll try to trample you or cover you with fire balls. His face is the weak point.
Mistral Winds: A storm cloud who knows what you are up to. Dodge its lightning bolts while hitting the eye of the storm as often as you can. Remember you can hit it as the cloud flies overhead.
The Slug: The key to beating this slimy bug is to hit the hearts lining the bottom of its body. Take out the two left hearts from the bottom left of the creature's body, firing straight across. Do the same from the right side. The last heart you have to hit while standing on top of the monster, firing down. Watch out for its maggot babies!
The Buzzing Bug: This critter is really disgusting! It's a big evil-looking bug, made out of a whole flock of little bugs. You can only hit it when it is whole. Both the flock of little bugs and the big creature can hit you, taking your armor and your life. You need the dagger to kill it the first time. Its abdomen is the weak point.

Ghouls'n Ghosts

Loki, Prince of Darkness: This is the guy causing all your problems. You have to defeat him to get your princess back. But remember... he's the toughest monster of all. But he does have a weak spot. Try to get between his legs and hit him in the head. Or stand on his foot and blast him when he raises it, but you'll have to dodge his shots. Nothing else will work.

STRATEGY SESSION
General Strategies

Before you enter the first stage, you will see a quick overview of the five stages you must clear to win the game. A tiny Sir Arthur will mark your place in the game. Then its on to battle!

Stage 1

The Execution Place. The entrance to the Demon's world. Your biggest enemy here are the skeleton murderers and vultures. The skeletons are easy to destroy. One hit will do it. You can turn the vultures into feather dusters just as easily. But don't turn your back because they'll fly at you with no warning! Try to get the Gold Armor from the second chest. The Magician is in the first one.

The Floating Island on The Lake. Cross the bridge and duck the Sickle Weasels as you brave the stormy winds. Remember you can only destroy the sickle weasels when you can see their body shape. Then you reach the ramps.

Watch out for the roots of the Poisonous Flowers and for the Pigmen's muddy breath as you climb for the heights. The Pigmen will try to impale you with their pitchforks. Time your move to get out of their way so you can strike them as they land.

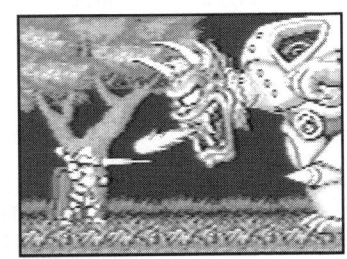

The first guardian of the gateways will be ready to lose his head over you. That's your target. Hit him hard and fast... and the Key to the next stage is yours!

Stage 2

The Village of Decay. Now get ready to face turtle power, dude! Only this time they are out to get you. Hit the Rock Turtles when they stick their heads out of their shells. You can't kill them when they are bouncing. It's best then to stay out of their way.

When you cross the bridges, look out for weak spots that will drop you into the ant lions below. Jumping will get you out and off of the moving sand paths—if you have not fallen too far in. The ant lions are virtually indestructible. Wait at the end of the last path. A chest will appear. Open it and you may find armor... or magic armor!

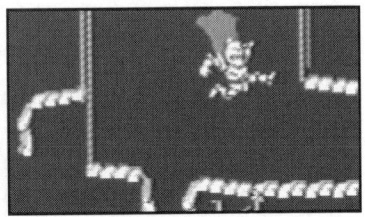

Ghouls 'n Ghosts

Town of Fire. Jumping off the last catwalk puts you in Fire Town. As you enter the stage, remember that you can duck under the spokes of the burning windmill. Just don't touch the flaming ends. A fire demon awaits you, ready to hurl fire to destroy your armor. Jump and fire as he drops to the ground. You need timing—and one good shot—to take him out!

Fire Bats and ground that falls away as you pass come next. Don't let the Bats knock you into the pits. One-eyed flowers spit poison at you as you try to jump from safe spot to safe spot.

Pass them all and you face Infernomo, the fire dog. His face is the weak spot. Don't let this hot dog drop flame on you!

Stage 3

Baron Rankle's Tower. This round scrolls vertically. The floor moves you up! In addition to the wall guardians and the rock bearing goblins, you have to make sure not to get trapped under a ledge or overhang. This is where firing up is your best chance for survival. Also, be careful here. Sometimes you'll accidentally get a weapon you don't want while trying to dodge a goblin.

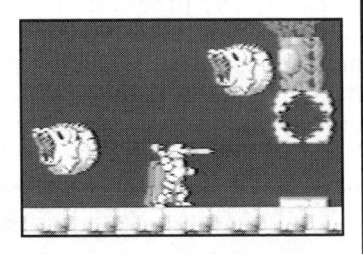

The most critical moment in this stage is at the top. Move to the right as soon and as fast as you can. At the other side of a whole cloud of Bi Fangs is a wall. You must knock it down and pass it before the floor traps you in. Pass this barrier and it's on to the next stage.

Horrible Faced Mountain. You have to get through this round by traveling on the tongues of monsters... yuk! Moving from tongue to tongue will require split-second timing. Some seem to move away just when you are ready to jump! Stay on a tongue too long and the demons will eat you. No fun!

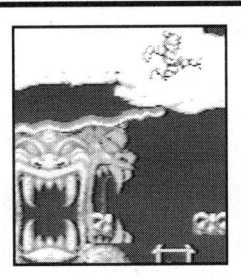

Moving from tongue to tongue or tongue to platform will require split-second timing. Don't let the chests or the Demon Dayflys knock you into the void! On the path of the moving stones, watch out for a Dayfly that flies higher than the others.

Demon Dayflys will try to knock you off. They are easy to kill. On the path of moving stones, however, at least one Dayfly will appear higher than the others. Don't let it catch you.

The last tongue will carry you to the rocky abode of the Mistral Winds. This storm moves quickly but can be dodged. However, you need one of the faster weapons to beat it! The dagger is best, followed by the discus. If you have the blue fire water in this round, you may continue many times before you actually beat it. Hit the eye of the storm. Get it? If you do, the key is yours!

Ghouls'n Ghosts

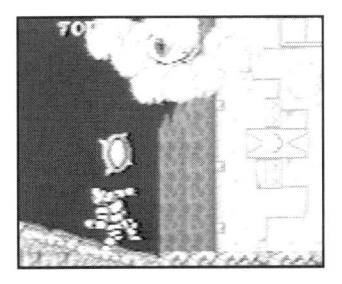

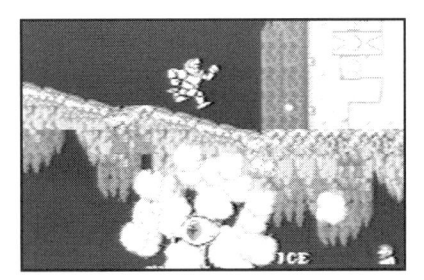

Stage 4

Use the Dagger Magic to double your fire power.

Better keep jumping. The flowers look hungry!

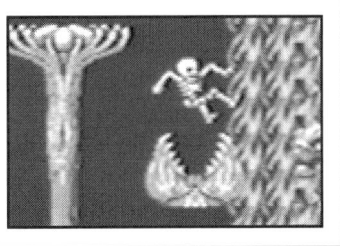

The Crystal Forest. This stage is a downward trip. Stand on the crystal ramps too long and blue snakes will try to lunch on you! Green, grabbing hands squeeze the life out of you it they get a chance! Don't get caught because you can't get out! The first chest you encounter in this round will contain a Magician. Open it and take your chances. The second chest, if you opened the first, will contain magic armor—or just armor if you need it. The third chest—if you opened the second—will contain a weapon. Just which weapon is impossible to predict.

At the bottom of the crystal ramps, green monster flowers carry you to the floor. Jump to another flower before the one you are on reaches the end! Clear the flowers and you reach the Slug. Ugh! Beat it for the Key to the castle.

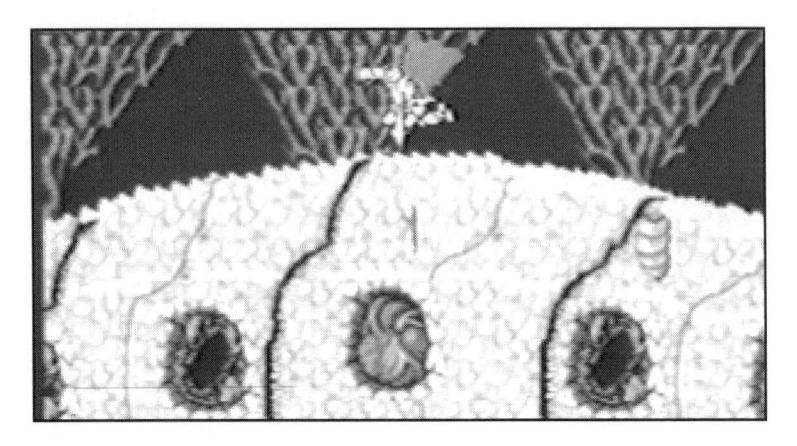

Stage 5

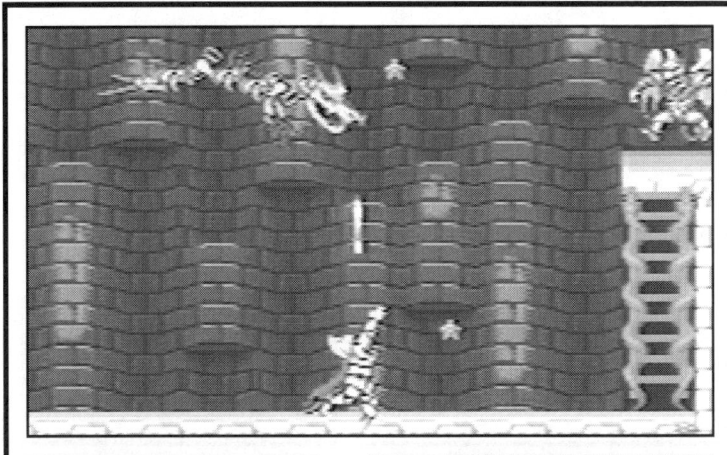

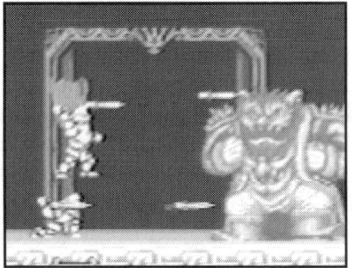

You can duck this guy's flames. Then jump up and fire at his head. Don't get caught, though. He'll change his pattern from time to time.

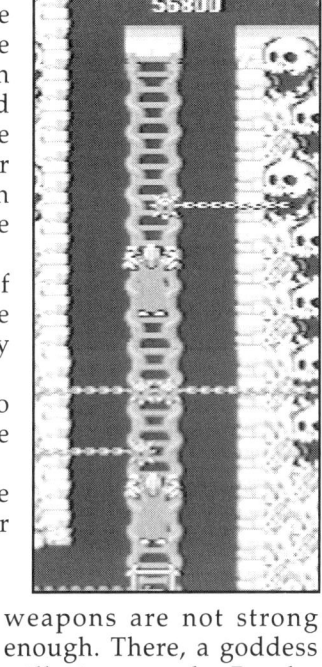

Castle of Evil Demons. This is the hardest stage of the game, aside from Loki. As soon as you begin the stage, skeletal dragons try to run you down. Climb the stairs and demons await. Use your magic here if you have it. If not, time your attacks to their up and down movements. You definitely want the Dagger in this stage.

As you climb higher, the size of the enemies grows larger. The Statue of Terror comes in pairs, followed by twin flame-spewing ogres.

If you reach the Doorway to Loki's throne room, a surprise awaits. The Wizard.

He will send you back to the beginning of the game because your weapons are not strong enough. There, a goddess will give you the Psycho Cannon. Now you must blast your way back to the throne room. Once there, your battle begins. Are you good enough to beat Loki?

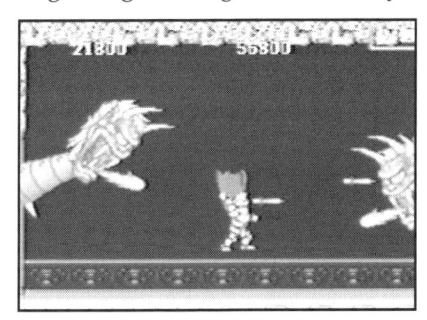

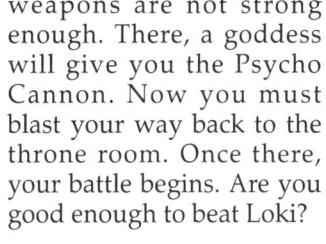

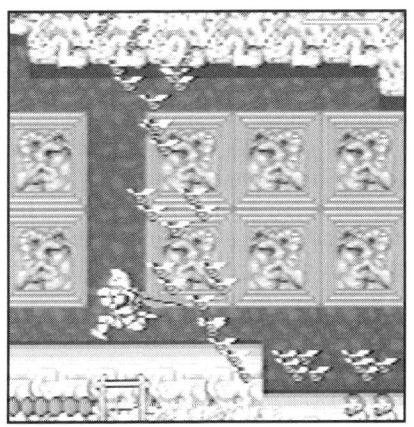

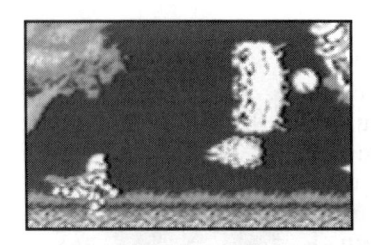

Go back to the beginning and use your new weapon. If you lose it, the Princess will return it. Keep it until you meet Loki himself. It's a long way. Was it worth it?

SHH... THE SECRETS

If you have the Psycho Cannon and your way is blocked by a weapon you don't want (that is any weapon!), backtrack on the screen for thirty seconds or so. The weapon you don't want will most likely go away. If it doesn't, let yourself be killed. It is worth a life to keep the Psycho Cannon. If you don't have it when you reach Loki's throne room, you will be sent back to the beginning again. That makes for a long game!

You want some real secrets? O.K. To go to any level in the game, press U D L R at the title screen. Keep doing it until you hear the tone. Then experiment with the direction pad and Start to choose a level. Press A to go to the second half of a level.

Invincibility? Shh. Don't tell anyone. Press U A D A L A R A B C Start at the title screen. Once you're in the game, thenpause and unpause. The trick will work. It's pretty cowardly, though.

CHAPTER 7

Golden Axe

Distributor: Sega of America
Game Type: Fighting

WHAT'S GOING ON?

It seems there's hardly a place left in our fantasies that isn't oppressed by evil magicians or threatened with extinction. The mythical land of Yuria is no exception. This time it's the all-powerful Death Adder himself who has kidnaped the King and his daughter. Not only that, but he's also stolen the legendary Golden Axe.

Death Adder is hiding in his palace. Can't someone go there and free the prisoners?

WHO ARE YOU?

Take your pick. You can be one of three mighty warriors:

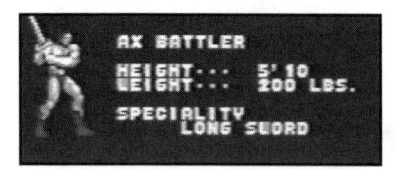

Ax-Battler is a powerful Barbarian. His mighty swings of the sword can fell the mighty enemies you face.

Tyris-Flare is an Amazon with a flashing blade and extra powerful magic abilities. She's nearly as strong a swordsperson as the Ax-Battler himself, but she's also faster.

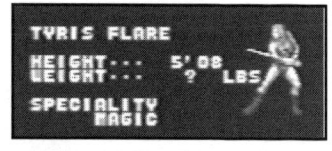

Gilius-Thunderhead is a strong, sturdy Dwarf whose flashing axe packs a lot of power. Gilius is also very fast and has the longest reach of all the heroes.

PLAYERS

Play Golden Axe with one or two players.

SCORING

The main goal of this game is to get to the end and defeat the final enemy. However, you do receive a rating at the end of the game which tells you about how you did (at least in the estimation of the programmers). As far as I am concerned, if you win the game, then you win the game. If you lose, then you have to try again. Don't you?

LIVES AND HOW TO LOSE THEM

You start out each game with three lives and three continues. That makes a total of nine lives (just like a cat). Use them wisely, for you'll surely need all of them.

You start each life with three to five health bars (depending on what you have chosen in the Option screen). Lose all of them and you lose one life. You can also lose a life by falling off certain parts of certain screens, so be careful where you walk.

CONTINUES

With three continues, you have a chance to make it...

WEAPONS?

Each hero comes equipped with his or her favorite weapon. Ax-Battler and Tyris-Flare both use a sword and Gilius-Thunderhead uses his axe. However, each character also has a specific magical ability that comes in very handy:

> **Ax-Battler** uses Volcano Magic to defeat his enemies.
> **Gilius-Thunderhead** has the weakest magic, though it does call down the Lightning on his opponents.
> **Tyris-Flare** has the most powerful magic. She rains fire down on those who would attack her.

Each character can charge up a certain amount of magic power. The strength of the spell they cast varies with the amount of magic power they have.

SPECIAL ITEMS

Getting special items.

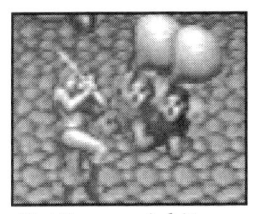

There are two special items that appear in this game. One is the magic Pot. To cast magic spells your heroes must have at least one of these magic Pots. The more you can collect (up to the maximum for that character) the stronger the spell you can cast.

The other special item is Meat, which can restore one bar of your health meter.

You obtain both Pots and Meat from thieves who appear at various points in the game. Kick or slash them to make them give you what they are carrying. Blue thieves carry magic Pots, and Green thieves carry Meat.

FRIENDS

In a two-player game, your partner is your only friend. The captives, when you free them, are friendly enough to tell you some important information, but otherwise, you're on your own.

Though not exactly friends, you can dismount certain enemies from their strange steeds and use the power of the mount to your advantage. These mounts (called Bizarrians) come in three varieties:

The **Chicken Leg** swings a mean tail and knocks the feet out from under you.

The **Blue Dragon** spits killer flame.

The **Red Dragon** shoots fireballs from its mouth.

Although these creatures are fitted with saddles, they are a bit wild still. You can ride them for a while, but eventually they'll split if you get dismounted too many times. And your enemies won't be content to let you ride in peace. They'll try to knock you off your saddle as fast as they can.

ENEMIES

Your enemies are a horrible crew of monsters, skeletons, giants, and magicians. It's lots of fun.

Each monster you face is rated for attack skill and movement. If you can win the game, you'll see a whole cast of characters. Each enemy race also comes in different colors. The colors can give you some clue about how difficult the enemy character will be. For instance, a Red Longmoan is more difficult than a purple one. On the other hand, there are the Dark characters. These appear to be made of some heavy substance like stone. Their weight is never listed, so we assume they are very heavy. Although they may not have as high a rating as another character, the Dark characters may be the toughest of all.. Here are the basic monsters you'll face:

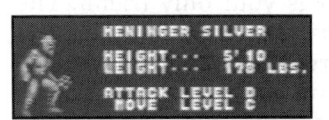

Heningers are club users. They come in several varieties: Silver, Purple, Red, Gold, Bronze, and Dark. Heningers are some of the easiest opponents you'll face. The Red Heninger is the most capable, with an Attack rating of A and a Move rating of B.

Golden Axe

Longmoans are another kind of club user who also come in several colors with varying abilities. The Red Longmoan is the most capable.

Some of your enemies will be deadly female warriors. They may not be built like giants, but they can waste you all the same. They sound like Russian ballerinas, but they dance with their weapons in hand. They are **Storchinaya** (purple), **Strobaya** (blue), **Lemanaya** (red), and **Gruziya** (dark). **Lemanaya** has the highest rating.

Skeletons are fast and very skillful. You may find that Skeletons give you lots of trouble at various points in your quest.

And then there are several types of giants: The **Bad Brothers** (blue), **Sgt. Malt and Sgt. Hop** (purple), and **General Heartland** (red) are all 8 foot tall giants who can bash you into the ground with their giant clubs.

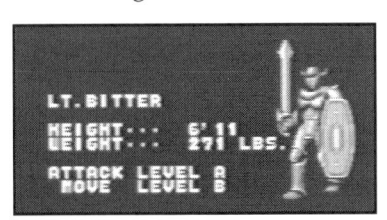

The sword-wielding knights in armor are the **Bitters**, (Lt. Bitter (silver), Colonel Bitter (red), and General Bitter (gold)). These guys only look like giants. After all, they're only 6' 11' tall. But think about it. That's still two inches taller than Magic Johnson. Their giant swords have a long reach. Don't get in their way.

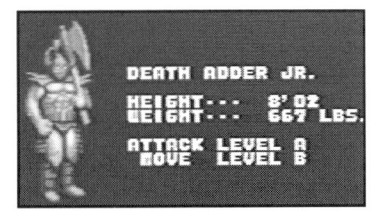

Finally, there's **Death Adder Jr.** and papa **Death Adder** himself. Not only will their slashing axe cut you to ribbons, but they cast nasty magic spells whenever they feel like it. And after Death Adder? Well...

CONTROLS

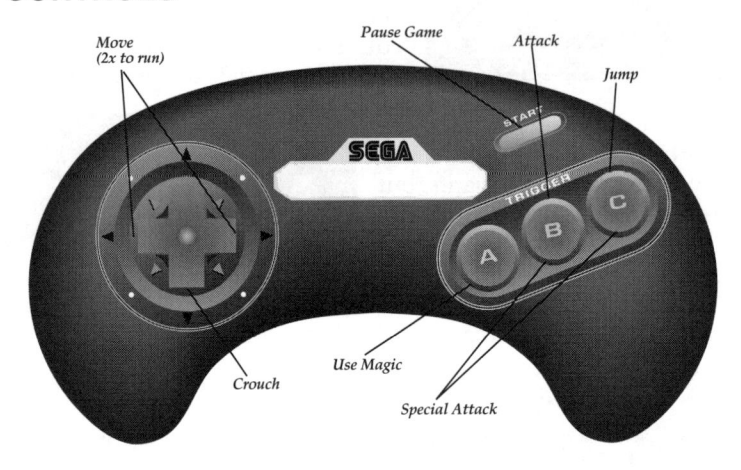

- Move (2x to run)
- Pause Game
- Attack
- Jump
- Crouch
- Use Magic
- Special Attack

One of the best aspects of Golden Axe is the great number of abilities your characters have. Each hero can deliver a wide variety of attacks, making this one of the most enjoyable hack'em slash'em type games.

As with other Mega Drive games, you can change the button assignments in the Option screen, but we'll talk about the default configuration (the one the game begins with if you don't change it).

List of Attacks:

Button B or **B (2x)**—Stab or slash once or twice (depending on distance from enemy).

B(3X)—
Special strong stab.
Poke weapon handle at a close monster.
Pick up near monster and throw it.

B(4X)—Poke close monster with your weapon handle.

B(5X)—Kick close monster.

Stab an enemy when he's down.

Press **Left** or **Right** twice quickly to start running. While running press **Button B** to attack with a head butt or flying kick (depending on the character).

Each character has a special move when you press **Buttons B** and **C**. Ax-Battler and Tyris-Flare both perform a powerful whirling slash with the sword. Gilius does a fancy somersault.

Tyris-Flare practices a spin move.

Another important move to master is the jump attack. Press **Button C** to jump and **B** to deliver a downward thrust with your weapon. The jumping attack can help get you out of a tight spot when you're surrounded by enemies.

GETTING STARTED

Before you start playing Golden Axe, you should know a few things. First, if you're going to play with two players, you want

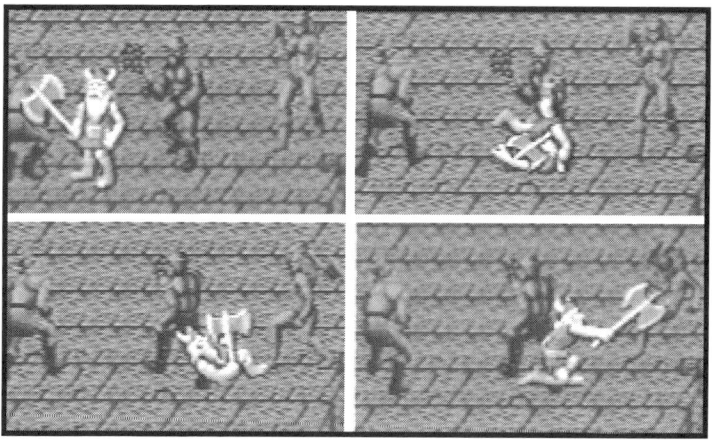

Surprise the enemy with a rolling attack.

to press Start on the second controller to tell the Mega Drive that you want the two-player game.

Next set the Options you want. You may want to make life easier at first and use the five-segment lifeline. Choose Exit when you finish selecting options.

Next, select the type of game you want to play:

The Duel allows you to fight against an increasingly difficult group of monsters to see how long you can last against them. This is great training. Or you can fight against a friend in a one-on-one battle.

The Arcade game takes you to the actual quest for the Golden Axe.

Finally, select the character you want to play. In a two-player game, each player must pick a different character. After picking your character, you're ready to start the game...

STRATEGY SESSION

General Strategies

You're probably anxious to start the quest and defeat Death Adder. But if you have the patience, you can get a lot of good experience in the Duel mode of this game. Here you can hone your skills and learn to master each of your techniques.

If you want to dive right into the adventure, however, there's no harm in trying. Remember that enemies only appear as you move forward. Once you've cleared an area, it's safe until you move on. At the beginning of the game, you're in a safe area. If you don't move too far forward, you can practice your moves unmolested. It's a good idea to get used to the timing of your techniques. Especially practice your jump attack and your special move.

Using the jump attack.

Be careful you don't press the Magic button by mistake! That will waste your magic powers and you'll have to wait to recharge them.

During the battles, don't get caught with an enemy on either side of you. They'll thrash you if you do. When you see you're about to be surrounded, do a jump attack to drive them off.

Another situation to avoid is more difficult to describe. There are places in the game where you may get cornered and you'll be unable to escape. You won't fall down, but you won't be able to attack either. If you're in a two-player game, ask your partner to come and help. Otherwise, you'll be pretty well wiped out.

When you get an enemy down, keep pressing the Attack button to do more damage. Finally, you'll either kick the enemy or pick it up and toss it. But be careful. Most enemies will come back for more.

Hit 'em high and low.

Some enemies are difficult to approach because they are fast and have a longer reach than you do. For instance, the Bitter soldiers have very long swords. Use a running attack to bash them down. The running attack isn't as strong as some, but you can often keep hitting an enemy with a jump kick or head butt again and again. Just as they get back to their feet, hit 'em again.

Look for special advantages. Death Adder's soldiers aren't usually very smart. You can fool some of them into falling off cliffs. That saves a lot of wear and tear on you. In other cases, you may be able to attack an enemy from below where he can't hit you. Also, use the Bizarrians when you can, but be very careful. In many cases, as soon as you get on the beast, one of the other enemies will knock you off again. They don't like the idea of being burned by a dragon's flame. Wonder why?

In two-player games, learn to use teamwork. You CAN hit each other. So stay out of each other's way. The best way is if you each take an area of the screen to fight in. Of course, enemy soldiers may all attack one player, in which case, you'll need all the help you can get.

Stage 1: The Woods.

You don't get to take more than a few steps along the way when... BAM! Some of Death Adder's minions. The Silver Heningers are pretty easy, but they're just a warm-up. Beat them and the purple characters who come

The attack of the killer drumstick?

The Bad Bros. eat some low-level fire magic.

after them, and you meet your first thief. Collect his magic by poking him. If you have Tyris-Flare in your party, let her charge up the magic. Hers is the most powerful, but at its sixth level of power, it needs six magic Pots.

Move on and get the Chicken Leg if you can. But don't worry about it if you don't get it. The Chicken Leg's tail thrash isn't all that spectacular and you can do just fine without it.

When you get to the outskirts of Turtle Village, you'll fight a couple more Heningers while the Bad Bros. stand by watching. The Bad Bros. won't step in until you've disposed of the Heningers—unless you attack them first. However, once you start fighting them, try to stay away from their hammers. The Bad Bros. will use all sorts of techniques. You can beat them with running attacks, though. Knock them down with a running attack, then hit them when they're still on one knee. They're helpless until they get back to their feet.

After you beat the Bad Bros., you've earned a rest. But watch out for that thief. Get some more magic before continuing your journey.

Stage 2: Turtle Village.

Defeat the first Heninger using running attacks and pinning him to the edge of the screen. Or send him and his buddy flying off the edge of the cliff just behind you. Then proceed into the village. But watch your back. You'll be attacked from both sides.

Right after you see the children running, you'll encounter a Blue Dragon. Get it if you can and burn your enemies. However,

Two ways to get rid of Heningers.

you'll have to be quick, or they'll get it back. The Storchinayas are fast on their feet, so you'll need to be faster.

Next, get the magic from the thief. He's hiding among the fleeing children. Now you'll meet another Heninger and some Strobayas. Beat them and along come a couple of Lemanayas with a Red Dragon and a Skeleton for company. If you can get on that dragon, you'll be able to take care of business with no muss, no fuss. Next, another opportunity to collect magic as more thieves appear.

Stage 3: The Crossing.

You're on the back of a turtle. You knew that, right? And now you'll have to cross over to the land. First fight off a small group and get their Blue Dragon. The Dragon can help you a lot in the next part of this stage.

Be careful when you jump the gap ahead. Jump at the last minute to make sure you make it, or practice a technique you'll need later. Tap the direction key twice and then tap the attack key to jump the gap. With a running start, a short jump like this is a breeze.

Ride 'em, axe man.

Collect more magic, then move onward to meet more adversaries. Right away, you'll run into some more Amazon women. If you have the dragon, use it. If not, you'll just have to fight your way past them. Move forward very slowly and you'll see a door with the word DEB. written above it. Sgt. Malt and Sgt. Hop will come out of there. If you ride the dragon along the wall, you can blast these two giants and never give them a chance to get near you. They'll try to rush you, but a bit of hot dragon breath will cool their jets (to mix metaphors outrageously). Of course, if you don't have the dragon, just use your best giant killing techniques.

More screaming children and more magic are followed by some gold Heningers and Longmoans. Before long, however, you'll meet Lt. Bitter, the first armored giant in the quest. Running attacks work pretty well. He may get you with his giant sword a few times, but you should be able to beat him. If you're feeling insecure, use magic. There's lots of it available once you beat Lt. Bitter.

Try an aerial attack.

Stage 4: Going to Eagle Island.

Well, you were in a village on the back of a turtle, so why not an island on the back of an eagle? Look out for the Red Heningers and Longmoans. They attack from behind. Take care of them and continue forward.

Here is a place where you can get caught, unable to move. But be careful. You're on an eagle, remember. Don't fall off the edge of the screen, or it's one life less.

Once you finish with the red guys, continue forward. Be on guard, though. A skeleton will appear from the ground behind

Trapped! Tyris tries to rescue Gilius, but takes a dive instead.

you. Skeletons are quick, so you'll have to bash them with any technique that works. Take care of the second skeleton before moving on. If you trap him on the upper level, you can sometimes beat on him from below, and he can't hit you back. That's fair play, isn't it?

The action heats up at the end of this stage. But you've got lots of magic if you need it.

Get some magic before you go on, then fight the Dark Heninger. Be careful moving forward. Two more Dark characters are waiting to attack. Then the message will tell you to go on. Immediately you'll be attacked by another Skeleton and another Dark Heninger. These guys just seem to be getting tougher and tougher, don't they?

Even tougher still are the two Skeletons and the Dark Longmoan who appear next. Will they never stop coming?

Somebody gave these guys some extra energy or something, because they really go to town on you. A little magic might help, though, because there are some thieves waiting for you if you can beat this last crew.

Stage 5: To the Palace.

Time to get off the eagle and get serious. But not before battling three more Skeletons, and these guys seem to be even tougher than the ones before.

Walk very slowly across the narrow causeway. You may be able to jump the Lemanaya on the Blue Dragon before she's

A surprise attack may earn you a fiery ride.

ready to attack you. Then you can get the dragon and really do some damage.

Perfect teamwork in action!

Get past the Lemanaya and there are some Red Heningers and Longmoans to defeat. They're followed by two Col. Bitters. Use your running and jumping attacks on the Bitters. And try to stay out of sword range. Use magic if you want. At the beginning of the next stage, there are several thieves to stock up your magic supplies.

Stage 6: The Palace Gates.

Once you collect the magic from the thieves in front of the gates, you'll meet two pals—a Red Heninger and a Longmoan. They're travelling with General Heartland, the toughest of the giants. His hammer flashes down on you pretty fast, so keep your distance. He'll succumb to some good running attacks. Remember, get him before he can get back up.

Cut the General down to size.

Well, that wasn't so hard, was it? So now you're ready for a good fight, right? Are you ready for two more skeletons and Death Adder Jr.? Sure you are. Treat them to a little dose of Flame Magic if you've got it. That will toast them to a crisp. All except Junior, who is a good deal tougher than anyone you've met so far. Treat him as you do the giants. Hit him when he's down. Constant running attacks, hitting him when he's still on one knee will do him in eventually. Don't let him cast any of his own magic spells, though. If you hit him just as he's about to cast a spell, you can stop the spell before it does anything.

But don't aim too high.

Junior is ready to rumble!

Once you've defeated Junior, you've freed the King and his daughter. But they'll tell you you're not done yet. These nice people send you to certain doom inside the palace dungeons. Oh well. Nobody told you it would be easy being a hero.

Tyris-Flare casts Fire Magic to soften up Junior.

Stage 7: The Palace Dungeon.

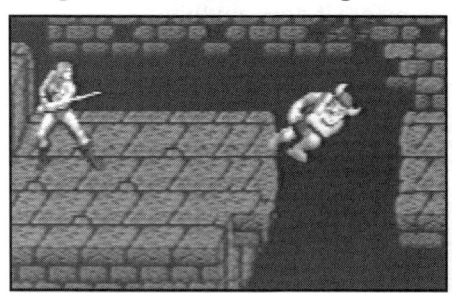

It's a long way down. Don't get careless.

As soon as you enter the dungeon, you're attacked from behind. Maneuver yourself so you get your enemies' backs to the hole and knock them into it. Now look at that gap in the floor! Don't just try to jump it. Play it safe and use your running attack to get across. And watch out that you don't jump and hit your partner or another enemy coming from the other side, or you'll have a long way to fall.

Once you're safely on the other side, defeat the Skeleton there and proceed. See that area that goes down to the front of the screen? It has no walls. Lure your enemies out of their hiding places and then walk down there. The Skeletons will simply fall off the edge. Then knock the dark enemies off the edges to make the fight short and sweet. But don't go over the edge yourself! Learn to dodge a running attack and watch your attacker fall into the blackness.

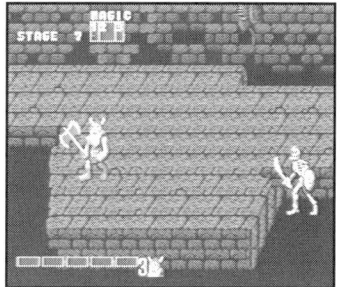

More attackers await you. Try to get behind them and knock them over the edge. You're going to need all your strength and all your lives, so don't fight any more than you have to. Keep on fighting and going ever forward. Get the magic after you take care of the dark soldiers. You're almost there. Just don't give up yet. The worst is yet to come, anyway.

Now you're in the Palace courtyard. Look out for the statues that come to life. Move down the screen to use the drop behind, and you'll make short work of this crew and the two General Bitters who appear next. Easy, isn't it?

Some statues can't keep still.

You thought it was easy, did you say? Well get ready for the most difficult encounter of all. Now you get to meet the Death Bringer. Not only does his flashing axe move like lightning... not only do his two Skeleton companions never die... not only that, but he also casts the wickedest magic spells every time he knocks you down. The best secret is not to let him knock you down. Barring that, come with plenty of lives left over.

To defeat Death Bringer, use any magic you have. Then concentrate on attacking him

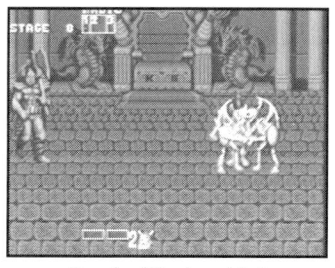

Looks like trouble!

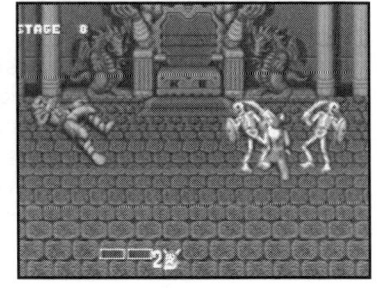

Try some magic?.....   *I think it helped... a little.*

without getting hit. You'll have to beat off the Skeletons, but don't bother trying to kill them. They just don't go away. If your timing is good, though, you can use the running attack the way you did on the other giant characters, but this guy is pretty fast, so you'll have to move even faster to succeed. Jumping attacks are also effective because you can keep the Skeletons away at the same time.

Death Bringer can cast all kinds of magic.

If you defeat Death Bringer, you've earned a reward. So stick around and watch the closing credits. They're worth a few minutes. Then check out how you rated in your game.

SHH... THE SECRETS

Golden Axe is a game that's lots of fun to play, whether you win or not. However, for those who can't make it to the end, there are some secrets that might help. The easiest is to start a two-player game and then kill off the second player, taking all his or her lives. Once the second player screen reads "Game Over," you'll have added an extra continue to Player One. That's three extra lives.

If you really can't get to the end, even with that trick, though, there's still a way. It's ultra top secret, though, so don't breathe a word. And don't read this if you want to keep the challenge of Golden Axe:

To select any level in the game, hold the B button and Start while pressing diagonally down and left on the pad. A number appears in the upper left corner of the screen. The direction pad selects the level number. Then press Start to begin playing.

CHAPTER 8

Insector X

Distributor: Taito
Game Type: Arcade Action

WHAT'S GOING ON?

Would you like to be treated like an insect? The Bagroids are getting sick and tired of it. The fact that they are insects doesn't seem to make any difference. They foresee a world of insects—ruled by insects, for insects! And they've already begun to realize their plan.

Enter the Insectors, a race of super-small humans. All but one of the Insectors has been killed by the Bagroids. Kait is the last Insector left. Realizing that he is Earth's only hope, he has donned the mechanical wings that his race once used for transport. He is now—Insector X!

WHO ARE YOU?

Kait, champion of the Insectors and of the Earth! You're small, but smart!

PLAYERS

There's only one Insector left.

SCORING

Kait racks up points by shooting Bagroids and collecting any items they drop. You get large bonuses for finishing each of the five levels.

LIVES AND HOW TO LOSE THEM

Start with anywhere from one to five Kaits, depending on what you select on the Option Screen. If you're hit by an enemy or an enemy's fire, you will lose a life. Run out of lives, and it's on to the Continue option below.

CONTINUES

When you continue, you'll start from (more or less) where you reached on the current level. You can continue three times.

CONTROLS

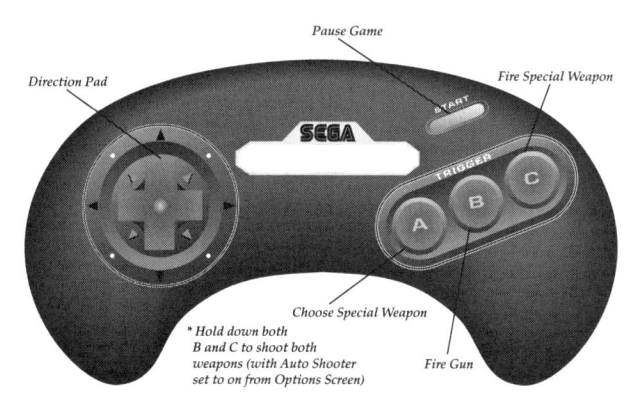

Pause Game
Direction Pad
Fire Special Weapon
Choose Special Weapon
Fire Gun

* Hold down both B and C to shoot both weapons (with Auto Shooter set to on from Options Screen)

WEAPONS

There are several weapons for the benefit of Mr. Kait:

The **P symbol** powers up Kait's gun, which gets stronger and covers a larger area of the screen as it gains power!

The **Insect Head** symbol equips Kait with the Special Weapon. You toggle between the two modes of the Weapon by pressing Button A.

The **Lightning Bolt** symbol is a bomb that will destroy every enemy on the screen! Being a Special Weapon, you select this with Button A as well. It has an effect on Bosses, but doesn't destroy them.

The **Red Mode** is a laser, similar to the gun. It is usually more powerful!
The **Blue Mode** drops bombs.

The more powerful Kait's gun is, the more powerful the Special Weapons will be. With all the insect enemies you'll face, you're gong to want a full-power gun as often as possible.

SPECIAL ITEMS

The **S** symbol is a Speed-Up; take this to speed up Kait's movements around the screen.
The **1000** symbol is not surprisingly worth 1,000 points!
The **1-Up** symbol gets you an extra life when you grab it. So grab it!
The **?** symbol is a mystery!

FRIENDS

None, unfortunately. That's why you're out for revenge!

ENEMIES

The Bagroids may know how to destroy a planet, but they don't have very good imaginations. Only the Bosses are named—and they are called Insect Bosses! Your other enemies may not have names, but they are out to destroy you!

STRATEGY SESSION
General Strategies

Rule number one: DON'T fly over to the right to grab Power-Ups! Let them float over to you. You should be at the far left of the screen about 95% of the time. If you're not, you're not playing smart, because the waves of insects will sometimes attack from the right so fast that you won't have any time to react.

Turn the Auto Shooter on; otherwise, you'll wear out your controller AND your fingers. And be sure to use the Option Screen to your advantage when you first start playing the game.

Round One—Desert Area

The first waves of Bagroids will be small Moths that attack in single file from the right side of the screen. Move up and down to catch both lines of Moths in your gun's laser-stream. A Large Moth will appear later on; these Moths carry Power-Ups. The

Insector X

Destroy the Laser Moth to get a Power-Up.

Power-Up you receive depends on your current Power-Up status; it should be a P symbol this time.

The next Moth will arrive with a head-mounted gun!!! This type of Moth takes lots of hits. Keep firing at it, and when it returns fire, fly above it. Get rid of it before the small Moths return, or you'll have to dodge all kinds of fire! A Large Moth will appear soon after this Gun Moth; this should give an S symbol to speed you up.

You should be in the trees now. The lake below you contains Fish that will emerge from the water to spit bullets at you! If you only have a single laser, you won't be able to shoot them when they're submerged. If necessary, fly down to water level and let them have it before they can shoot at you.

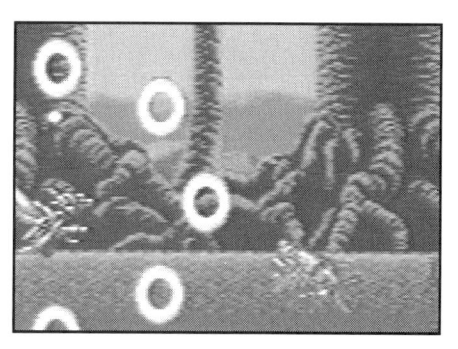

A Gun Moth will appear when you're almost past the water; then another Large Moth will appear when you're just past the water. Power up! Shoot the next few waves of small Moths and you'll come to a door. Kait will fly inside automatically.

The first attack is a wave of Laser Moths! These guys fly slowly, firing Lasers right at you! If your gun is powered up to the point where its fire is spreading, you won't have to dodge their lasers. Otherwise, you'll have to dodge and weave madly if you want to shoot all the Moths. A safer strategy is to stay toward the bottom of the screen, keeping one or two rows of Moths clear while the others fly harmlessly over you. One of the later Moths in the wave has a Power-Up, and then there will also be two Large Moths to follow. So if you haven't powered up at this point, now's your chance!

Two Gun Moths will appear, and Laser Moths will also attack! Stay at the extreme left and you can dodge their fire easily. Another Power-Up appears during their attack.

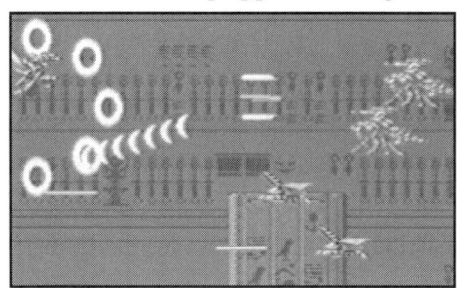

You should now see some Mushrooms. These fungoids fire Lasers diagonally. Fly right up to them, hugging the ground, and fire away. Get ready to do the same thing for the rest of this tunnel, because you'll run into several more Mushrooms. A few Laser Moths will appear as well, but you will get them if you're getting the Mushrooms.

Now the small Moths will return. Are you wearing a bug light or what? After you blast your way past a row of four Mushrooms, hug the ground again and blast away at the Snails that will

Insector X

appear. You'll have to fly upwards a couple of times to shoot the small Moths.

When you reach a wall with three large guys holding even larger swords, the Insect Boss has arrived! It looks like something that you don't want to find in your garden, doesn't it? The Boss Bug will slowly come onto the screen from the right. Its head is its vulnerable spot, so shoot at it.

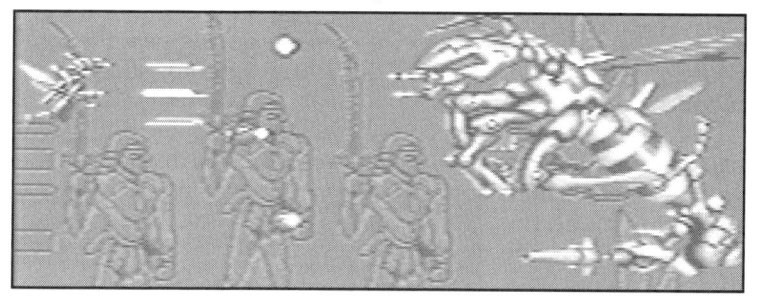

When the gun on the Boss' head starts to glow, it's getting ready to fire. When it does, a spread of three bullets comes out. Dodge between the upper two bullets. This way, you'll hit the head even while you're dodging.

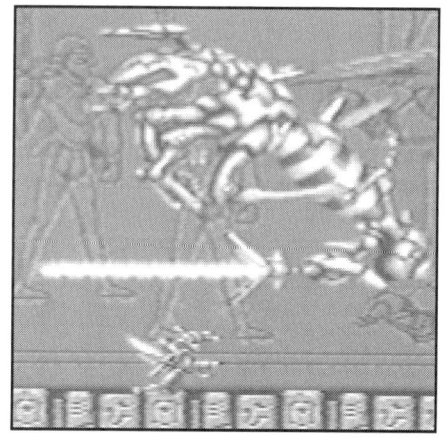

When its tail comes to life (the Laser Stinger), QUICKLY fly to the bottom of the screen and underneath the Boss, because it's going to come to the left. Then hang out behind it while it's at the left side of the screen. When it starts moving back to the right, fly back in front of it and start shooting again. Repeat this pattern, and he'll be exterminated soon!

Round Two—Plateau Area

The Bagroids are cruel; they've sent Ladybugs to attack you! War is hell, though, so shoot them (they attack in a zig-zag formation, so shoot between the zig and the zag). The small Moths are also here, and being their usual pesky selves.

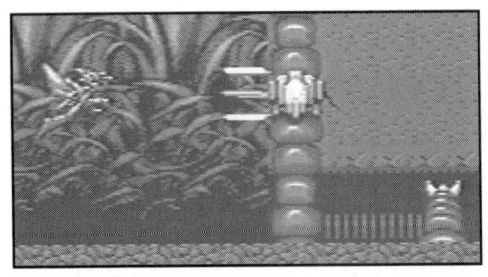

A Large Moth will appear just past the first wall you fly past. Then you'll see huge red things wiggling in the ground. These are the Borers. There's a trick to getting past them (of course). When a Borer comes out of the ground, shoot at its robotic middle. Boom!

Not much of a trick, you say? Well, the first three Borers will come out in time for you to shoot them. The fourth one, though, won't come out until it's almost all the way to the left side of the screen—not enough time for you to do anything! So fly past the Borer until it comes up. Then you can safely return to the left.

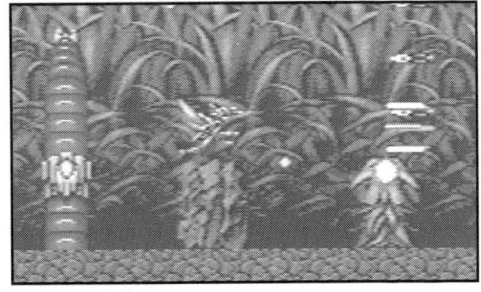

Shoot the two Flowers just past the Borers; their spores are very painful! A Large Moth (and hence a Power-Up) will appear after them. Then it's the return of the Ladybugs. Shoot straight at them! It's all you can do, after all.

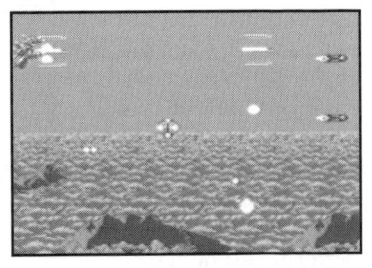

Just before the grass comes to an end and you reach the sky, a Spore Moth will arrive. This guy is similar to the Gun Moth, except he takes more punishment and shoots more rapidly! Use the same "dodge-above-the-bullets" technique and you'll get rid of him. He'll leave behind the Special Weapon symbol! Take it and start holding down Button C immediately. Check out that extra firepower!

Insector X

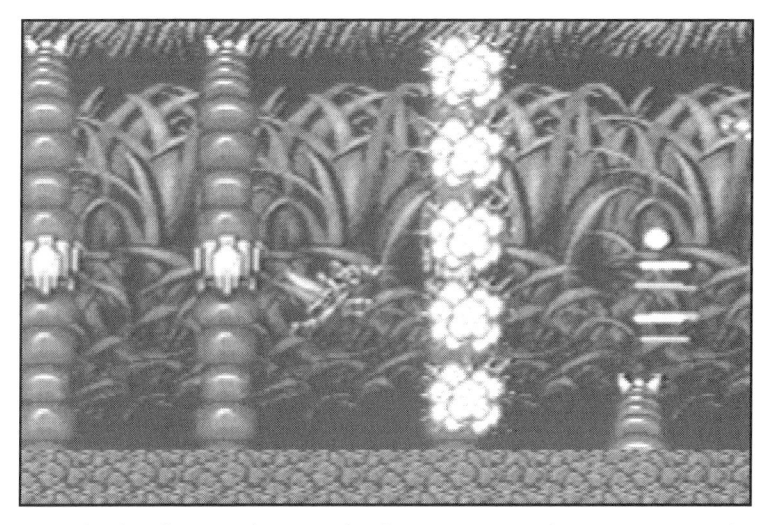

The landscape changes back to grass, and some extremely tricky Borers appear. Fly past the first two, but stay behind the third one. The first two will spring up, then the third. Shoot! Quick! Then fly between the next two and wait for the fourth and fifth to pop up. You'll be destroying the fifth one.

Back in the sky; you'll encounter three Large Moths. One of them will drop the Lightning Bolt symbol. Take it. These small Moths are getting a lot peskier, huh? And faster!

Stay toward the bottom of the screen. Why? A Bomber Moth will soar from the left side of the screen! Fly back up and attack. Two more Large Moths will appear; one should have a 1-Up token. Now hang out towards the top of the screen, because a Bomber Moth will soar from the bottom left.

Two Spore Moths will attack with the Ladybugs; concentrate on the Moths. Two Large Moths appear after that. More Borers? Stay to the left of the first; shoot it; fly between the second and third; shoot the third. Did you make it? Sure you did. That's why the Boss is here to make sure you don't make it any further!

This Boss' weakness is his body; but his head has a cannon that fires straight ahead. If your weapons don't fire with a spread, this is going to be tough. It's tough anyway!

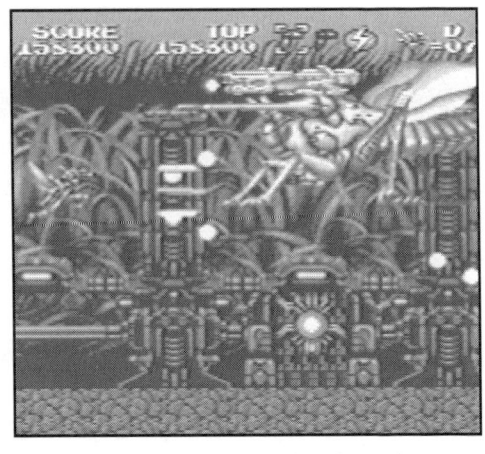

Stay at the upper-left of the screen. Let the Grasshopper jump at you. Sometimes when he jumps, he'll stop firing until he either lands or reaches the top of his jump. This is when you want to strike. You can also dodge between the head's bullets, but this is more dangerous. It's up to you; just keep in mind that both techniques still take a while to destroy the Boss.

Round Three—City Area

A big clock! What time is it? Time for you to whip more Bagroids!

This round starts out simply; small Moths that you've blasted before (and will blast again). Two Large Moths appear after them. But are you ready for the Spheres? These electrified balls don't shoot, but they'll absorb laser fire better used on the

Insector X

Laser Moths that will be attacking. Your dodging skills had better be good!

We'll stop mentioning the Large Moths at this point; you should know to shoot every one you see. Okay? Okay! Your next attackers are three huge Locusts. Their bullets zig-zag with the Locusts' movements! Spheres will also appear while you're shooting at the Locusts. Stay above them, as with all the firing Bagroids.

If you manage to get all the Locusts, an Insect Head will drop. You'll need it! A few small Moths later, you'll arrive at a hole. Kait, let's go inside!

The Large Moth is the first thing you see; then you'll see a Crab swimming in the purple liquid below you. Handle this Crab like the Fish; zoom down and shoot him! The Spider will appear next; hug the roof as you shoot it to avoid its spread of bullets.

A few Mushrooms will appear; hug the tunnel as you shoot them and their lasers won't clip your wings. There will be a short interlude with some small Moths, and then you'll fly down a long Mushroom tunnel. Keep firing, whatever you do!

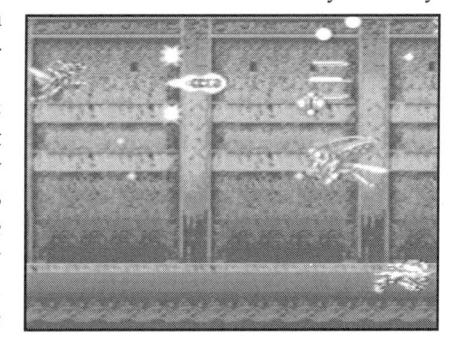

Next are four Crabs; then a Mushroom that you can't immediately shoot. Dodge between its lasers (it will fire three before it pauses). Now two Locusts will arrive. Stay toward the top of the screen as you fight them; this will make it easier to dodge the incredible number of bullets that will be on the screen, fired from the Spiders and Crabs. A Lightning Bolt may be required here.

You'll now be flying down another narrow tunnel; shoot the Laser Moths. When you emerge from the tunnel, the Insect Boss will arrive.

Its head is the weak spot. Concentrate your fire on it. Dodge between the white bullets it shoots; don't get in front of its head or the cannonfire will take you out! When it comes towards the left side of the screen, don't panic! Keep firing and get ready to dodge a bit faster.

This Boss is the strongest yet; keep firing and you'll win!

Round Four—Jungle Area

The foliage is thick, but the Bagroids will be thicker. If you've had problems up to now, you'll be having fits in this round.

You'll start out under siege from Fish and Ladybugs. The Ladies will be attacking in a much larger formation; without a spread weapon, you won't make it past them unless you're very lucky. The Fish also require a Power-Up of some kind to be taken out quickly.

About this time, the Zigzag Moth will appear. It shoots double lasers that zigzag (hence the name) at you! Stay above it;

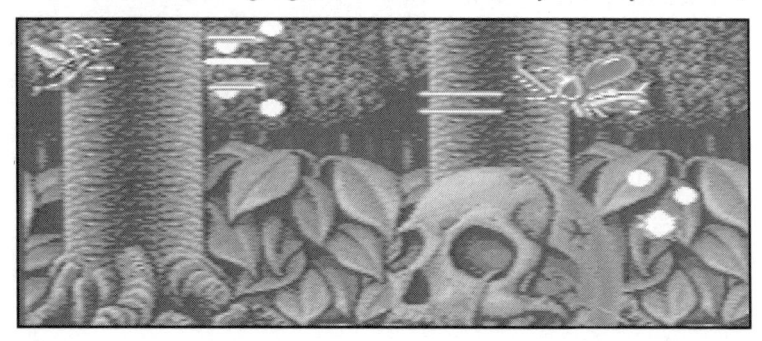

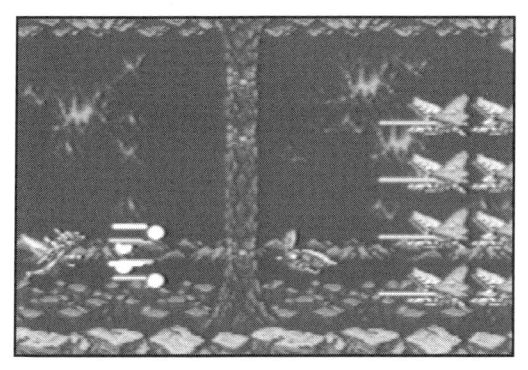

It's a major bug brigade!

you know this by now! After it are some Ants; they march along the ground slowly, but take a ton of punishment. Get low and fire until you can't.

You'll fly over a pond with some Fish and small Moths, then reach land again. Ladybugs will attack again; you'd think they would have learned by now not to attack you!

Now two Zigzag Moths will arrive. This sequence is extremely difficult; there's no one position on the screen that's safe. Staying low will help, but not much. Lightning reflexes are your only hope to make it safely past the Moths and to the hive.

Laser Moths introduce you to this humble abode. The Spiders will now spin webs and drop down to attack! And there's a new enemy—the Frog. It will spin to attack you if you fly past it, so you must shoot it to be safe. Stay toward the bottom of the hive to make this easier.

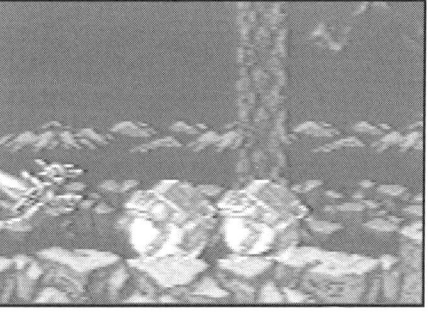

I thought frogs ate bugs!

A Zigzag Moth will attack; but you'll have to stay toward the bottom of the screen to shoot the Frogs. Dodge back and forth at the bottom of the hive. You'll soon reach a cave.

Each of these caves will have some Spiders and Frogs inside it; you'll be attacked by Laser Moths as well. Fly in the middle of the screen; with a spread weapon, you can take out Spidey and Froggy without putting yourself in peril. But get ready to dodge the Moths at any moment!

When you arrive at an extremely large spider web, you've arrived at the next Insect Boss. It's a huge spider, of course!

Believe it or not, stay in the middle of the screen. You'll only have to make very small movements to avoid the spider's bullets. But here's the catch; sometime during its attack, it will bound to the left side of the screen. You must VERY quickly dodge under it until it returns to the right. The attack is almost instantaneous, so be on your toes.

This Boss seems less tough than some of the others; if you keep shooting, you'll only have to dodge a pounce once or twice before the spider is chowder.

Round Five—Their Empire

All right, Mr. Kait. This is it. Are you ready? Yes? Good! Let's go!

You'll start out in the honeycomb tunnel. Small Moths are your only attackers; while they're speedier, they're still easily killed. Stay toward the middle and zoom up or down as you need to.

Once you come out of the tunnel, the Moths will start to come from the top and bottom of the screen. Still not that bad, right? Oh, it gets worse. A little more flying and you'll stop—you're heading into the next part of the Empire.

The start of this portion is ultra-difficult. A Spread-Gun Moth is your new enemy; it fires five bullets at once! You can

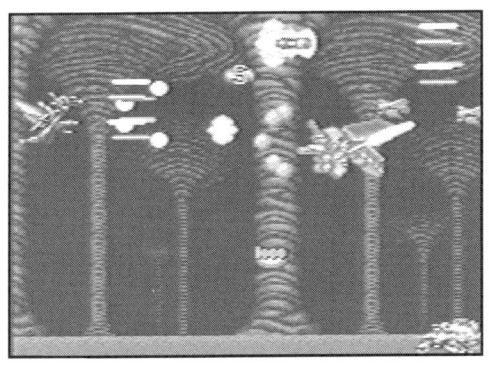

Insector X

dodge between two bullets, but it's often safer just to dodge all of them by flying under them. There are also Crabs on the floor of this cavern. If you have the Special Weapon (and if you don't, you're in serious trouble), you should switch to the Blue Weapon and bombard the ground. This way, you only have to worry about your airborne opponents.

If—I mean when—you destroy the Moth, he'll leave behind an Insect Head. Where was it before?!? Oh well. Take it and you'll be arriving at a tunnel. Kait will go inside, brave guy that he is.

This tunnel will have a few Spheres, but they're easy. The three Spiders are not. Dodging between their fire is difficult at best; try jumping from Spider to Spider, hanging out underneath each one. If you stay at the bottom of the screen, you'll have to dodge the fire of all three. Pass them somehow and two Spread-Gun Moths appear! How nice! Stay toward the top of the screen as you fire. Beat them and you'll be headed into more tunnels.

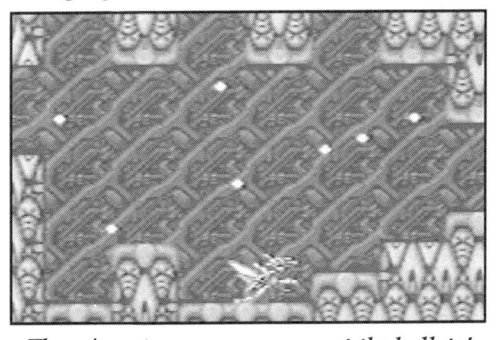

These insects can sure pump out the bullets!

Those walls that look like they're formed with arrowheads don't fire at you; but they take a lot of laser fire to destroy. So get as close as you can to them, to do maximum damage. Pass about half the walls, and three Frogs will be behind a ledge so that you can't shoot them! Fly past them in between volleys of bullets and stay low, so they can't hit you. Make it and you're off to the final battle!

Stay at the bottom of the screen. There will be too many airborne attackers to dodge. At the bottom of the screen, all you have to do is shoot the Snails and dodge the occasional bullet. The Spread-Gun Moths almost never get bullets down to your level.

Here it is! The final Insect Boss! You can destroy him with your own technique, or use the one in The Secrets. But choose quickly! The Earth depends on you!

SHH...
THE SECRETS

How do I defeat the final Insect Boss? His weakness is his chest.

Insector X

His arms will cover it half of the time, and not cover it the other half. So concentrate on that area! The pods he shoots in the air are easy to dodge if you know their attack pattern, which is this: Most of them fly high into the air before dropping down, but the occasional pod shoots horizontally at you. Dodge the pods upwards and to the left so that you stay in firing range of the Boss' belly.

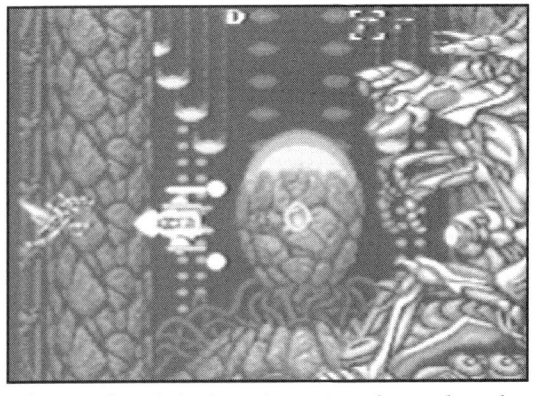

When his belly starts to glow, that means he's getting ready to fire his laser! Dodge up, because it's a big one! He'll take a LOT of laser fire, but he'll be beaten. Don't give up!

Special Note: We based this chapter on a preliminary version of Insector X. It is possible that the game will change slightly before it comes out. Most of what we have written should remain accurate, however.

CHAPTER 9

Michael Jackson Moonwalker

Distributor: Sega of America
Game Type: Arcade Action

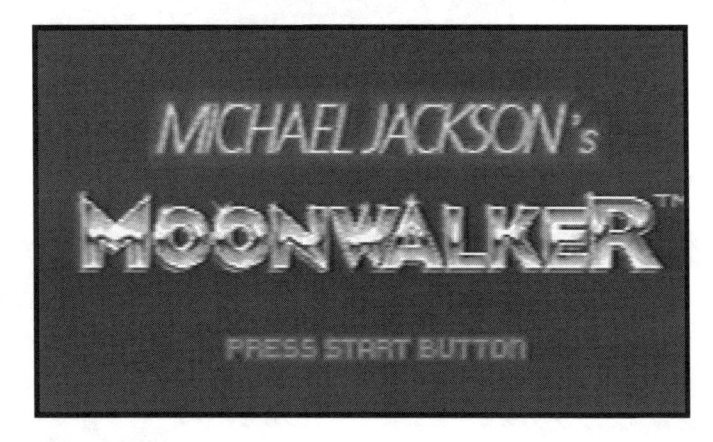

WHAT'S GOING ON?

Oooo! It's Michael Jackson. In a video game? Yes. Michael has been digitized and now resides somewhere in the silicon chips of your Moonwalker game cartridge. He's spinning and dancing his way right onto your screen.

Of course we all know Michael. He's the ultimate performer, and his string of hit songs, his videos, and his amazing dance talents have won him the love and loyalty of millions of fans, young and old.

Now the evil Mr. Big has captured a bunch of Michael's young fans, the fans that give Michael his energy and strength. Michael must rescue his fans from a variety of hidden locations, defeating Mr. Big's henchmen along the way. And if Michael frees all the hostages, he'll take on Mr. Big himself!

Michael's adventure takes him through six levels of action. As he explores each level, he listens to some of his most popular songs. And so do you.

WHO ARE YOU?

Michael Jackson! You've got to dance your way past Mr. Big's defenses, using every move in your repertoire! You'll beat Mr. Big, but you'll do it with style!

PLAYERS

One or two players can play. With two players, you alternate turns, with each player taking his turn when the other player loses a life. The first player's Michael is dressed in a perfectly tailored white suit. The second wears a salmon outfit (for those fashion buffs out there).

SCORING

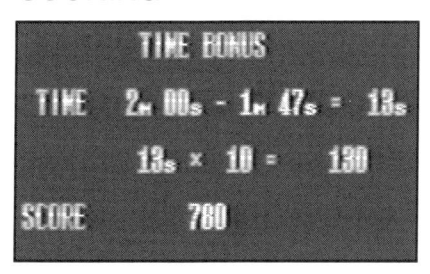

You gain points by beating Mr. Big's henchmen. The higher the difficulty level and the more advanced your dance move, the more points you'll score.

You also receive a Time Bonus at the end of each level. You have to finish the level quickly, though. For every extra second that you beat the time limit by, you'll gain ten points.

LIVES AND HOW TO LOSE THEM

Begin with three lives. You have a Power Bar at the bottom of the screen, and you lose Power when you execute spinning attacks, or when you're hit by any of Mr. Big's henchmen.

The Power Bar shows one of three colors to indicate your current strength. If the Bar is Blue, your attacks will be their most powerful. If the Bar is Yellow, your attacks will be less powerful. If the Bar is Red, your attacks will be weak and short-ranged. If you run out of power, you lose one of Michael's lives.

Michael regains some of his Power every time he finds and rescues a child.

CONTINUES

If you lose all your lives, you can continue from the start of the last level you reached. You can continue three times.

CONTROLS

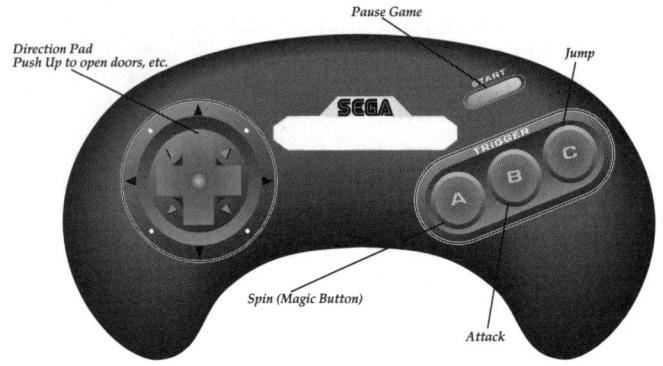

- Direction Pad — Push Up to open doors, etc.
- Pause Game
- Jump
- Spin (Magic Button)
- Attack

Use the Option Screen to change the configuration.

WEAPONS

Michael's got lots of ways to beat the bad guys. When you press the attack button, Michael has several attacks. If the Power Bar is blue or yellow, Michael's aura expands from his hand or foot, adding to the range and power of the attack. The lower the Power Bar, the weaker the attack.

If he's standing up, Michael will kick.

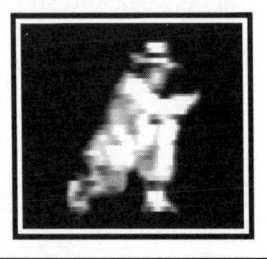

If you push up on the control pad, Michael will thrust his hand into the air.

If he's jumping and attacking, Michael will throw his hand out to the side.

If he's ducking, Michael will "shoot" at an enemy with his hand!

Michael has a few other special moves, too.

If he's on the stairs in Level One, he can slide down them, at the same time ridding himself of baddies unlucky enough to be on the stairs at the time.

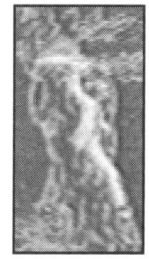

On Level Three, Michael can launch himself at high speed off the branches, blasting his way through any zombies in his path.

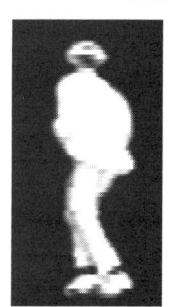

Tap on the Magic Button and Michael spins away anyone nearby.

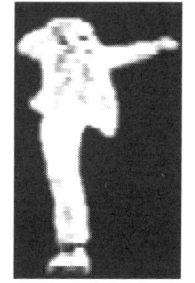

Hold down the button for a moment and he'll throw his hat. The longer you hold the button, the farther he throws his hat (and the more power the move will use).

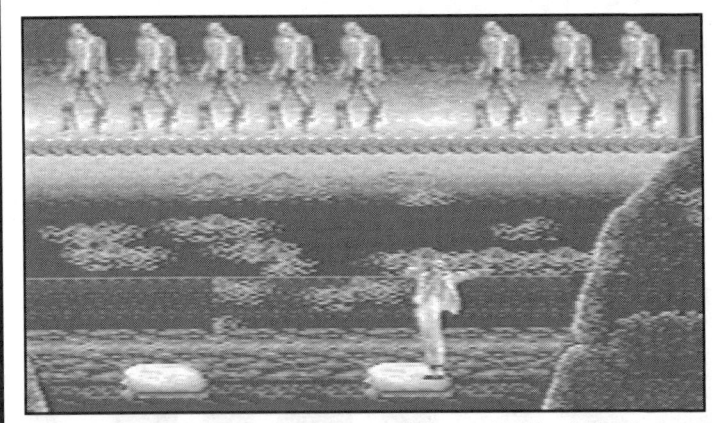

If you hold down the button without releasing it (and if you have enough energy), Michael starts the High-Power Dance. Anyone on the screen will start dancing with him and will drop from exhaustion! The dance Michael executes depends on the level he's on.

Finally, if Michael catches a Shooting Star, he'll transform into a Robot! Then he can fly, shoot lasers, and even launch missiles! This power only lasts for a short while. Also, even though he can see the captured kids, Robot Michael can't rescue them.

SPECIAL ITEMS

Besides the Shooting Stars, Michael is the most special item. However, there are a few other surprises—the folding stairs in Level One, for instance, or the manholes on Level 2.

Michael can also use some objects as weapons. If he kicks a chair or garbage can, he'll get any bad guys within range.

FRIENDS

Michael's friends have been kidnaped by Mr. Big! That's what this is all about. You've got to help Michael rescue them!

ENEMIES

Each level presents a different array of foes for Michael to defeat.

Level One

The **Gangsters** dance around, trying to knock Michael out.
The **Pool Players** wave a broken cue at Michael!
The **Dancing Girls** grab Michael and stop him.
The **Cat** pounces out of windows.

Level Two

Hoodlums hang around and cause trouble.
Dobermans attack Michael with razor-sharp teeth.
Militia Hitmen wear helmets and carry riot guns!
In one round, the **White Dog** and its pack will attack.

Level Three

>Zombies rise from the grave to thrill you.
>Redbirds roost and wait patiently to bite you!

Level Four

>Spiders are eight-legged web-makers!
>Stalactites fall from the ceilings.
>There are also more Militia Hitmen and Zombies just to keep life interesting.

Level Five

>Homing Lasers fire at you from the ceiling.
>Dangerous Sparks run along electrical wire.
>More Militia Hitmen. In fact, lots more.
>A whole company of Soldiers will appear at the end.

Level Six

>The Showdown! It's just Michael and Mr. Big.

STRATEGY SESSION
General Strategies

Conserving your energy is important. This means that you shouldn't use your Magic too much. The regular attacks are enough to keep almost everything at bay.

When Mr. Big appears at the end of a round, don't touch him! You can't hurt him, but he'll really deplete your energy. When it's time to take on Mr. Big, you'll know.

Search everything! Mr. Big has hidden the children in all kinds of places. Windows, car trunks, tombstones, you name it.

Club 30
Music: Smooth Criminal

Round 1-1. Michael gets the music started, but you have to do the rest. This first level will introduce you to the Gangsters and the Dancing Girls. Some of the children are on the floor and are easy to rescue; a few of them have been hidden behind the doors.

When you're on top of the table, press the A Button to pull down the

Rescue the first kid.

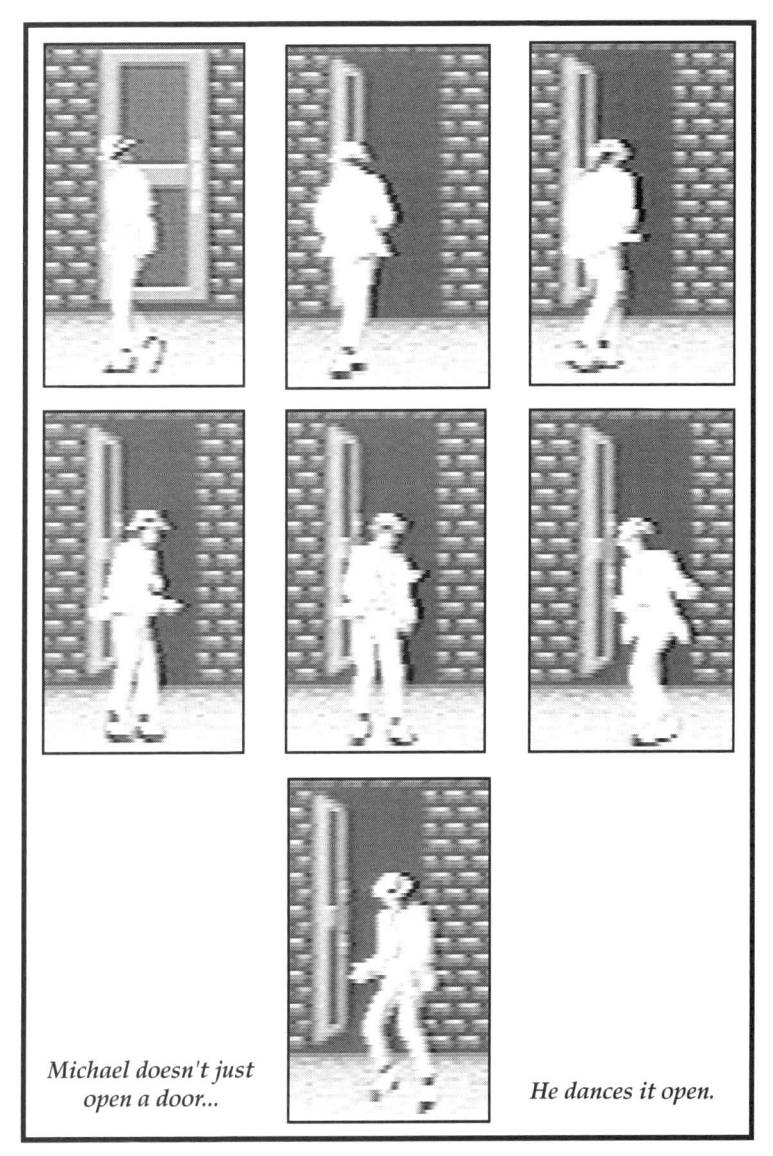

Michael doesn't just open a door... *He dances it open.*

ladder. This will help you later on in the round. On the top floor, you'll see a Cat if you open a certain window, and a Pool Player next to the pool table. Try kicking the chair to see what happens.

When you've rescued all the children, Michael's pet chimp Bubbles appears. He'll get onto Michael's back and point in a direction. Walk in that direction. When you reach the right spot

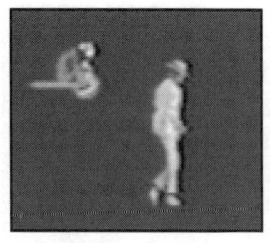

When you've rescued all the children, Michael's pet chimp Bubbles appears.

(which is the piano), Bubbles will hop off and Mr. Big will appear! Don't try to hit him; stay away from him and he'll soon leave the screen.

Now a group of Gangsters will start attacking you from both sides! Stay on the piano and use your kick against the Gangsters. If you have a lot of energy, you might want to hold down A and do a High-Power Dance for extra points!

Mr. Big appears! Don't try to hit him; stay away from him and he'll soon leave the screen.

Now a group of Gangsters will start attacking you from both sides! Stay on the piano and use your attack against the Gangsters.

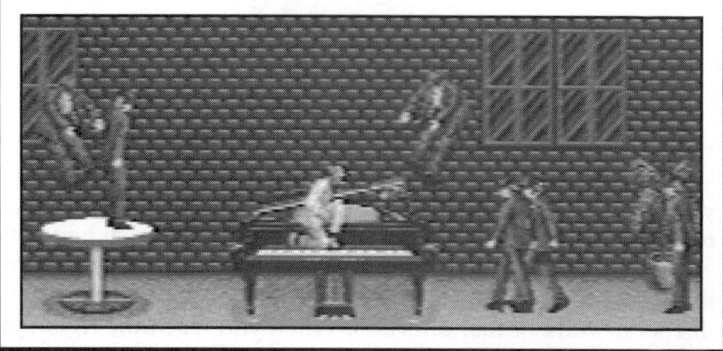

When all the Gangsters have been defeated, another kid will appear at the right side of the screen. Walk over to the kid and you've finished the first level!

Round 1-2. This level has kids on every floor. You should walk to the bottom floor and work your way up to the top, searching along the way. On the top floor, you'll find some pinball machines. But Michael doesn't have time for pinball now. He's on a mission!

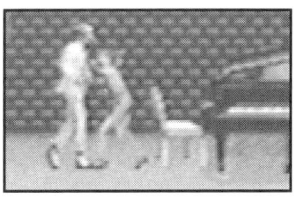

The girls slow you down.

Duck the shooters.

This level is quite similar to the first; Bubbles will point you to the top floor for the Gangster wave. Stand on the pinball machine and use its height to stand above the Gangsters as you kick them.

Round 1-3. You should walk all the way to the bottom floor and search, then return and pull down the ladder to climb up to the top floor. Don't be afraid to open some windows. Your final opponent will be a tough Gangster who will jump as he attacks. Jump up and hit him as he's jumping. Time your jumps to his, and you'll defeat him easily.

The Streets

Music: Beat It!
Round 2-1. You're out of Club 30 and onto the Street. Try opening the window to the left of the door, but be ready to run quickly! That was a Bomb in the window, and there are more of them. So when you open a window, quickly jump away.

That was a Bomb in the window, and there are more Bombs. So when you open a window, quickly jump away.

111

Jump to the rooftops.   *Fight the punks at the dumpster.*

    After you find the children on the street, jump up from the top of the car onto the wall and come back to the Club to search the higher floors for kids. Find them all and Bubbles will point you to the right side of the street. When the Hoodlum attack starts, move slightly to the left of the garbage dumpster and duck. This will be the safest place to attack from.

Round 2-2. The Hoodlums in this garage have been fooling around with the cars. Some of them contain Bombs in their trunks. Others contain kids. You should search all the cars except the red ones. They almost always contain a Bomb—or nothing at all.

The garage is very easy to nagivate; there are five cars on each floor, and five floors to search. Find kids on every floor. Your final fight is against a squad of Riot Police. Stay low and keep turning and attacking!

112

Round 2-3.

You'll have to search on the street, above the street and below the street. Start below the street and work your way up. Don't open the second door from the right, on the ground level, until you've collected the other kids. Your final attackers will be a pack of dogs!

Don't worry about the black dogs; they just keep coming, anyway. The white dog is the one you have to get.

It'll dodge you, so you'll have to do some fancy maneuvering to get it. Don't waste Magic trying to make the white dog dance; it won't tire him out.

The Woods
Music: Thriller

Search the tombstones and the bushes.

Round 3-1. There aren't any Bombs, so you should search everything—and that means the bushes... and the tombstones. Michael is not afraid of ghosts. Don't worry about falling into the grave or the water; you won't be hurt.

Walk all the way to the right, finding kids along the way. Jump up the cliffs and walk across the bridge. There's one section of the bridge towards the left that will break. This is okay. In fact, it will help you get to Mr. Big faster. When you get the final kid, fall through the hole and walk to the water. Jump to the stone on the right.

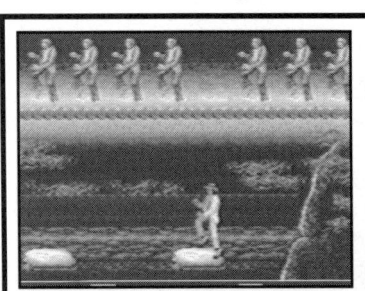

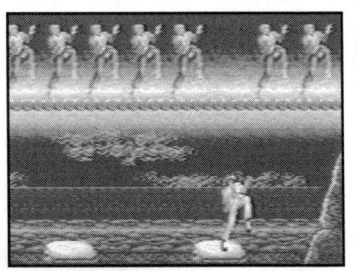

Kick all the Zombies coming at you from the sides. When they stop coming, start a High-Power Dance with all the Zombies on the bridge. They move pretty well for having such stiff muscles!

Round 3-2. You'll need to swing like a chimpanzee to succeed in this round. The trees have branches that you can grab onto by jumping up at them. Then you can swing on the branch, and leap off, knocking Zombies off the ledges as you soar.

Almost all of the kids are on the right side of the screen. There's only one kid to the left, on the second ledge from the top. You should get the kids on the top last, because Bubbles will direct you here.

The first wave of attackers will be Zombies. Duck down in the middle of the screen and pivot quickly to catch the Zombies as they jump at you. Keep fighting them off and you'll defeat all of them—except for two.

These two will split into half, with the top half flying at you while the lower half stays put. While they're split like that, you can't touch them. But they sure can touch you! Use your Magic! If you don't have enough energy for a High-Power Dance, a strong hat throw will destroy the Zombies. If you aren't strong enough to use Magic, you'll have to duck and jump the invulnerable halves and attack the zombies when they're whole.

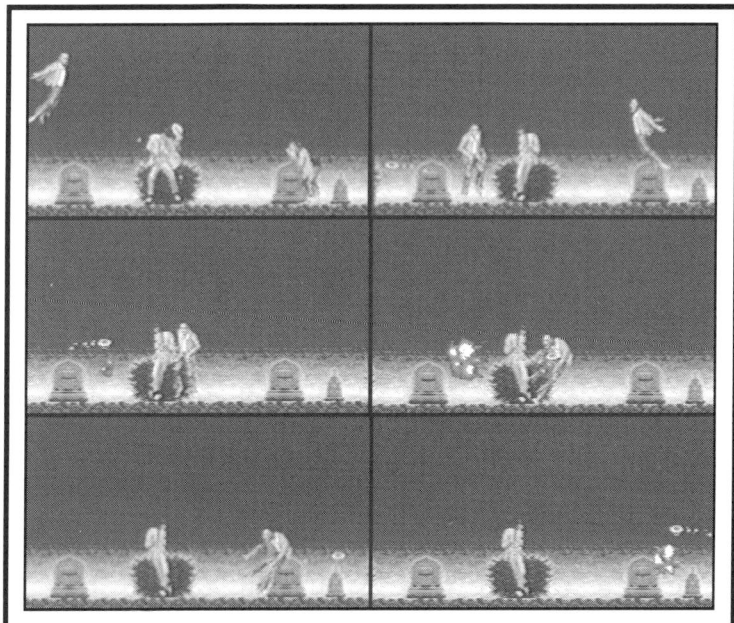

A perfect hat throw. It gets the Zombie on the left, then loops back around to get the one on the right twice.

Round 3-3. There are more trees to swing on, and a huge waterfall that splits the level in half. There are kids on both sides of the falls, both hidden and in bushes. You'll have to explore almost the entire level to find them all.

Once all the kids have been found, jump to the bottom of the waterfall. You'll be attacked by two Zombies again. This time, their upper halves will soar high in the air and drop knives down on you! Wait until both halves of a Zombie are together, and then kick it to the edge of the screen. As it tries to come back to attack you, keep kicking it back.

The Cavern

Music: Billie Jean

Round 4-1. This cavern is full of smaller caves. Some of them contain kids, but most of them contain danger! A lot of enemies from previous levels will be back, like the Zombies and the Militia Hitmen.

There are hidden caves behind the spider symbols that you can open by spinning in front of them. You don't want to do this on this round, however, because there aren't any kids inside!

Some of the caves have stalactites on the roof. These will fall if you get close to them, or if you kick them. Some of these are placed so that you can drop them onto your enemies!

There are hidden caves behind the spider symbols that you can open by spinning in front of them. You don't want to do this, however, because there aren't any kids inside! You DO want to go into the caverns behind the spider webs; these always have kids inside.

After you collect the eight kids, Bubbles will direct you to the spider web to the left on the bottom floor. Jump onto the ledge to the right of the web and duck down to shoot the attacking Militia Hitmen. Use your High-Power Dance when there are only a few left.

Moonwalker

Some places are hard to reach.

Round 4-2. This cavern is very maze-like. There's only one path to find all the kids. If you take a wrong turn, you may lose track of which caves you've looked inside.

Just to make things tougher, some of the hidden doors contain kids, and some of the ones behind webs don't. So you'll have to explore every cave! The techniques you used in Round 4-1 will work here as well; it's just a matter of finding your way around.

When you reach Mr. Big, move behind the right edge of the web and duck down, facing to the right. Keep using your Attack to knock away the Zombies and Spiders. They'll eventually stop attacking.

Round 4-3. The cavern returns to a slightly simpler pattern. There are ten kids, scattered around the entire cavern. Don't be afraid to part the waters in your search for children. And be sure to open every hidden door. Except for the one near the start of the level, they all contain kids.

The end of the level sends the Militia Hitmen and Zombies at you. Stand on the bottom or jump on a ledge. There's no perfectly safe spot on the screen, so keep moving.

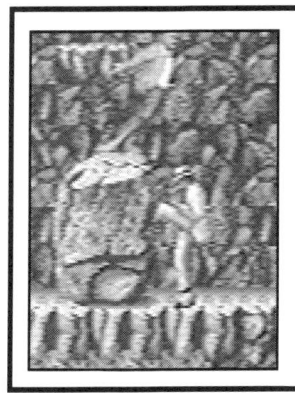

Kick the big rock and use it to get up.

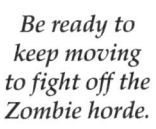

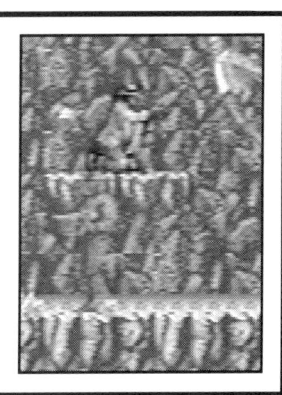

Be ready to keep moving to fight off the Zombie horde.

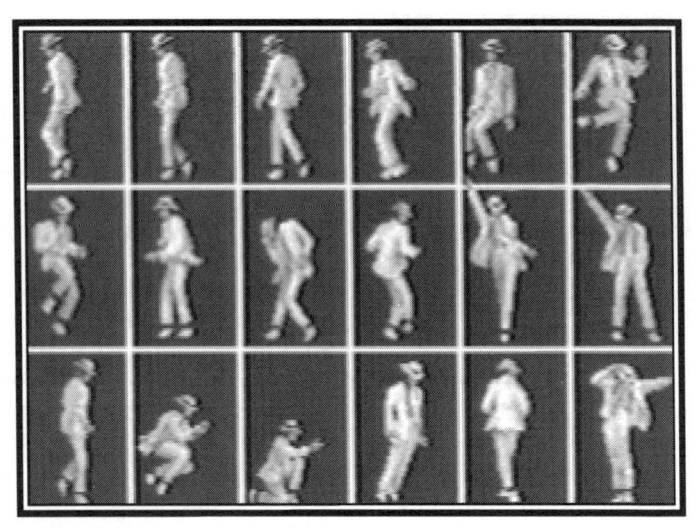

Michael's Moves.

Mr. Big's Hideout

Music: Bad
Round 5-1. Mr. Big's hideout is scattered with high-tech equipment. There are computers that you can blow up and teleporters that you'll need to use to move among the level. And

Rescue kids, wreck computers, warp, and destroy lasers. It's fun!

the enemies are high-tech, like the ceiling-mounted laser! Jump up and use your Attack to knock this out. That should be your first priority.

Keep track of where the teleporters send you, because once you collect all the kids you'll want to use them quickly to get to the final attack of the level. This area has a high ledge; use the computer to jump up to it and let the Police come onto the screen. Then start a High-Power Dance. If you're weak, on the other hand, you'll have to fight them on the ground, which is more difficult. Most of the time, you can stay low, but some of these guys will kneel down and shoot low, too. So be on guard if you can't use your dance.

Dance 'em til they drop!

Round 5-2. The teleporters are gone in this round. In fact, this round is fairly small and easy to figure out. The new obstacles are trap-doors that will drop you down a level, and conveyor belts that you'll have to jump across to make any progress across them.

Bubbles will direct you to a fight against three very tough Militia Hitmen. Stay on the left side of the screen, ducking under the small ledge when you need to, and whacking the guards with your attacks.

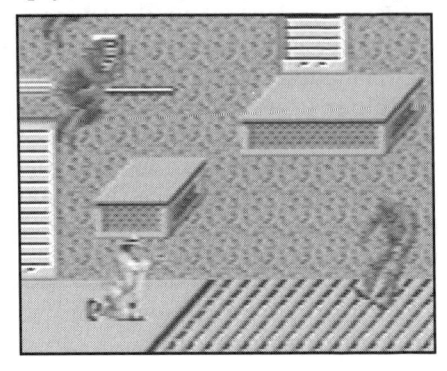

Round 5-3. It's the final level before Mr. Big! You start at the bottom floor; search your way to the right and use the elevator to get to the higher levels. There aren't any new surprises; in fact, most of the kids will even be visible on this level! There will be a tricky jump or two, but that's about it.

When you've rescued the final kid, and been directed by Bubbles, you will automatically get a shooting star! In your robot form, fly all around the screen, shooting Mr. Big's soldiers constantly. You don't have to worry about changing back into your human form. When you shoot enough soldiers, you'll be whisked off to the final battle!

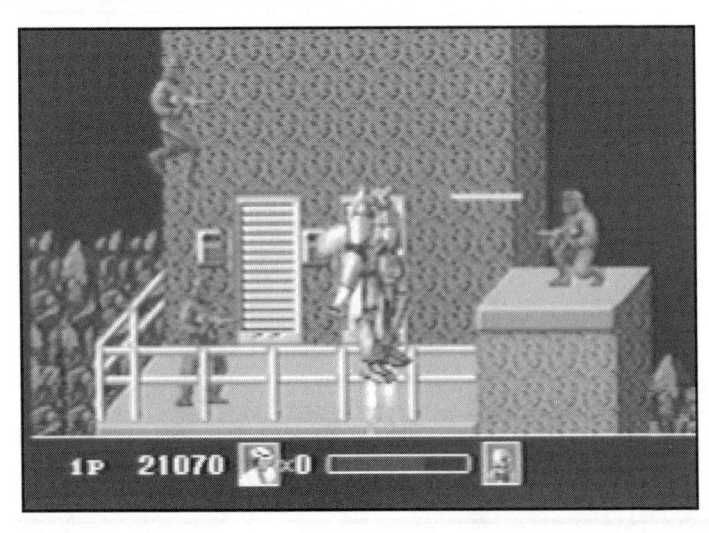

Moonwalker

Michael's Battle Plane

From the cockpit of this Battle Plane, you'll take on Mr. Big! At first, he'll send waves of spaceships at you. They look like anchors! Avoid them and concentrate on shooting Mr. Big when he flits onto the screen. When he tires of the anchor-ships, he'll attack by himself, ramming you and shooting at you!

When Mr. Big rams you, there's not much you can do. You can dodge his lasers by watching his ship; when it starts to blink, dodge quickly! You'll need a steady hand and a good trigger-finger to beat Mr. Big. You can do it—for the children!

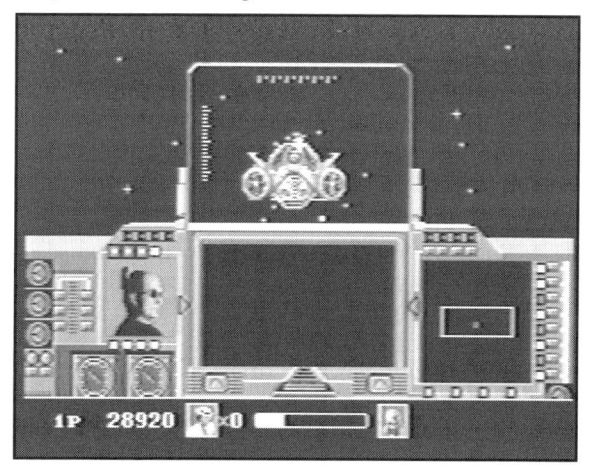

SHH... THE SECRETS

So, you probably have done pretty well at this game, but just in case you want to practice getting the best time bonuses, here's a guide to help you find the kids:

Round 1-1: The bottom floor has three kids. Open the door on the far right of the floor, under the stairs. The top floor has two kids. Open the door to the left of the pool table.
Round 1-2: There are kids on every floor, all hidden behind doors. Search the doors in the middle and on the right except for the top floor, where the kid is in the leftmost door. Rescue this kid last so that you save time moving to the Gangster wave.
Round 1-3: There are kids on all the floors, and one of them is hidden behind a window on the second floor. The last kid to collect should be on the top floor, behind the far right door.
Round 2-1: Don't open the windows on the bottom floor of Club 30. Walk to the right and collect three kids. There is a kid in the

garbage dumpster, but leave him there. Jump up to the wall and walk back to Club 30 for two kids. Go back to the dumpster and rescue the last kid.

Round 2-2: On the first floor, open the fourth car from the left. On the second floor, open the first and fourth cars from the right. On the third floor, open the second car from the left. On the fourth floor, open the first and fifth cars from the right. On the fifth floor, open the fourth car from the left.

Round 2-3: Go underground and pick up two kids. Come back up and walk to the car garage. On the first floor, open the third car from the left; on the second floor, open the second car from the left. Leap off the second floor and rescue the kid, then leap again to the next building and open the window. Jump down to the door and open it.

Round 3-1: Push the first tombstone and the fourth tombstone from the left. Get the kid on the stone, then look behind the bush just to the left of the cliffs. Climb up and go left. Get the kids left of the bridge, then fall through the bridge.

Round 3-2: Push the right tombstone on the ground, and then jump up a level. Open the bush at the far right of the screen. Jump up two more levels and open the bush at the far right again. Jump to the top and collect two kids at the top. Drop down to the left two levels and open the bush. Jump back up and collect the final kid.

Round 3-3: There are two kids on the bottom level, both behind bushes. Jump up to the next level. Get the kid to the left of the falls, the one on the falls, and the one hidden in the bushes to the right of the falls. Go up to the next level. Get the kid right of the falls, and open the bushes on the far left. Jump up to the highest level and get the kid on each side of the waterfall. Drop down to the bottom of the falls.

Round 4-1: Walk right and enter the cave behind the spider web. Walk right two caverns. Then walk right another two caves to another web. The fourth kid is in the cave just right of the web. Walk right, to the waterfall, and jump up above it for the kid. Now jump over to the left. Enter the cave left of the hidden door. Then walk left all the way to the web. The final kid is two caves left of the web.

Round 4-2: Go right and leap over to the cave. Then drop down below the cave and go into the web cave. Drop down again and go inside the hidden cave. Jump up and left to another web, another cave, and another kid! Now drop down, staying left, until you reach the bottom of the cavern. Open the hidden door just right of the web. Then walk right until you reach a boulder.

Moonwalker

Kick it against the right wall. Enter the hidden door right of the web and left of the boulder. Hop onto the boulder and up to the next web. Pass the next web above and leap up to a hidden door. The last hostage is in an even higher hidden door.

Round 4-3: Kick the boulder and jump up to the hidden door left of the web. Come back down and walk right to an open cave. Walk right again and search the waterfall. Leap up and walk left to the hidden door left of the open cave. Come back to the right and leap over the falls to another hidden door. Hop up another level and walk left, opening the door right of the web. Beat it down to the left and look behind another web. Walk left and jump up to the final level. Open the door right of the web. Leap to the right and open the next hidden door. The final kid is all the way to the right in an open cave.

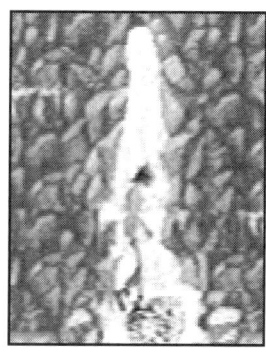

Round 5-1: Climb down the stairs. Walk to the right and go down the stairs again. Walk left to the leftmost teleporter and use it. Pick up the kid and open the door. Use the teleporter to get back down. Walk right and use the next teleporter. Walk left and open the second door you come to. Use the teleporter to the left of the door. Walk left and grab the kid. Go all the way to the right, past all the teleporters, for another kid. Use the teleporter to the left of the kid. Open the second door to the right, then walk all the way to the left and open both doors. Walk back to the right and use the rightmost teleporter. Walk right, teleport, walk left, and teleport again. Walk right for the final teleport. Walk right and climb up the stairs, then walk to the door under the stairs to the left for the final kid.

Round 5-2: Open the door just to the right of you. Leave the kid on the ledge. Go across the conveyor belt and pick up the child on the ledge above it, opening the door as well. Get the kid on the right end of the belt. Open the second door past the kid. Climb up the stairs to grab another child. Jump up to the ledge and open the right door. Move to the left and open the door on the ledge above the belt. Keep going left and open the left door on the ledge above the stairs. Climb down the stairs and grab the final kid on the ledge.

Round 5-3: Walk all the way to the right and take the elevator. Drop below the elevator and grab the kid. Walk left, past the three doors. Jump the trap-door and rescue the kid. Walk left and open the leftmost door. Now jump up to the ledge on the right and pick up the two kids. Go back to the left and jump across. Rescue the kid and jump up to find the kid at the top. Leap across to the right and open the door to the right. Get the child on the ledge and drop back down two levels. The final kid is in the rightmost of the three doors passed earlier.

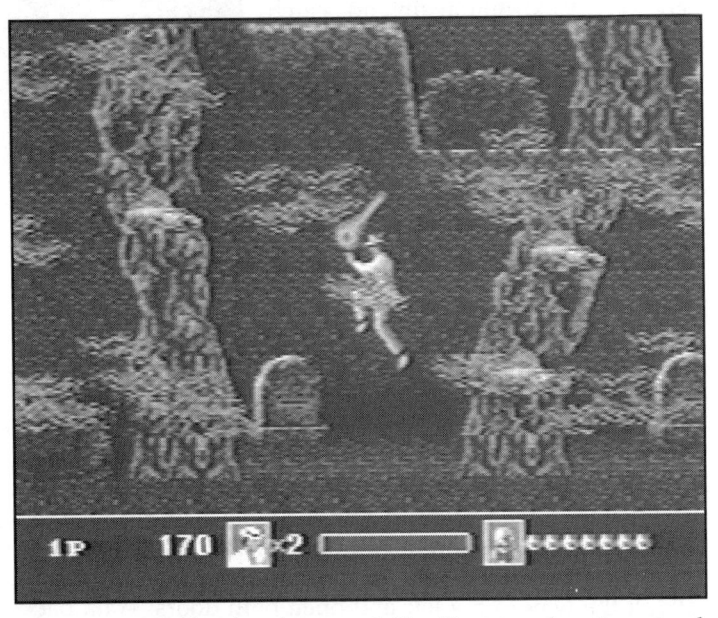

How do you get the shooting stars? You'll get a shooting star by collecting a particular child first in the round. There's a shooting star in every level except the first and the last, but only one round in each level has the secret. Here's how to get the star in two of the rounds.

Round 2-1: Rescue the child on the roof of Club 30 first. Move to the right and catch the star!

Round 3-2: Push the tombstone on the ground, and then move to the left. When you first turn on the Genesis, let the game demonstrate the various levels and it will show you exactly how to do it!

CHAPTER 10

Mystic Defender

Distributor: Sega
Game Type: Arcade Action

WHAT'S GOING ON?

Zareth isn't a very nice guy. In fact, he's the Devil's Disciple. And now he plans to bring Zao back to life. You know Zao, don't you? He's only the most evil, most powerful wizard that ever was—and ever will be! He'll turn the world into a personal slave reserve.

You never would have known about it until it was too late, but Zareth needed a soul to sacrifice to get Zao back. And he chose your girlfriend, Alexandra. Now you've got two goals—save the world and save Alexandra!

WHO ARE YOU?

You're Joe Yamato. You're fortunate enough to have extensive knowledge of magic. It will come in very handy on this mission.

PLAYERS

Mystic Defender is a one-player game only.

SCORING

There are no points in this game; your only goal is to get through all eight levels alive.

LIVES AND HOW TO LOSE THEM

Use the Options Screen to start out with anywhere from three to five lives. Each life has three Life Packs. As you're hit by the enemy, you lose Life Packs. As usual, lose all the Packs and you've lost a life. During the game, increase your life total by finding special items.

CONTINUES

You can continue three times, each time from the start of the last level you reached. You can't continue if you die on Level One, for obvious reasons.

CONTROLS

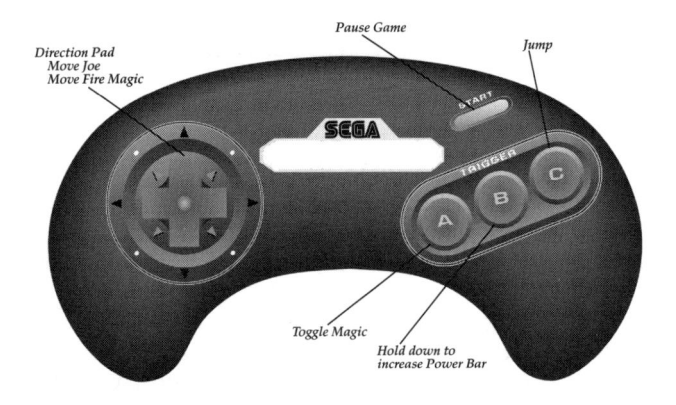

Direction Pad — Move Joe, Move Fire Magic
Pause Game
Jump
Toggle Magic
Hold down to increase Power Bar

WEAPONS

Joe will obtain different types of Magic during the game:

Psycho Magic is what Joe starts with at the beginning of the game. It's a ball of power. If the Power Bar is full, the ball will split into three!

Find the **Flame Magic** at the end of Round One. You'll be surrounded in a fiery cloud as you charge up this Magic; release it and you get a huge streak of flame. Move the flame with the direction pad to wipe out enemies in any direction.

Find the **Sonic Magic** in Round Two. It shoots out six balls of power. At full power, four of the balls will ricochet around the screen to cause maximum havoc.

Find the **Thunder Dragon Magic** in Round Three. Use it to destroy everything on the screen! Disappears after one use.

SPECIAL ITEMS

There are three very useful special items.

> The **Strength Item** will give you an extra Life Pack.
> The **Life Item** gives you another life.
> The **Power Item** will cause the Power Bar to fill more rapidly, giving you quicker attacks.

FRIENDS

None in this game. If you did have any, you wouldn't want to bring them along on this trip!

ENEMIES

There are many; unfortunately, only a select few have names. We'll make appropriate ones up as we go along. Here are the few enemies who are named.

> The **Spectre** is actually many Spectres. Kill one and another appears! Make sure to get rid of them quickly—dead Spectres have a habit of coming back.
> The **Six-Faced Phantom** looks a lot like a metallic ball, but who are we to disagree with the name? It's only vulnerable to attack when open—which isn't very often.
> **Spiders** aren't too bad—unless they become Death Worms!
> **Death Worms** are, well, deadly.
> **Ghosts** are tough to catch and hard to beat. You've got to kill them all—not easy when they're already dead!
> **Zareth** is Zao's right-hand demon. He'll do anything to protect his master.
> **Zao Zao** is evil personified! Destroy him or it's curtains!

STRATEGY SESSION
General Strategies

The Options Screen lets you tweak the game to your liking. Adjust the controls and select a Difficulty Leve—Easy, Normal or Hard. We suggest using the default controls and setting the game to Easy (which might as well be Hard when you start playing the game).

When you first get a new Magic, start fooling around with it—there's no time limit, so there's nothing to stop you. And you'll often need it very soon after you get it.

You can't charge up your Magic when you're moving; therefore, the best strategy is to kill an opponent, stand still and charge the Magic to maximum, and start moving again. This technique will be more necessary on later levels, thanks to the tougher foes.

Round One: The Forest.

These trees are the keys to your survival on this first level. By jumping onto the branches, you can safely travel to the right without danger of attack.

Climb into the trees and jump to the right. Snakes will be crawling up and down the trees, but your Psycho Magic will take care of them. Continue until you see a man guarding a Red Power Item. Jump down to the branch and take it. Eventually, the branches will run out and you'll have to return to the ground. There will be a large metallic head shooting multicolored balls. A full-power Psycho destroys it.

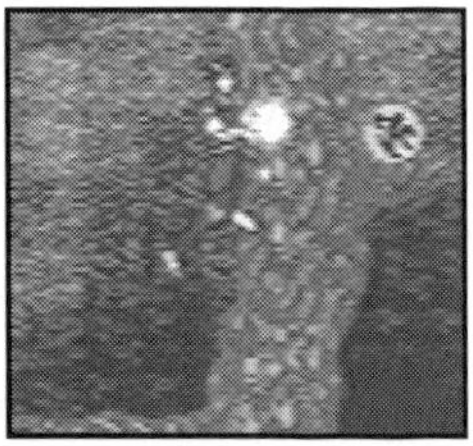

Get back into the trees and you'll soon find the Blue Strength Item (which you'll probably need by this time). There's another one later on. If you hit the ground, men will appear and attack; even the weakest Psycho blast will defeat them.

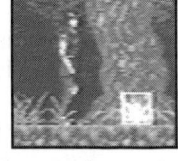

You'll reach a large Worm; keep moving or it will fire at you. A full-strength blast to the head will take it out. Pick up the Flame Magic and walk off the screen for your close encounter of the Boss kind.

This metallic monkey will jump around the trees a while, and then roll into a ball. You can only hurt it when

128

Mystic Defender

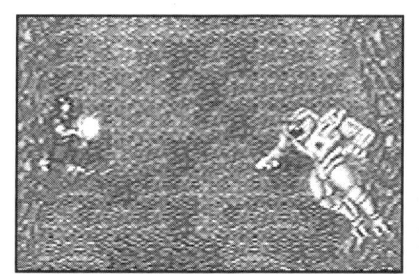

it's in monkey form. Two full-strength blasts of Psycho Magic will destroy it; but odds are you'll need to avoid it a lot more than shoot at it. Stay in the trees, but watch out for it when it lunges up at you.

One technique that we've found successful is to jump up to a high branch and charge up the magic. When the monkey appears, blast him. Sometimes you can trap him with short blasts that keep him trapped. If you succeed in doing that, he won't last long at all.

Round Two: Staircase Maze.

Run to the right and get onto the first staircase. At the top, you'll meet the main enemies for this round—the Rolling Head Creatures and the Slime Babies. The Creatures can summon Flaming Moths onto the screen, and can also turn into Heads and start rolling at you. The Slime Babies, if they're not hit hard enough with your magic, will mutate into puddles of slime!

Continue up these stairs until you see the Blue Strength Item. You can jump up and get it if you need it. Climb back down to the Slime Baby dispenser and run to the right. Jump across the gap.

Jump up and use the Psycho Magic to clear the stairs before you climb them.

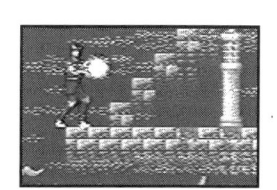

Then you'll make it to the second set of stairs.

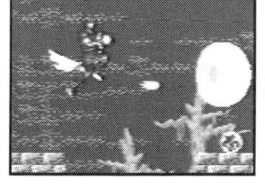

You'll need to make several long leaps from platform to platform.

The Intersection.

129

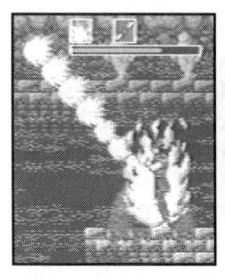

Now start up several steps, dealing Psycho death to the Babies and Heads. The stairs will take you to the left, and to the intersection of two sets of stairs—up and down. Go up to find a Red Power Item. Grab it and go

Use the Fire Magic to clear the path so you won't hit a Slimer on the way across.

back to the up/down intersection. Go down the stairs. Walk right and you'll be on a ledge. Jump across again.

Climb up several staircases; there will be a Blue Item to grab, then keep going up. The next gap you come to will be a tough jump; miss it and you'll have a long climb back up to this point. Use the Fire Magic to clear the path so you won't hit a Slimer on the way across. Go up and you'll be going to the right. Use the Fire Magic again to clear away the Slimers. One more leap and you'll receive the Sonic Magic. Go through—or rather, out—to the right.

Keep heading right. What are all those spinning guys? They are the Spectre. They'll disappear—but not for long. Select the Sonic Magic and get ready to use it! You'll have to move around this screen, looking for Spectres. When you see one, use the Sonic Magic! If you take too long to kill them, the dead Spectres will turn into huge spiders! When you've killed all the Spectres, you will automatically run off the screen and to the next round.

Round Three: The Fiends' Machine Room.

Run right and scale the wall. Watch out for the flame-thrower as you jump down. To blast the Wormy Wall, use Psycho Magic on full strength. Shortly after it is another Wall. Destroy it and run to the right. Jump up, timing your leaps to avoid the flames.

When you reach the top, wait for the floating platform to appear and leap onto it. Don't miss or you'll need to climb all the way back. Ride it to the left and jump onto the ledge. Avoid the flames again as you scamper left. You'll come to a vertically floating platform. Jump aboard.

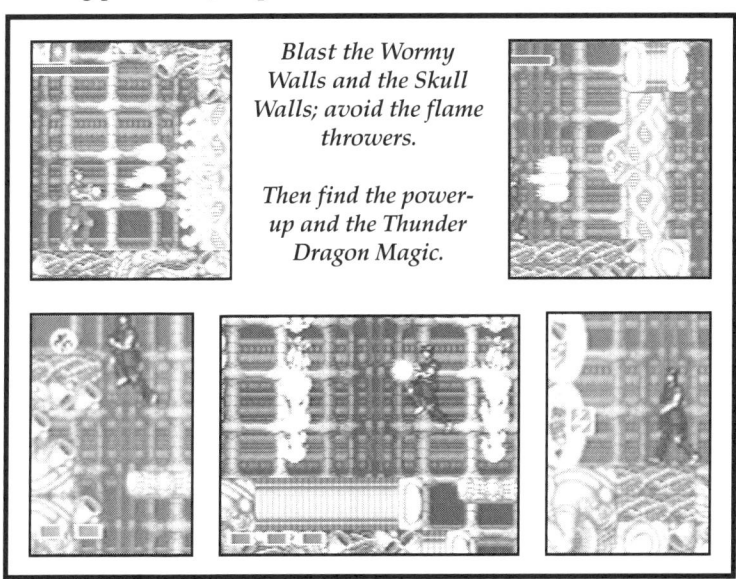

Blast the Wormy Walls and the Skull Walls; avoid the flame throwers.

Then find the power-up and the Thunder Dragon Magic.

Take it down and waste the Wormy Wall. Then ride it up and grab the Red Item. Now leap to the right and onto the next ledge. Go up and destroy the Wall to your left and head in that direction. Now you'll have to kill the Skull Wall. What ever happened to mild-mannered walls?

Run to the right, past the now-dead Wall. You'll reach another Skull Wall. Pass it and plummet all the way down to a Wormy Wall. Shoot it and you'll get the Thunder Dragon Magic! Ride the floating platform up, and exit the screen to the right.

Round Four: Lava Lake.

Yes, the lava is fatal. Jump into it and—well, you won't be teaching magic, that's for sure. Run to the right (as you will be for this entire round). Select the Flame Magic.

You're going to have to leap from rock to rock. Some of the rocks raise

Standing on a low rock.

and lower, but only quickly dip into the lava, so that you can jump off them briefly. Some of the rocks don't move until you jump onto them, and then lower all the way into the lava. You can tell which is which, so they shouldn't take you by surprise. The enemies, on the other hand, can definitely surprise you.

The Lava Pods will shoot Lava Moths at you. The Flame will hopefully kill them as they appear on the screen. If you miss them, maneuver the Flame to destroy them. The key to this level is to use the Flame magic to clear a path ahead of you, then move forward. If you move too fast, you'll run right into an enemy or three and probably lose a life. When you get past all the lava, and jump onto a flat platform.

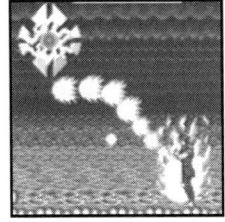

The Six-Faced Phantom will randomly move around the screen, occasionally stopping to open and fire a bullet at you. When it does open, try to be there with a full-strength Flame to burn it. It will drop a Dragon Magic when destroyed. Just past it is a Blue Item.

You'll have to pass some more lava again, and then you'll reach another Phantom. After you defeat the second Phantom, switch to Psycho Magic.

These two rather huge Lava Worms aren't too tough to beat. When they go into the lava, they will usually turn around. When they first appear, they're facing left. They'll sink into the lava; when they re-emerge, they're facing right. Their heads are their vulnerable spots; shoot the head of the left Worm. If it goes into the lava, be ready to leap onto the rock between them, because it might end up facing left. Destroying the left Worm first makes your job a lot easier. Then you deal with the Right Worm from a safe distance.

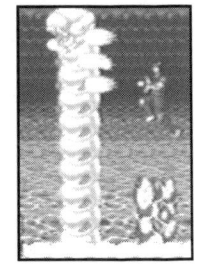

Round Five: The Spider Pit.

There's nothing too challenging here—select the Psycho Magic and walk to the right. The Spiders are easy to kill. The Leaping Ghouls could give you problems—but it's doubtful. Eventually, the enemies will stop coming but this only signals the

Mystic Defender

appearance of the Death Worm!

You'll have to dodge the rainbow of spores it shoots while you shoot it in the head—its only weak point. The Worm aims its spores at your position, so wait until it begins to shoot, then move. When the Worm blows up, walk up to the next level.

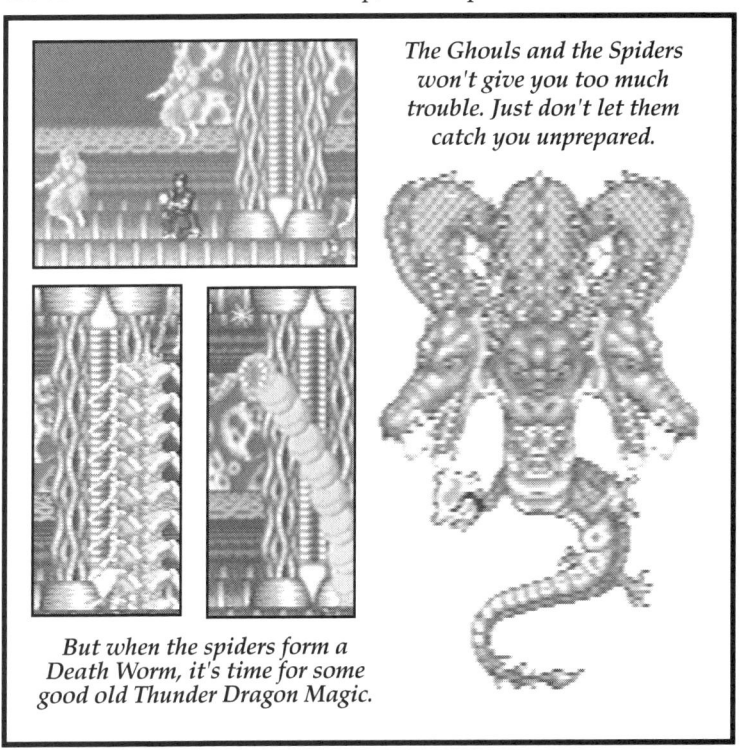

The Ghouls and the Spiders won't give you too much trouble. Just don't let them catch you unprepared.

But when the spiders form a Death Worm, it's time for some good old Thunder Dragon Magic.

Use Sonic Magic here. Walk along the ground until you reach the Blue Item. Then walk along the platforms until you reach the Red Item. Watch out for the Spiders and Ghouls. There will be one more Blue Item to collect, and then another Death Worm. But this Worm is a lot more deadly!

Now is the time to use the Thunder Dragon Magic you've been holding. After that, return to Psycho Magic and keep blasting away at the Reaper Head. Stay to the left and stay on the move. You'll beat this thing!

Round Six: The Ghosts' Machine Room.

From Fiends to Ghosts. This round heavily resembles Round Three—and therefore, the strategies are mostly the same.

Run to the right. Get past the flames and then jump upwards. At the top, a Skull will emerge to your right. Fry him and then leap onto the platform. Kill the Wormy Wall and go up. Kill the next Wall and jump up to get the Red Item. Leap back down and go right and down. Collect the Blue Item. Climb back up and head right. Kill the Wormy Wall and leap down.

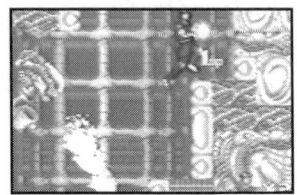

You'll need to get past a lot of flame-throwers; when you reach the bottom, go right and pass even more flame-throwers. At the far right, kill the Skull. Now jump onto the platforms and ride up. Jump onto the right platforms. Work your way to the right and you'll find a handy 1-Up. Walk back to the platforms and jump onto the far left one to go up.

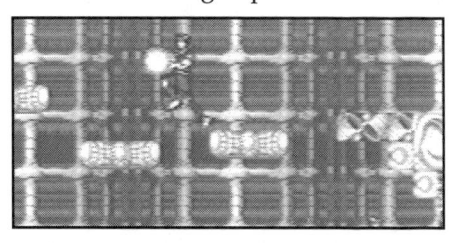

Walk right and total the Wall. Go up onto the platform, kill the Skull, and make the jump to the left. This next trip is past a convention of flame-throwers; watch your timing! When you reach the floating platforms, leap over to the left one that floats vertically. Fall and you've got quite a trip back—past the flame-throwers again. So don't fall!

Destroy the Skull Wall to your right and head that way. Watch out for the Hand. Fall down and collect the Red Item. Pass some flame-throwers, destroy another Skull Wall, and a short walk later you're done!

Round Seven: The Elevator Maze.

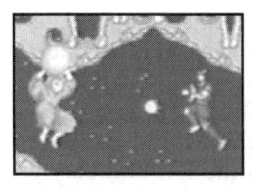

Prepare your Psycho Magic for some action; the Leaping Ghouls are thick here. Walk to the right and go up two levels. Walk left and go down. Walk all the way right and go up. Walk left. These Throwing Ghouls are easy to kill, but the pods they throw aren't. Dodge them instead. Or switch to Sonic Magic here. It does a good job on ghouls and pods. Go up once you reach the elevator.

Use Sonic Magic to destroy the shooting thing on the ceiling. Walk all the way to the right and go down two levels. Move left

Mystic Defender

and collect the Red Item. Go left, then down two levels.

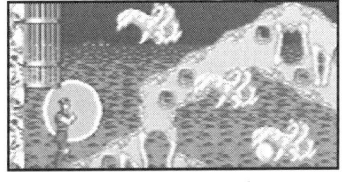

The Floating Claws are best disposed of with the Sonic Magic; destroy them all before you start moving to the right. Move all the way to the right and go up. Move left to collect the Blue Item. Then move right. Go down the elevator. Move left, dealing the Hands some destruction. Get onto the elevator and up two levels. Run to the right, then up, then left. Almost there!

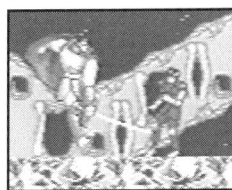

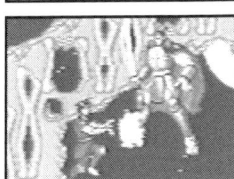

Run left until you reach yet another elevator; go up and right. Collect the Thunder Dragon Magic and continue. The Boss is here! Call him the Flying Flamer. He'll hover above you, flying down only to slash you or shoot fire.

Use Thunder Dragon Magic at the start to weaken him. Then switch to the Psycho Magic. Now wait until he comes down at you, then jump up and let rip with the Magic. He'll keep flying backwards; keep moving towards him. Eventually, all that Magic will be too much for him and he'll blow up!

Round Eight: Zao's Lair.

Run to the right, and use Psycho Magic to kill the Wiggling Demons. You'll come to Zao more quickly than you'd expect.

SHH... THE SECRETS

How do I defeat Zao? If you have any Thunder Dragon Magic left, use it. After that, use your wits. Avoiding Zao's single shots is easy; avoiding the spread of fire isn't. Run all the way to the left and the bullets should just pass by you. Use the Psycho Magic and stay toward the left side of the screen. Jump and fire, and Alexandra will soon be free!

CHAPTER 11

Phantasy Star II

Distributor: Sega of America
Game Type: RPG

Phantasy Star II is a remarkable game, as anyone who's played it can tell you. However, because it comes with an in-depth hint book full of maps and hints (which range from vague clues to actually telling the story), we decided not to do our usual chapter on this product. It is a very big game, and would take many hours (days, weeks...) to complete. So we decided to help you out by filling in some of the gaps the hint book leaves.

In this chapter, you'll learn how to negotiate most of the mazes in the game. You'll also learn a few tricks and techniques to make the game go easier. With the hint book in one hand and this book in the other, you should be ready to embark on a fabulous, but challenging journey in another solar system—somewhere near the Phantasy Star!

SECRETS OF PHANTASY STAR II
Getting Started

To begin with, you need to build up your characters. At the beginning, there are only you and Nei. Soon, however, you'll

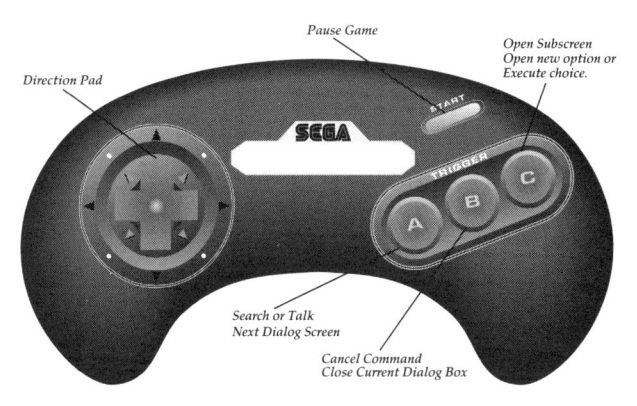

Controller diagram labels:
- Direction Pad
- Pause Game
- Open Subscreen / Open new option or Execute choice.
- Search or Talk / Next Dialog Screen
- Cancel Command / Close Current Dialog Box

meet Rudo and after that the cast of characters continues to build. Charging up the characters with experience points is a must. If you use the maps (and the secret techniques in this chapter), you'll be able to cruise through the mazes quickly. The drawback is that you won't gain many experience points in those mazes, and therefore you won't gain levels (and their associated hit points and technique points). So you need to get used to charging your characters out in the overworld.

As you move from city to city in the story, you'll find that the monsters that attack get stronger and are consequently worth more points. So fight near the latest city to earn the most points. Stay close, though, and you can duck inside to get healed if things get rough.

You'll need to save up money quite often, and this character charging is also the best way to gain the money to buy important items. Try to carry a few Dimates to heal your characters so you can save Technique Points for casting other spells. Later in the game, you'll want to carry all the Trimate you can. You'll probably need most or all of it, too!

Also remember, each time you add a new party member, he or she starts out very weak. Immediately go to a lightweight area and charge them up slowly at first. If you attack the heavy monsters with undeveloped characters, you might lose them very fast.

Also, be sure to save the game at regular intervals. You don't want to spend hours charging characters or exploring dungeons only to lose it all in an unexpected battle. Remember, even if you usually handle the monsters fairly well, some battles are just unlucky and your enemies will hit you first, and maybe get some lucky shots in. So be prepared. If you have money, clone your characters at the Cloning Station.

How the Story Works

The Dream.

The story line in Phantasy Star II controls your actions fairly well. Even though you can explore the world around you freely, the plot is designed to prevent you from getting too far without taking care of business. For instance, you can't get past Darum until you've rescued Teim, and you can't do that until you've gotten the dynamite from Shure dungeon to blow open the door to the Tower of Nido where Teim is imprisoned. You see? It may seem that you're making the choices, but someone else is at the controls.

Anyway, if you invest your time building up your characters, you'll be able to roam around without fear of sudden demise. Then you can get to the work of solving the many mysteries that surround you. Don't be surprised by anything. This game is full of plot twists that you wouldn't expect in a video game. Get used to the unexpected.

Special Techniques

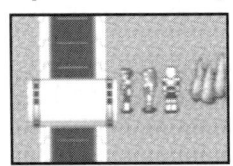

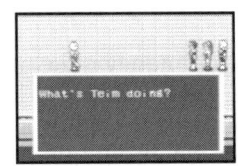

Here's a technique for those of you who want to keep your risks to a minimum: This is the so-called invincibility technique. What you do is alternate pressing Button C and Button B as you walk. Button C opens the subscreen menu; Button B closes it. For some reason hidden deep in the programming of the game, walking this way prevents monsters from attacking you—much. It isn't 100% reliable, but it does work. In the end, it will save you time since you won't have to fight very many battles or go back to the beginning when you become weak or die. The best way to do it is to get into a rhythm: step forward, Button C, Button B, step again, and so forth. Eventually, you get good at it and it almost doesn't seem like slow motion.

Speaking of which, there is a way to play the game in slow motion or single frame mode. Press the Pause button, then hold down B for half speed or C for frame-by-frame mode. I can't really think of a reason to use this technique, but it works.

Questions and Answers

How do I get the Jet Scooter? In Roron, walk around the first dungeon. Go to the left (yes, you can walk on the black area), and you'll find it in the bottom dungeon. By the way, the scooter will always be parked nearby, even if you teleport to another town. It follows you like a good scooter.

How do I get to Piata? Piata is hard to reach the first time. You have to park the Jet Scooter over on the Eastern edge of the map, in the bay there near some mountains. Then trek it overland to make it to Piata. The way is hazardous. Fortunately, after your first visit, you'll be able to use the Transporter to get there in the future. Don't worry about losing the Jet Scooter (see the note above this one).

How do I get the Visaphone? To get the Visaphone, take Shir to the Baggage Room in the Central Tower of Paseo. Keep going in and out until she steals it. She'll meet you back at your home. You can also get Moon Dew and Star Mist the same way by taking Shir to the Tool Shop in Paseo and doing the same thing. Moon Dew revives a fallen party member. Star Mist heals the whole party.

How do I get the Megid and Nasar techniques? Your character (call him Rolf for convenience, though you may rename him) gets Megid when he reaches experience level 35. The Doctor learns Nasar when she reaches level 30. By the way, Megid is the most powerful offensive technique Rolf can learn. It drains half the party's hit points when used, though, so you'll want the Doctor in your party if you expect to use it.

What is the best party to use? The best party may vary from one situation to another, but toward the end of the game, you'll probably want to use Rudo, Anna, and Kain. Amy and Hugo do have their uses, and some players may want to use them in place of one of the others. Shir is almost useless, unless you need to steal something, of course.

How do I beat Neifirst? Go in with all the best equipment and plenty of Trimate. Use the Laser Knife in both hands. Nei should have the Laser Bars, Rudo has the Laser Cannon, and Anna has the Laser Slashers. Neifirst has about 1400 hit points—far more than any enemy so far. So be prepared to fight to the death.

Is there anything I can do about Nei? Sorry. You can bring her back DURING the battle with Neifirst, but after that... well it's as the man in the Clone Labs says. Listen to him.

How do I beat the Dark Force? Try using Nathu (or Megid) and the Neisword. Use lots of Trimate. If you have Star Mist, have one of the characters use it as needed. Of course, your party should have all the Nei items.

How do I fight the Mother Brain? It's pretty much the same as fighting the Dark Force. Do your best, hit it with your best techniques, and hope you're strong enough to prevail. If you got this far, you'll do fine.

Corrections from the Hint Book

There are a few inaccuracies in the Phantasy Star II Hint Book. Not many, though...

It says in the hint book that the Biosystems Lab has two basements, but it only has one. It's marked as the 4th Level in the book and you get to it by falling down the pit in the center of the 3rd Level.

Also, there's no Shotgun on the 3rd Level of Shure dungeon, and there aren't any Laser Boots for sale in Zema town.

On the big, fold-out map, the locations of the Blue and Yellow Dams are reversed. However, they are correctly portrayed in the hint book.

In the hint book, it sometimes says there's a powerful enemy awaiting you. In fact, there's no special enemy. The book refers to the more powerful monsters that you encounter normally. There are only three major enemies in the game: Neifirst, Dark Force, and Mother Brain. However, there's a veritable parade of weird creatures—both biological and mechanical—to fight. You will not be bored.

Another strange event may confuse and bother you if you get that far. If you get the Nei Sword in Esper Mansion, the game will lock up in Noah Dungeon. To avoid that, get the sword, then go outside the mansion and save the game. Now

Reset and start the game from the save. By the way, to get the Nei Sword, you have to have all the other Nei Items (see the maze walkthroughs below).

Walking Through the Mazes.

From here, we'll leave it to the hint book to get you into the plot of the game. For the rest of this chapter, we'll give you walkthroughs of most of the mazes. Some are just too easy, and we figure you won't have any trouble with them. We suggest that you have the hint book handy while reading these walkthroughs. We'll refer to it from time to time. For the most part, we'll let you find your way to the mazes. With the hint book and the fold-out map, you shouldn't have any trouble. Once inside, though, it could be a different story....

Bio Systems
1) Head East at first, then go North to the chute at the top of the map. Go down the chute there and get antidote from the chest.
2) Then go East and walk into the black pit. You'll fall down to the 1st level. If you use this pit, you'll skip the long walk around Level 2.
3) Now go to the chute to the Southeast and return to Level 2.
4) Walk North to the next chute and go to the 3rd Level.
5) Go South and get the Dynamite. Now walk North and all the

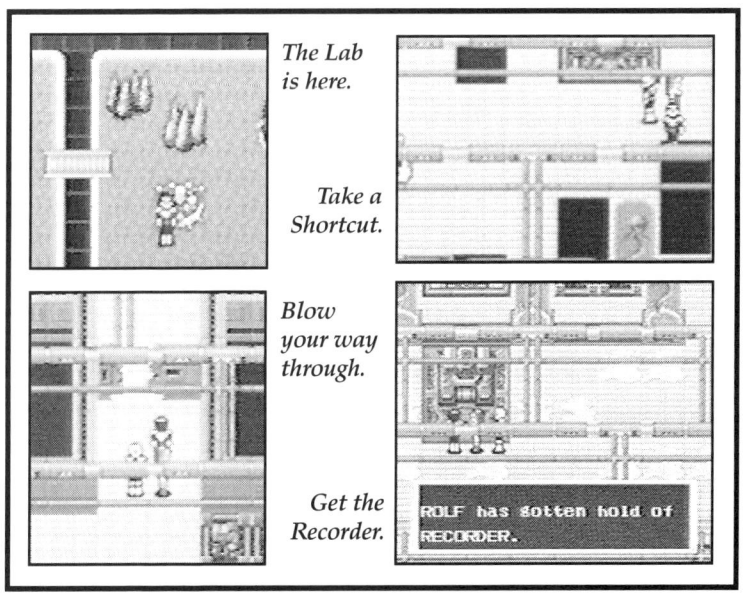

The Lab is here.

Take a Shortcut.

Blow your way through.

Get the Recorder.

way around the level until you find the wall to dynamite. Blow it open and then walk down the pit in the middle.

6) To get the Recorder, you have to find the correct block in the Northeast area of the map. See the picture to give you a good idea. Press Button A when you get there.

Uzo Island

This maze can be tricky... especially when you don't know which tree is the real one (it's the third from the right). To get there:

1) Go East and Up. 2) West and Up. 3) Straight Up. 4) West and Down. 5) West and Up. 6) West and Down. 7) East and Down. 8) West and Down. 9) East and Up. 10) West to Hole. 11) East and Up. 12) East and Up. 13) East and Up. 14) East and Down. 15) East and Down. 16) East to Hole. 17) West and Up. 18) This is it—the Maruera-Tree.

Enter the 1st cave.   *Enter the 2nd cave.*

Exit 1st cave.   *Exit 2nd cave.*

Scenes from the Uzo Island Maze.

Climatrol

Stairs on first level are in the Southwest corner of the maze. They're easy to find by following the map.

1) Level One is basic. Go to the chute far to the West.
2) Levels Two, Three, and Four are also basic.
3) On Level Five you can take more than one route:

The East Route. 1) Go Northeast and take the first chute heading up. 2) Now take the next chute up (it's to the Southwest). 3) Go East, then turn South to the chute leading down. 4) Take the chute to the South. 5) Go East and chute up to the Eighth Level. Head for the center to meet Neifirst.

The West Route. 1) Start with the first chute to the Northwest. 2) Take the up chute right next to the one you just exited. 3). Head East, then South to the same chute as step 3 in the East route. The rest is the same.

Jet South from the false Uzo to find the Climatrol.

The Climatrol is full of new encounters like the Firia above. But nothing has prepared you so far for Neifirst.

Control Tower
The Control Tower is easy enough.
1) Go all the way North to the top of the maze, then turn West.
2) Count the chutes along the top and take the sixth one.
3) Walk South as far as you can go. Pass two chutes along the way. Turn West at the bottom and take the chute.
4) Go South to the chute.
5) As the hint book says, go up and down until you reach the seventh chute along the bottom, then head North to the chute above it. Now your path to the center of the Level Two is clear. Don't touch the keyboard! Use the Musik technique. The door behind will open and you can get the four cards you need.

Red Dam
Use Red Card to open door.
1) Go to the Northwest chute.
2) Now go South and West to the next chute.
2a) To get the Fire Slasher, go up the chute almost directly South, open the chest you find, and then go back down.
3) Now go down the chute in the Southwest corner of Level 1.
4) Go North and East to the next chute.
5) Back to Level 1, go West and take the chute there.

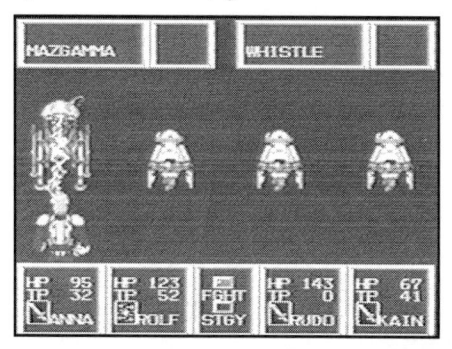

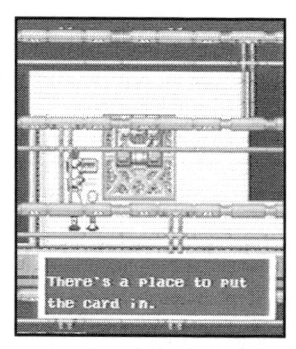

6) You're on Level 2 again. Go East and get the Fire Staff from the chest, then keep going to the chute on the Eastern edge.
7) You're back on Level One... again. Go South to the chute.
8) The Sword of Ang is almost directly North. Get it, equip it, then head to the Northeastern chute.
9) Almost there. Go West and South to the next chute. It takes you to Level Two and the way is clear now to the computer. Use the Red Card to open the locks.

Yellow Dam
1) Once you get through the door, go all the way to the Eastern edge of Level One and go in the lower chute.
2) Now use the chute directly West of where you come out.
3) Back on Level One, now you're in the middle area. Go to the chute to the West and go back up to Level Two.
4) Go up the chute to the Northwest.

144

Phantasy Star II

5) Only one way to go—up to Level Four. The chute is South.
6) Walk around the spiral and go up to get the Amber Robe from the chest.
7) Now go back down and all the way to the East end of the level. Go North and follow the path to the middle spiral. Take the chute there. It leads to the computer. Do your thing with the Yellow Card, and Hinas out of there.

Blue Dam
The beginning of this dam is pretty simple.
1) Go to the Northern chute on Level One.
2.) Then go East to the chute on Level Two.
3) Now on the Third Level you have a long walk to the chute. Take the first one you come to.
4) Now you're on the Fourth Level. Go up the chute directly East.
5) Walk South to get the Storm Gear and give it to Kain. Then go to the chute just South of the chest.
6) Walk East and fall down the middle pit.
7) Get the Snow Crown, then walk South to the chute.
8) Now back on Level Two, go to the Northwest chute.
9) Finally, walk all the way North, then South to get to what looks like a computer on the map. It isn't the right one, though. Take the chute just East of it.
10) Go up the next chute to the North, get the Wind Scarf, and go back down.
11) Now head East and then North to the next chute.
12) North to the next chute.
13) South, then East to the next, which takes you back to Level 3.
14) South to the chute back to Level 4, and there's the computer! But you can't go right to it. Of course not!

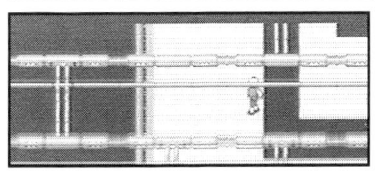

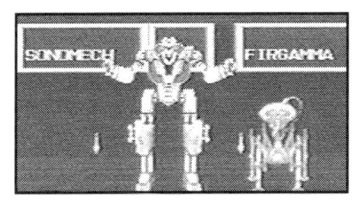

You need to find the right pits fo fall down.

Jump from Level Five to land near the Computer.

15) Head East and around the edge to the next chute.
16) You're back to Level Five. Go South, West, and South again to the chute down.
17) To get the Star Mist, take the Eastern chute, then come back and use the Western chute to go up.
18) Walk North and fall in the hole. Here you are.

Green Dam
1) Go through the entrance and go South to the chute.
2) Walk North, then West to the first chute you come to.
3) West to the next chute.
4) Get the Truth Sleeves from the chest, then head North and West. Go in the Northern chute.
5) West to the next chute.
6) Now walk West and then East along the outer corridor. It's a very long walk, but you'll need to go until you find another gap leading into the main area. Walk back in and head West, then South. You'll find two chutes side-by-side. Take the left-hand one (the one that leads down).

Monster!

7) Walk West and take the chute there.
8) Walk West and then North and you'll find the computer... and Army Eye.

Gaila (or Gaira?)

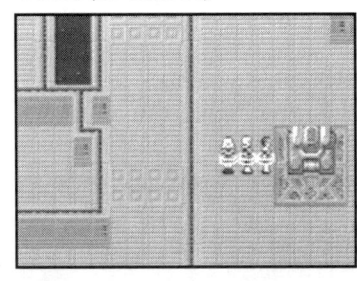

In the game, it's called Gaila. In the hint book, it's called Gaira. Take your choice. Either way, the maze is pretty simple. Just go as far East as you can. Don't worry about anything else. If (when) you're attacked, run. You can't do anything else, anyway.

Skure
First of all, there is no special secret in Skure, despite what the hint book says. However, there is one very important item and there's also lots of money. But the hint book reverses their locations. We'll let you find the money you need, but here's how to get the Magic Cap and find an exit...

146

1) From the start of the maze, walk North, then take the second turn to the West. Go to the stairs and walk down to the second basement level.
2) From there, walk East, then take the first South turn and use the stairs.
3) From here, walk North and find the room full of chests. Help yourself.

There are actually several places where you can exit the maze. For instance:

1) Starting from the beginning again, walk North and take the first turn West. Follow the path all the way around until it turns back to the East and take the stairs you find.
2) From here, you can go either North or South. You'll end up in the same place eventually. If you go North, get the chest, then take the next stairs.
3) Go South to another set of stairs.
4) Go North and turn East when you come to the T intersection. Keep going and you'll find the exit.

Try other routes if you're adventurous.

Crevice
In the Crevice, the maze is pretty simple.
1) Head East, then North to the chute.
2) Walk all the way around to the second (most Eastern) chute you come to.
3) Then walk West, North, and East to the next chute.
4) Finally, walk South to a chute, then West to another chute. You're out!

Menobe

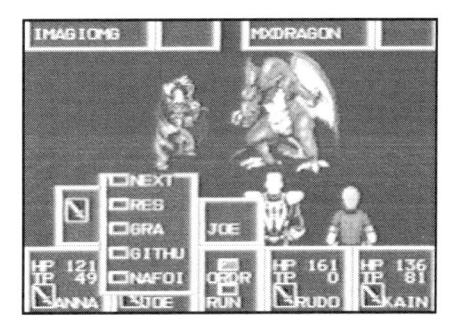

1) Begin this dungeon by walking all the way to the Northeast corner of the maze, then walking through the gap. Take the first West turn you can, then walk to the stairs just South.
2) When you exit the first staircase, look around you. See the downward stairs just Northwest of you? Find a safe way to them, and go downstairs to get the Nei Crown from the chest. Then go back up the stairs.
3) Return the way you came, then head North through the gap to the outside path. Then turn West and follow the path all the way to the Western edge of the level. Once you start heading South, pass the first gap, then turn East at the second gap. Go North at the first opportunity, and walk up the stairs at the end of that path.

Heading East.

4) Go East, walk all the way to the Eastern edge, then take the first turn you can Westward. Go North and to the Stairs.
5) Take the Eastern path to the South, then walk West along the edge of the area. When you must, head North, then West, then South again. Now turn West at the first gap you come to. To the South is the next stairway. Get the Nei Met and go back up. Rolf should equip the Nei Met, then Hinas out of there.

Guaron

1) First, walk North, through the gates, then to the second turn West. Go to the first Northern turn and walk to the top, turn West again, and follow the path until it turns South. Head out the first Western gate and into the trees. Just Southwest of you, there are two gates back into the dungeon. Find your way through the Eastern-most gate, then walk to the East and up the stairs.
2) The next levels are easy enough. Walk up six more flights of stairs, avoiding the pitfall in the center.

The Eighth Level looks different.

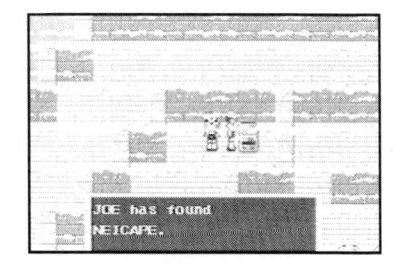

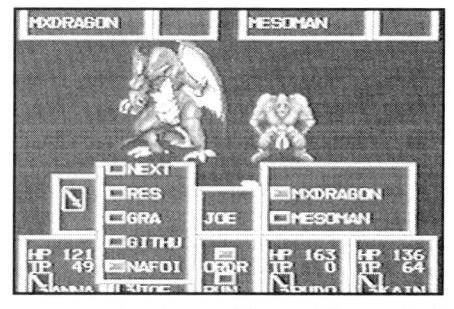

3) Now you're on the Eighth Level. Walk West and then around the spiral until you get to the chest containing the Nei Cape. Head back the way you came and find the stairs up (just North of the stairs you used to get here).
4) Now climb eight more stairs. Don't goof here! If you fall down the center pit, you go all the way down to level one again. You can stop on the Ninth Level to get the Cryst Cape, or continue up to the Sixteenth Level.
5) If you've been getting plenty of exercise, you'll make it to the Sixteenth Level. See that chest? Go get it. It contains the Nei Armor. Let Rudo equip the Nei Armor and split the scene.

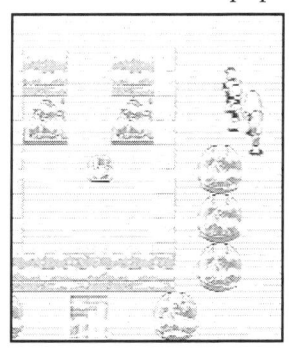

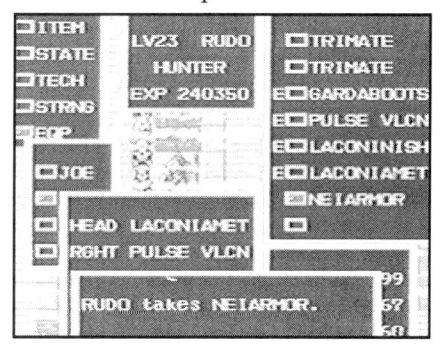

Ikuto
If you follow these directions carefully, you'll avoid wasting your time in the dreaded Sixth Level basement:
1) Walk to the West and into the first pitfall.
2) Walk South and into another pitfall.
3) Walk West to the second pitfall.
4) Walk North and into another pitfall.
5) Walk North again and into a pitfall. 
6) Get the Nei Shot from the chest just Southwest of your landing point. Equip Rudo with the Nei Shot, then use Hinas to get back out again.
7) Back from the beginning again, walk due North and into the middle pitfall.

8) Walk South and into the middle pitfall.
9) Go North, then West and into another pitfall.
10) Walk East and, yes, into another pitfall.
11) North again, and into a pitfall again.
12) You'll land in a square area bounded by four "rocks." Head East until you get to another, identical-looking area. Keep going East, but turn South as soon as you can and keep going South. The Nei Slasher is at the end of this path. Give the Nei Slasher to Anna and let her equip it. Replace the Fire Slasher. Now you're done here, so it's Hinas time again.

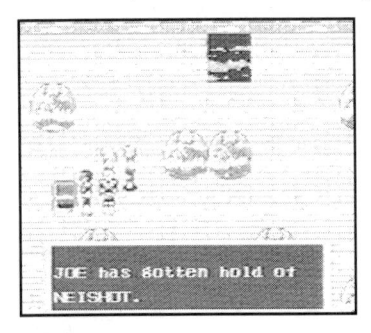

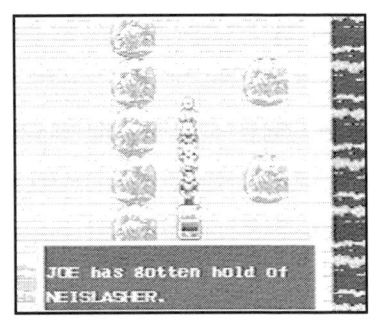

Naval

On this level, you have to figure out where and when to jump off the pitfalls. Also, look out for some fearsome enemies. For instance, the Fiend can wipe out a character in one attack!

1) Walk Northeast to the maze entrance, then head North to the first stairs.
2) Walk South and around to the next stairs. Don't fall off the edge.
3) Walk North and around to the next stairs. 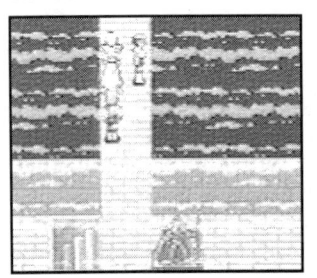
4) Walk South and around to the next stairs.
5) You're on the Fifth Level, and as the hint book states, your choices now are critical. Walk North about three steps past the wall and walk off the Eastern edge of the pitfall.

Phantasy Star II

You'll fall two floors. Now walk due West and off the pitfall on that side. There you'll find the Neimel in a chest.
6) Walk due West from the chest and drop down to Level One. Here we go again.
7) Walk to the Southeast stairs and go up them.
8) Go back to the Fifth Level and this time head South about two steps past the wall and walk off the pitfall to the East. Walk off again to the East, and once more walk off to the East. Get the Nei Shield and let Kain equip it. Finally, use Hinas to leave Naval.

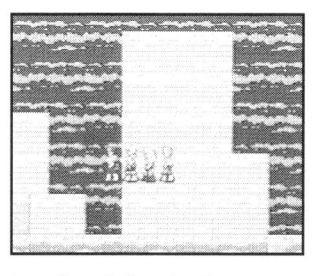

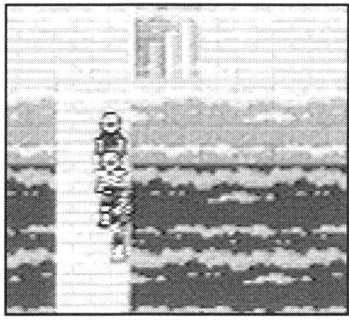

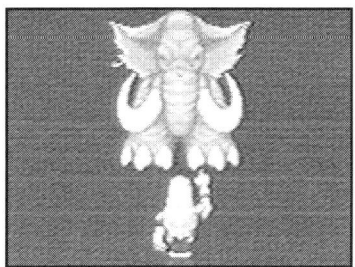

Find the place to jump to get the Nei Shield. Keep your techniques handy to battle enemies like this Wizard or the fearsome Eletusk.

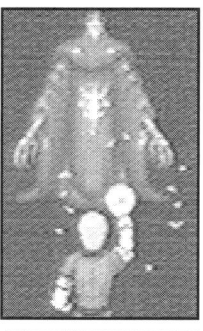

Noah
1) Level One: Head East, then North to the first stairs.
2) Level Two: Take the first stairs West next.
3) Level One: Head West, then North and East until you reach the wall. Turn North and take the first turn West. You'll find a stairway ahead. Take it.
4) Level Two: Go North to the next stairway. It's your only choice.

5) Level One: Walk West and take the first stairway you reach.
6) Level Two: Go North and East, pass the first stairway, and take the next one.
7) Level One: The next one is due North.
8) Level Two: There's only one choice here.
9) Level One: Again, there's one choice only.
10) Level Two: Again, it's obvious.

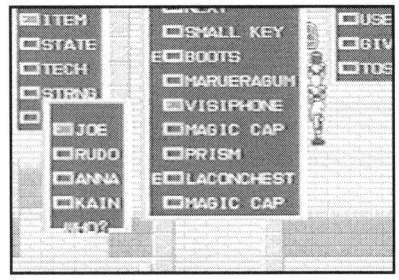

It's a good time to use the Visiphone.

11) Level One: Go South and East.
12) Level Two: Go East and South.
13) Level One: Walk East, then North, but beware. It's about to get hectic. You're about to meet the Dark Force. Are you ready? And after that?!?!!! You're on your own now.

Are you ready for this?

CHAPTER 12

Populous

Distributor: Electronic Arts
Game Type: Strategy

WHAT'S GOING ON?

Since the beginning of time, the battle between Good and Evil has raged on. Sometimes Good has been more powerful, sometimes Evil. Yet the cosmic scheme of things always balances the two forces again. Now you get to try your hand at changing that balance.

You are Good. Your opponent is Evil. Your battle will take place across nearly five hundred worlds—each populated by followers of Good and followers of Evil. As a god of Good, you must help the Good people to settle; raise crops; advance technologically; and ultimately destroy the Evil people. Of course, Evil is doing the same thing for his followers—and they will destroy your people if you let them.

Will you win and insure happiness throughout the universe? Or will Evil succeed and cast its blackness upon every life form in the cosmos? Only your wisdom will decide!

WHO ARE YOU?

The force of Good. You are all for peace, love and happiness. Hopefully, you feel this way when you're not playing the game!

PLAYERS
Populous is for one player only.

SCORING
If you conquer a world, you receive points based on the number of battles you won, and the number of Knights and settlements you have left. So it pays to rout the opposition completely.

LIVES AND HOW TO LOSE THEM
Populous is played out over a series of worlds. Each world pits you against Evil. If you destroy all the Evil followers in a world, you advance to a new world. If all your followers die, you will have to try the world again.

Your people are called Walkers. The number of Good Walkers determines how much power, or Manna, you have. So if you use Manna to flatten land for your Walkers, they'll settle more easily, and you'll get more Manna to flatten more land.

The Leader and the Ankh.

Walkers will go through lifespans; they will weaken and eventually die. In the more hostile worlds, they will die very quickly if they cannot settle. Walkers can also die in combat.

One Walker is the Leader. This Walker is similar to the others, except that he can be transformed into a Knight. Without a Leader, you cannot move the Papal Magnet.

CONTINUES
Every time you defeat a world, you advance to a new world. It is not always the next one in sequence; you may advance several worlds (depending on how well you did on the previous one).

You'll receive a password for each world you complete. When you start the game, you should select NEW GAME, and enter the password for the world you were on. Now you'll start at that world.

Even if you die on a world, you'll be allowed to play that world again.

CONTROLS

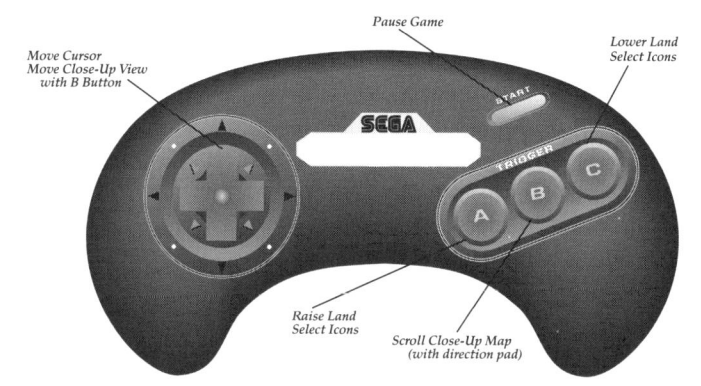

Move Cursor / Move Close-Up View with B Button — D-Pad
Pause Game — START
Lower Land / Select Icons — C
Raise Land / Select Icons — A
Scroll Close-Up Map (with direction pad) — B (Trigger)

The Populous screen may look complex, but it's really simpler than it seems:

The **Book of Worlds** shows an overview of the entire world. It also shows Good settlements (white dots), Good Walkers (blue dots), Evil settlements (dark grey dots), Evil Walkers (red dots), rocks (light grey dots), and the location of the Close-Up Map (white crosshair).

The **Manna Bar** is an indication of your current strength.

The **Info Shield** gives you information on the Walker or settlement currently selected by the Shield (the Shield Bearer): The bars on the sides of the Shield indicate the populations of Good (left bar) and Evil (right bar).

The upper-left corner shows the Alignment (Good or Evil) of the Shield Bearer.

The upper-right corner shows the Advancement of the Shield Bearer, with a picture of one of the Walker Weapons.

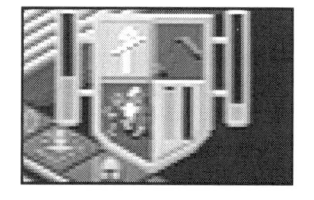

The lower-left corner shows the Shield Bearer: Walker, Knight, Leader, or settlement.

The lower-right corner shows the strength of the Shield Bearer. For a settlement, the yellow bar shows strength and defensive power. The green bar shows the population. If this is full, a new Walker will emerge. For a Walker, the bars show the strength of the Walker.

The **Close-Up Map** is a small area of the current world. It's like a zoom-lens view of the crosshair location on the Book of Worlds. It shows everything within the area in detail. You also raise and lower land with the Close-Up Map, by moving the pointer to a location on it and pressing Button A (to raise) or Button C (to lower).

The Command Symbols control most of the game. Move the crosshair onto a symbol and press A or C to activate it. Some symbols change the crosshair itself into another symbol. For instance, the Question Mark changes it into a shield. Place that shield on a Walker or settlement and he or it becomes the Shield Bearer. Click on the two arrows (the Raise and Lower Land symbol) to return the crosshair.

The rest of the commands are described well in the manual, so we won't repeat all that information. However, in the Strategy Session, you'll learn the best ways to use these symbols.

WEAPONS

Since you perform the role of a god, your weapons are truly awesome. They range from simple earthquakes to devastating floods and volcanoes. In the Strategy Session, you'll find some tips for how to use these weapons effectively.

Your ability to use weapons depends on how much Manna you have. Much of your time as a god is spent arranging the land for your worshippers, but when the Manna Bar begins to rise, so does your taste for retribution. All evil followers beware!

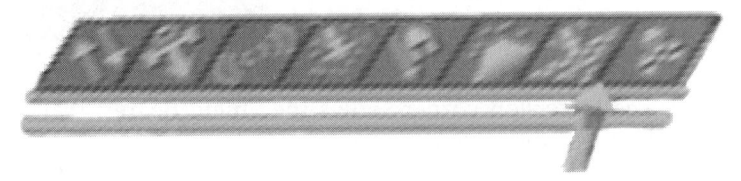

The Manna Bar.

Walkers use weapons as well—modest weapons, of course, for they are only Walkers. Walkers may use (in order of effectiveness): Fists, Rocks, Clubs, Spears, Axes, Short Bows, Balls and Chains, Long Bows, or Swords—depending on their level of cultural advancement.

Depending on the terrain of the world, there may be a limit to cultural advancement. On Desert terrains, for example, Ball and Chain is the highest weapon attainable.

SPECIAL ITEMS

There really aren't any special items in the game, other than the various command icons and the ankhs, or holy symbols, of each side.

FRIENDS

You are the Walkers' friend, and they are yours! Be good to them and you'll have power beyond imagination.

ENEMIES

Evil is the enemy, always has been, always will be. He will take actions to insure that his people prosper, while yours suffer horribly. Evil can, depending on the world, create Knights and use Divine Intervention just like you!

Another kind of enemy appears from time to time. These random enemies destroy the land they touch, and they don't discriminate. There's nothing you can do about it when a Swamp Creature cuts a swath through your carefully tilled fields leaving swamps in its wake. Random enemies are simply another problem for a god to deal with.

STRATEGY SESSION
General Strategies

Populous is a very open-ended game. You can try literally any type of strategy you like, although certain ones work a lot better than others! Here are some basic hints to get you started.

Flatten the land so that your Walkers can build castles as quickly as possible. This will start your Manna building, which is important since it is so low at the beginning of each world.

Don't try to attack Evil at the beginning of the game. You should concentrate on flattening land for quite some time.

Here's a trick to produce Walkers faster than normal; create a castle and then lower the land near it. The castle will shrink to a smaller settlement, and a Walker will usually come out. Then fill in the hole you created to rebuild the castle.

The Volcano is, without a doubt, the most destructive Intervention. Try several Volcanoes to really mess Evil up.

Use your Shield to keep an eye on Evil's Leader. This way, if he gets too strong you can wipe him out.

Building

The technique used to get the Walkers out of castles is called Sprogging. Remove one square of land next to a castle, and it will turn into a smaller settlement. This usually means the smaller settlement's population is too big, and a Walker will be ejected. With several castles next to each other, lowering one square can sprog three castles at once! Don't forget to replace the land you've removed to rebuild the castle.

If you don't have enough Manna for a volcano, here's a tricky way to simulate one: have a Walker settle in enemy land. Then scroll the Close-

Sprogging the castles.

Up map so that you can just see your settlement, but lots of Evil settlements. Then build the land up as much as you can!

You can also create flat land, and then "nipple" the land by creating small hills around it. The Walkers will create smaller settlements. Then you remove the hills, and castles will be created, releasing a large number of Walkers at the same time!

The only way you'll ever defeat Evil in the later worlds is by building as fast as possible. In fact, you'll often have to build while he attacks! If you can fend off his attacks and build, you can win.

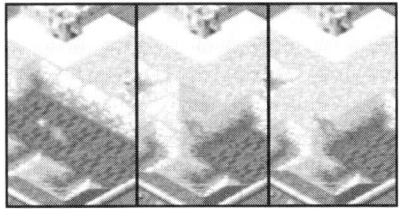

Two up and one down.

To build land quickly, raise the land twice, then lower the remaining lump. You'll fill in four squares of land with three button presses.

Divine Interventions

Earthquake: This lets Evil know you're getting stronger, but it generally doesn't do too much except distract him. For proof of this, Earthquake your own settlements and then rebuild. Didn't take much, did it?

The Volcano is the best Intervention. It will create lots of rocks and ruin the land around it. Do this to an area two or three times to really destroy! If, on the other hand, you are the unfortunate recipient of one, use an Earthquake to flatten it out. Then rebuild the best you can. Don't ignore a Volcano, because it will devastate your population.

Swamps can be very effective against castles and Leaders. They will only work on flat land, but that's where Evil's castles will be! Swamping an Evil Knight or Leader is always good for your confidence (and your Manna).

Knights can really do a number on the enemy. They'll burn the Evil settlements and make them unusable unless they're lowered into the ocean. Before you create a Knight, make sure your Leader is very strong and has an excellent weapon. You can have multiple Knights rampaging at the same time if you have the Manna to create more than one!

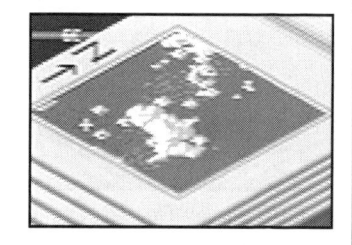

A hard Knight's day!

Floods can reverse the tide of battle with a click of the button. For this reason, it's a good idea to build your settlements about two or three levels high (if Evil can use floods). If you're flooded, and the water is harmful (as opposed to deadly), move to your Walkers and build land under them as fast as you can.

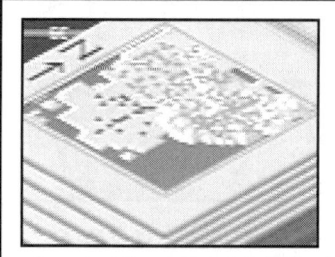

Armageddon is a mixed blessing. On the one hand, it will call the battle to a final conclusion, which you will certainly win if you have more followers. On the other hand, it won't get you as many points as you get by destroying each Walker with other means. If progress matters to you, use Armageddon; if points matter, play fully through each world.

The swamp can be a very important part of your attack. With it, you can eliminate Evil's most powerful Walkers and Knights. This Intervention will be very important in the later worlds, when his population will grow by leaps and bounds.

Defensive Strategies

When an Evil Knight attacks, you can: ignore it, and clean up the damage it creates; try to kill it by swamping or lowering it into the water; or create a strong Leader to defeat the Knight.

Another defense against Knights is to build small settlements in the hills between your castles and Evil's. This way, attacking Knights will spend their time (and their life) attacking the houses and huts while your castles remain safe.

Evil will try to swamp your Leaders quite often. Here's a defense: place the Papal Magnet in a lumpy area that can't be swamped. Now you can bring Walkers to the Magnet and create Knights to attack Evil. He'll try to swamp you, but as long as the terrain won't allow it, he'll merely waste Manna.

Offensive Strategies

A double or triple volcano will often destroy the area where it's used. A double volcano is better than two volcanoes in separate areas.

Getting in among the Evil settlements is good for several reasons. You're safe from swamping and other disasters, and you can build settlements from which to launch attacks.

The Leader

Building up your Leader can be the difference between winning or losing. There are several ways to achieve this.

The most obvious way is to use the Go To Papal Magnet or Gather Then Settle options. This will get the Leader strong and ready to rumble.

Heading for the Ankh.

Move the Leader to a settlement with a high level of cultural advancement. He'll be equipped with a powerful weapon. Weaker Walkers with better weapons will usually win battles.

Use the Leader as a pseudo-Knight by moving the Papal Magnet onto Evil settlements, and then using the Go to Papal Magnet mode. The Leader will go to the settlement and rout it! Using the Leader in this manner, along with a few Knights wandering about, will finish off the enemy in no time.

Remember that when you turn a Leader into a Knight, the Papal Magnet will be moved to the location where the transformation took place. Create another Leader quickly, or else you won't be able to move the Papal Magnet.

Miscellaneous Tips and Tricks

Watch how Evil attacks you. Learn when it switches from a building mode to an attack mode. Check out how it flattens its land. Then use this knowledge for your own devious purposes.

Evil will not often let you eliminate its Leaders and Knights by lowering land; it will just build it right back up again. You can do it with practice, but it costs a lot of Manna—that can often be better used elsewhere. On the other hand, if water is fatal in the game you're playing, lowering a very powerful knight or leader is often worth the Manna it takes.

If you and Evil start a world close together, use the Fight Then Settle mode. Your Walkers will work toward the enemy slowly, settling along the way.

Each terrain allows only so much cultural advancement. Here's each type of terrain and the level it allows:
    Grass—Sword
    Rocky—Sword
    Ice—None
    Desert—Ball and Chain

In addition, your Walkers will die faster in the Ice and Desert worlds.

All the settlements produce the same amount of Manna in the Ice worlds, so don't waste space with castles; build as many settlements as possible.

By the way, there's a limit to how many worlds you can advance by playing the game normally. If your performance in the previous game is truly divine, you'll skip five worlds.

Populous

SHH... THE SECRETS

So you want to try some of the later worlds? Here's a trick that will get you anywhere! Select New Game and Start to enter the password. But hold down the B button while you scroll through the letters—and numbers will appear. Good. Now put in a number five times the number of the level you want to play. For instance, put in 150 to play level 30! That's it. You're on your own now.

Don't try these passwords until you've become pretty experienced with the game; otherwise, you'll lose so quickly and easily that you'll become disheartened and not want to play the game anymore!

    World 100: CALEOLD   World 300: BILQAZOUT
    World 200: EOAMPMET   World 400: BADMEILL

    World 494 (The final world!): WEAVUSPERT

CHAPTER 13

Rambo III

Distributor: Sega
Game Type: Fighting

WHAT'S GOING ON?

It's not your average day, is it Rambo? You wouldn't go to Afghanistan with Colonel Trautman. You were sick of war, you said. So he went alone, and now your friend and teacher is in enemy hands. That's bad. You can't sleep at night thinking about that. There's only one solution for a man like you. It's time to act. It's Rambo time, again!

Your ultimate goal is to save Colonel Trautman, but you'll soon learn that you'll have to cause some diversions, destroy a lot of enemy soldiers, and obliterate tons of weapons and equipment.

WHO ARE YOU?

You're Rambo, the meanest, toughest, and (maybe) the luckiest S.O.B. ever to carry an automatic weapon.

PLAYERS

Up to two players can play, but only one at a time. Sorry. Rambo goes it alone.

SCORING

You gain points for every act of destruction. You also gain bonus points for completing each round in record time. For instance, if you complete Mission One in under 150 seconds, you gain 10,000 points! So even after you complete the game, you have something to shoot for (pun intended). For specific scoring information, see Enemies, a little later.

LIVES AND HOW TO LOSE THEM

You start the game with three lives, but you can also use the Options screen to give yourself as many as five. There are actually three ways to gain lives:

1. Pick up extra life happy faces left behind by soldiers you waste.
2. Certain soldiers will give you an extra life if you knife them (more about that later).
3. Well, technically it isn't an extra life, but if you're really messed up, you can just die and start over. You can continue this game endlessly up until the sixth and final mission. Then, it's do or die!

You lose a life every time you get hit by a bullet, blown up by a grenade, or wiped out by a truck or tank. However, you can run into other enemies without taking damage. It's not a good idea, though. They generally shoot you at point blank range.

Whenever you're shot, you are invincible for a few seconds. If you're into knifing enemies, that's a good time to do it, since they can't shoot you until you stop blinking.

CONTINUES

You'll get endless continues for the first five missions. You always start each new game with the same number of weapons as you ended the last one with (unless you turn off the machine, of course). The endless continue feature allows a very interesting strategy, as you will see.

CONTROLS

Before you begin the game, choose Options to set the difficulty level you want (Easy, Normal, Hard, or Hardest), then set the

Pause Game *Fire Machine Gun*
Direction Pad

Select Special Weapon *Use Special Weapon*

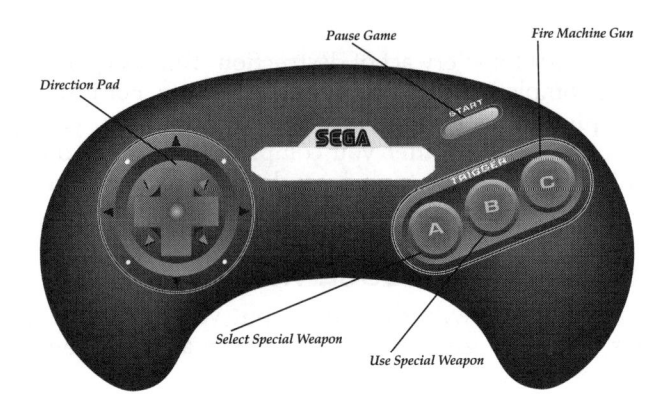

number of lives you want (listed as Players). If you don't like the way the controls work, you can reassign the buttons to different functions:

SEL stands for Select. Use the Sel button to select which special weapon is active.
SPE stand for Special. Press this button to use the special weapon you've selected.
MAC stands for Machine Gun. Press it for continuous rapid fire.

Now try the sound test to listen to the various game sounds.

Start pauses the game. It's not a bad idea to press the Start button if you get overwhelmed. It gives you time to decide how you're going to get out of the situation you're in. But remember, as soon as you press it again, you're in the action!

WEAPONS

Use the **Survival Knife** to kill enemy soldiers in hand-to-hand combat. But don't expect them to use knives. They'll shoot at you as you try to approach, so pick your victims with care. And remember, this isn't a Swiss Army Knife. You have a pretty hefty reach with this poker, so use it. Don't wait until you're right on top of an enemy to use the knife. That's a good way to get killed. Instead, charge up fast and hit him from a slight distance. You'll be amazed how effective this technique can be, once you learn to judge the distances.

Rambo III

The **Machine Gun** is your basic weapon of destruction, you can fire an endless stream of bullets. Somehow you never run out. Isn't that nice? Oh, and if you stand still and keep shooting, you'll lay down a deadly pattern of bullets.

The **Explosive Bow**: Yeah! When you really want to take down something heavy and stay out of the way at the same time, try using this killer bow. Just get a good pull on the string, and you can blow up tanks and jeeps and helicopters with one shot! The bow will also kill soldiers, but it does have some limits. It won't take out the guard towers or the massive gates that block your way. For that, you'll need bombs:

You'll get to know Rambo's **Time Bombs** pretty well before you're through. They come in handy in lots of situations.

SPECIAL ITEMS

There are three: One-Ups, Extra Arrows (marked with an A), and Extra Bombs (marked with a B).

FRIENDS

As you might guess, there aren't many. In fact, there are only two, and they're no help at all. One is a secret agent you have to find in Mission Two, and the other is Colonel Trautman himself. Oh well, Rambo doesn't need any help.

ENEMIES

As usual, Ram, baby, you're surrounded. Guys with guns seem to come right out of the woodwork. You blast ten or twenty, and thirty more come at you. And they don't fight fair, either. They throw grenades over walls, shoot you any time, and they'll even run you down in jeeps. But you'll take care of them, won't you?

A **Common Soldier** is worth 100 points if you use your machine gun, but knife him for extra points. In the first two levels, the first soldier you knife is worth 200 points. Each one thereafter (if you don't die) is worth 200 extra points, up to a maximum of 1000 points. By the third mission, soldiers are worth 300, 600, 900, 1200, and up to 1500 points. If you're good with the knife, you can gain lots of extra points in certain parts of the game. But you'll have to be fast.

A **Jeep** is worth 100 points.

A **Tank** is worth 1000 points.

A **Helicopter** is worth 1200 points. Like the Common Soldiers, Helicopters are worth more for each one you destroy in a row.
Each Guard Tower is worth 100 points. Destroy them with bombs.

STRATEGY SESSION
General Strategies

You'll notice that enemy soldiers don't have automatic weapons. That's fortunate, because if they did, you'd be toast. But you're the only one with the really good toys, and, I guess because of your superior reflexes, everyone else's bullets seem to move in slow motion. Duck and weave. That's your motto. There may be a lot of them, but they're slow as molasses at the North Pole.

Practice running while swinging the gun back and forth. This is the best way to clear a path through enemy lines. Be careful, though. Sometimes you'll be standing in front of a soldier and shooting, but you'll miss him on both sides. Don't get caught in that position.

Bombs. Use bombs to take out the guard towers. They can be a nuisance, but they're easily eliminated. One bomb near the base is all it takes.

You'll come to huge gates that block your path. Some will require several bombs laid out in a pattern along their width. Be careful, though. Snipers often hide behind the gates and shoot you down.

Bombs will destroy just about anything on the ground. Use them to destroy troop trucks before they can unload their cargo.

For the most fun, use bombs to eliminate whole groups of enemy troops with one shot. There are several places during the game where you are attacked by maybe ten or more soldiers at once. A well-placed bomb can work wonders.

Caution: Don't stand around after placing bombs. They'll kill you, too!

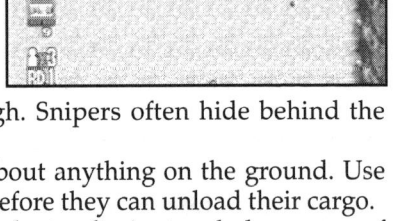

Charging Up. In some missions, you'll need lots of bombs, and the best way to get more of them is to knife lots of soldiers. However, if you try to knife soldiers in a crowd, life can be short. True, you'll get a lot of them, but they'll get you, too. On the other hand, if you just pick out solitary victims, it will take a long time.

The best way to charge up on arrows and bombs real fast is to go on what we call suicide missions. Since Rambo has more lives than an army of cats, you can simply find a nice crowded area and knife away. Sure, you'll die, but you continue right where you left off. It's brutal, but that's the nature of this game.

Once you're charged up, then you can continue with the current mission with plenty of bombs and arrows.

First Mission.

Mission One is a good place to learn how to use your weapons. Your object is to infiltrate enemy lines, but the mission is pretty easy. That doesn't mean it's useless, though. Practice using the bombs and the arrows. See those little gray cylinders? Try shooting one with an arrow from a safe distance. A little goes a long way! And you don't have to pull back far on the bow. Any arrow will set them off.

This is also a good place to practice your knifing technique. Right from the beginning, you can knife three soldiers who come out of the truck. Or you might try bombing the truck and moving on. It doesn't matter.

This is also a good place to practice a skill you'll need throughout the game: weapons selection. You always have your trusty machine gun, but get used to changing special weapons on the run so you can quickly move from knife to arrows to bombs. Later on, you don't want to be thinking about it. It's best if switching weapons becomes automatic. So practice a little bit.

Get rid of the first guard tower by shooting the gray cylinder with an arrow. Or use a bomb, if you prefer. You can also get rid of another troop truck with the arrow-to-cylinder technique. Keep shooting the machine gun, though, to get rid of any other enemies, and don't get blasted by a grenade thrown by those guys behind the bunkers.

The real test of this level is to bomb the two guard towers, then bomb the front gates. You'll need to move fast and stay one

How Rambo Opens Gates: First bomb the guard towers so you don't get shot while you're working. Then drop some bombs next to the gate, run back and watch the fun.

step ahead of the bullets to succeed, but with fast movement you can blast your way through the gate and into enemy territory. Lay three or four bombs in a line in front of the gate, then run for it.

Tip: The snipers behind the gate fire in a pattern. Count four consecutive shots, then move in and lay down bombs. Run back and wait for the blast.

Now you're into enemy territory, but you're not through Mission One just yet. The enemy has one more test for you—a helicopter right in your way.

To blast the helicopter, hide behind the rocks for safety and plan your attack. If you're quick, you can dart out from behind the rocks, pull part way back on the bow, and let fly an arrow. You'll know when you connect, because the copter will glow briefly from the hit. However, it will take several shots like that to skrunch the whirlybird. The other way is to wait until your opponent goes behind the rocks, then take a good full pull on the bow and release. One shot like that and the copter is scrap metal! You'll need to practice the technique of darting out from cover, drawing the bow and aiming the crosshairs at the same time. It's a useful skill as you'll find out in future missions...

Second Mission.

In this mission, you have to find the secret agent. He'll be the third prisoner you find, no matter which order you look in. So don't get fooled. You'll have to explore the whole maze. Then, once you find the agent, you'll have to get out of there fast, before the place blows up. The trick here is to find the agent in the place closest to the exit. Since the exit is to the Northeast and there's an agent almost directly North of your original position, it might be best to save him for last—for two reasons. One, because you have to get to the exit fast, and two, because suddenly you'll be greeted by a horde of enemy troops intent on giving you grief. So do it the hard way if you want, but I'd save the Northern agent for last.

The other two agents can be found by heading East, then South. One is to the Southwest, and the other is to the Northeast, but you have to go down the Southern corridor to get to him.

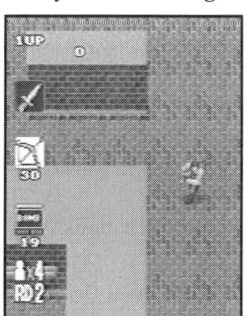

The maze isn't very tricky, and there aren't all that many enemies along the way, so you should be able to complete this mission without much trouble.

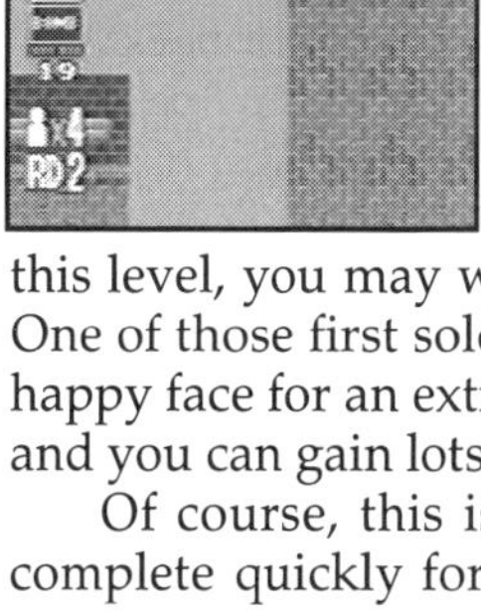

At the beginning of the mission, there are lots of enemies. You can destroy them with bombs or shoot the ammunition dumps with arrows to send fireballs up and down the corridors, but once you get good at this level, you may want to use the knife. One of those first soldiers may give you a happy face for an extra life. Strike quickly, and you can gain lots of extra points!

Of course, this is a mission you can complete quickly for extra bonus points, so you may want to ignore the beginning soldiers and simply run away from them. Head Southeast and go straight for the first two agents. Then come back to the last one and on to the exit and Mission Three.

Third Mission.

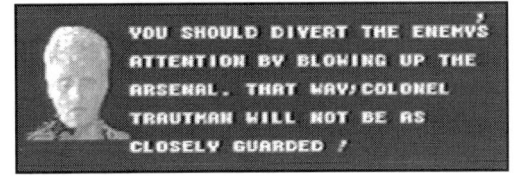

You'll never get to Trautman. He's too well guarded even for Rambo. Maybe if you create some commotion... A little well-placed diversion... How about blowing up all the enemy's weapons? Good idea.

In this mission, you have to get to the arsenal. Here, you have to contend with camouflaged soldiers, guard towers, jeeps, narrow bridges, and enemy time bombs. You'll need all your agility to get through this one.

First, head East, past three guard towers. Ignore them, though. They won't bother you if you just keep moving. If you're quick, you can bomb them just for points. Now turn Northward and over a bridge. Here you'll encounter jeeps and enemies with time bombs. Don't get run over by a jeep. Oh, and this might be a good place to pick up extra supplies if you're into a knifing session and don't mind starting the mission over when you die.

Once you're through playing with jeeps and time bombers, make your way as quickly as you can to one of the narrow bridges. Keep that machine gun smokin' and lay a few well placed bombs to cover your back.

Now head East again, past the two barracks buildings. You'll pass a guard tower on your left. Bomb it, or it will give you trouble later. Once you pass it, you can't go back to it.

Now you'll come to the gate. Bomb the second guard tower and then bomb the gate. You can also stand back and shoot the gate with

Rambo III

the machine gun, but it takes a while, and bombing it is more fun. If you use the machine gun, you'll know you're succeeding because the gates will glow for a second with each hit. You may have to find the right position to shoot from, but if you took out both guard towers, it is pretty easy.

Now you have to destroy the tank. This is pretty much the same deal as you had after Mission One, only the tank is a little easier since it can't fly. Just time your shots. It's probably easier to take a lot of potshots at the tank than to try to get him with a full charge. With patience and good timing, you'll prevail.

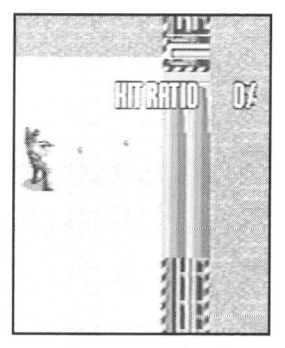

Fourth Mission.

OK. Now you're inside the arsenal, so you might as well cause as much destruction as you can. First, head East and blast your way through the first gate. If necessary, replenish your supplies by knifing the enemies at this first part of the stage.

Once you're through the gate, head East, then down through the automatic door. Immediately turn West again and head across the railroad tracks. Keep moving West, past the tracks and through the narrow opening. Head North through a narrow corridor, then turn to the East. A

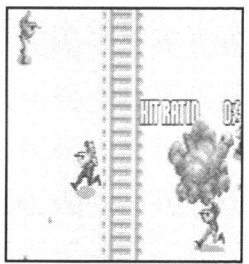

Creative use of bombs: Get your enemies; cause chain reactions.

little further, and then turn North. You'll come to a room full of small explosive boxes labeled "Sega." Set a bomb on the left-hand one and you'll start a chain reaction that blows them all up at once. Or take care of them one at a time with machine gun or bombs.

Next, head back the way you came and find the other Sega dump to the Northwest of this section. Blow up the Sega boxes there and then head back the way you came—back over the tracks, and almost straight East. You'll find another room full of ammunition. Blow them up with bombs or machine guns, then exit the room and head North to the first automatic door you used. Notice that your Hit Ratio now reads 56%. That means you're more than half way there!

Head out the automatic door and almost directly North, go through another door. Head up the Eastern corridor in this section and don't worry about the enemy soldiers. Most of them won't bother you. Just shoot the ones that get in your way.

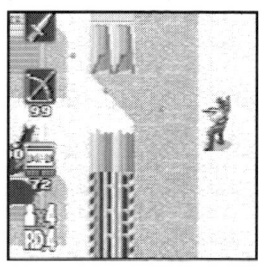

Now blast your way through the door to the next ammo dump. However, this one is especially easy. Just stand outside the room and blast with the machine guns. If you don't go too far forward, no enemies will appear. Watch out for stray grenades, though. Once the first two ammo containers are powdered, move up a little and take out the next two. Four more containers await you in the next room, then you head back the way you came, your Hit Ratio up to 88%.

Once you are out of the long corridor, head West as far as you can go, then turn North. Head West again at the top and cross the tracks. Slightly to the North is another gate to blast. You'll probably be pursued by enemy soldiers, so shoot the gate as you run toward it. You shouldn't even have to break stride. Now run quickly and drop bombs next to the helicopters. When you have blasted enough of them to rubble, your Hit Ratio will disappear and the

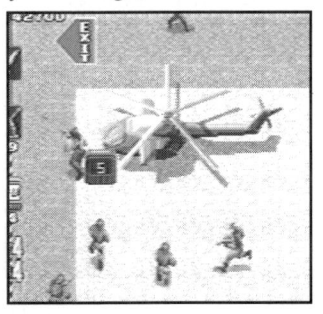

Rambo III

message will tell you to head for the Exit. Run to the Northwest corner of the room and out you go! On to Mission Five.

Fifth Mission.

In this mission, you have to penetrate the fortress where Colonel Trautman is being held. You'll want to have plenty of bombs here, so you may want to do some knifing. There may also be an extra man here.

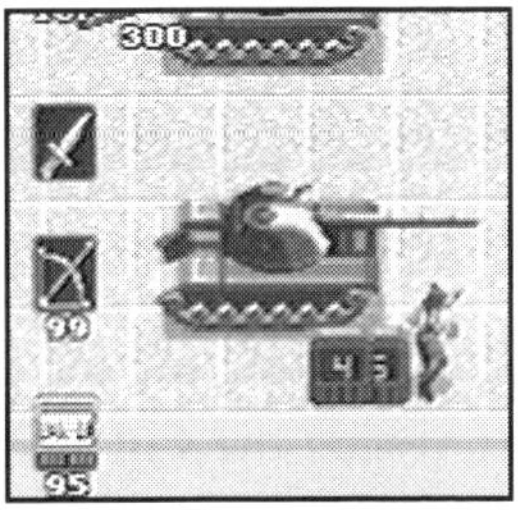

Time to charge up!

Once you're ready, run East, avoiding the tanks. Bomb them if you wish. Then head Southeast through the helicopters. Optionally bomb a few of them, just for fun. Now East again, then to the North, being careful of the tanks. You don't have to mess with the tanks, however, just run by as fast as you can.

Now blast the gray cylinder with an arrow, then get ready to use bombs and machine gun to wipe out a lot of enemy soldiers who keep coming out of the doors straight ahead. Eventually, they'll stop coming. Lay a bomb or three in front of the middle door and then you're through. Except for the two helicopters waiting for you! You might have guessed there was more.

Get the left helicopter, then the other is easy.

These copters aren't all that hard. Remember, they can't shoot when they're behind the buildings, so if your aim is true, you can take a long pull on the bow and let go as they come out from behind the walls. One shot like that for each of them, and you're on to rescue the good Colonel.

One additional note: Since you can't continue past this mission, don't even bother to complete Mission Five if you will only have one or two men left for the next mission. The chances of blowing it big time are too good. If you really get wiped out in Mission Five, it's probably wiser to start over than to risk getting killed in the next one. You can complete Mission Six with one man, but it's very risky!

Sixth Mission.

In this mission, you finally have your chance to rescue the Colonel, but it won't be easy. The maze in this mission is more complex than the others, and, to make matters much worse, you can't continue if you lose here.

First, head East as fast as you can. Then turn North and keep going until you get to the checkerboard floors. Immediately turn West, then South. At the bottom of the corner, turn West and immediately go back North. Go through the first opening to the North and continue along the twisty corridor until you reach the railroad tracks. Watch the openings along the West side of the screen. Count four full openings and head into the fourth one.

South, then West.

Keep shooting until you've shot out the prison bars. Colonel Trautman will come running and you'll both escape out the North exit. Whew. You did it!

At last, the Colonel!

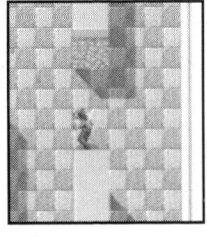

Well, you're almost done. Just one more minor obstacle. Yes, this time it's a tank and a helicopter together!

176

Rambo III

Escape!

The secret to this encounter is to shoot the helicopter. It will fall on top of the tank. So don't bother with the tank, just the bird. Use the same techniques you used before. Luckily, the two machines fire at you simultaneously, so you can time your shots in the ordinary way. That's it, though. Now you've earned your rest.

SHH...THE SECRETS

One tip we've heard about involves Mission Two. After you reach the third agent (the one in the Northeast), blast your way right through the wall leading West. You can save yourself some time that way.

This trick can save you time and earn a better bonus score.

Sorry, Rambo III doesn't have any other real juicy secrets that we know of. However, it's a pretty easy game given the endless continues and the many weapons at your disposal. So you don't really need secrets, do you?

CHAPTER 14

The Revenge of Shinobi

Distributor: Sega of America
Game Type: Arcade Action

WHAT'S GOING ON?

I am Musashi. Since my birth, I have studied the ways of the Ninja. My sensei taught me slowly, first teaching me basic physical skills such as leaping and somersaulting. Then I learned to throw the Shurikin. But not until I was ready did I finally learn about Shinobi—the art of stealth. And with Shinobi came Ninjitsu—Ninja Magic.

Now my sensei is dead, killed by the treacherous Neo Zeed clan. And my beloved Naoko has been kidnaped. My sensei must be avenged, my lover rescued—and the Neo Zeed destroyed!

WHO ARE YOU?

I am Musashi. Do you get the feeling of deja vu that I do?

PLAYERS

My mission is not the concern of others. But one player—he with the magical Control Pad—may assist me on my mission.

Revenge of Shinobi

SCORING

The true Ninja is not concerned with points. But he with the Control Pad is. Most of the members of the Neo Zeed are worth anywhere from 200 to 1,000 points. The Power Villains (or "Bosses" as my sensei said they were also called) are worth more points (see "Enemies" for each).

Finally, the patient and skillful Ninja will obtain bonus scores. If you do not use Ninjitsu in a Scene, you are awarded 10,000 points. If you finish a scene with 11 Shurikins for every life remaining, you are also awarded 10,000 points. (My sensei never did explain the reason for this—perhaps the three numbers have a cosmic significance beyond a mere Ninja's understanding.) There is also a secret bonus—worth 50,000 points—but only the best user of the Control Pad will find this.

LIVES AND HOW TO LOSE THEM

The Control Pad user can select the number of "lives" I am given for a game. There are four Game Difficulty levels: Easy, Normal, Hard and Hardest. For the Easy level, I am given 10 lives. For Normal, I am given three. For the Hard and Hardest levels, I am given but one life in which to defeat the Neo Zeed.

Within each life, I have a Life Bar. This Life Bar is slowly shortened as I am injured by the weaponry and physical attacks of the Neo Zeed. (I have noticed this always seems to be the result of unskillful tactics by the user of the Control Pad.) If the Life Bar runs out, my life is ended. If I do not have another life, my mission is a failure—and I will not see Naoko until she reaches the spiritual realm.

Every time I complete a Scene, I am awarded two lives. At 50,000 points, I gain an extra life. At 100,000 points, my Life Bar is extended by two segments. And for every 100,000 thereafter, I am given an extra life.

CONTINUES

If the Control Pad user hinders me and loses all my lives, the Continue Game screen will appear to him. From this screen, he can continue up to three times—each time from the first Scene of the last District I reached. If all three continues have been used, the mission is truly finished.

CONTROLS

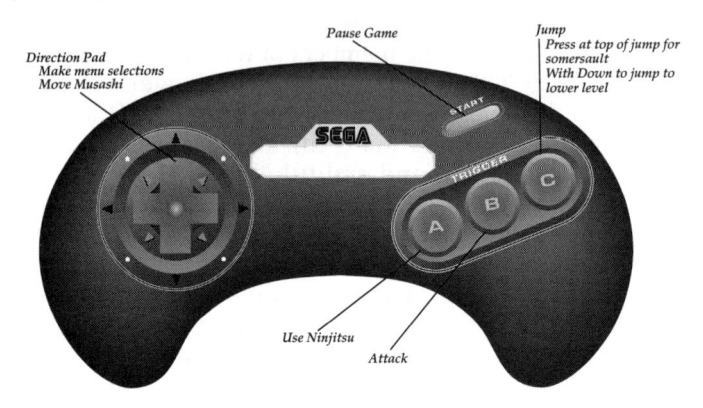

- **Direction Pad**: Make menu selections / Move Musashi
- **Pause Game**: START
- **Jump**: Press at top of jump for somersault. With Down to jump to lower level
- **Use Ninjitsu**: A
- **Attack**: B

WEAPONS

Although Ninja such as myself prefer not to use weapons, they will be required to fight the Neo Zeed on their own terms. The Shurikin is the weapon I use. You may select the number I start with on the Options screen (anywhere from 0 to 90 Shurikin). Additional Shurikin are found inside crates. There are both 5 Shurikin and 20 Shurikin symbols.

During a somersault, press the attack button to throw eight Shurikin at once—a wasteful attack, but often necessary.

There are several other weapons to be found inside crates.

> The **Power Pack** increases my Life Bar, makes the Shurikins faster and more accurate, gives me a deadly sword, and allows me to Cross Guard. This technique allows me to deflect Death Stars with my Shurikins. However, if I am hit, I will lose the benefits of the Power Pack.
> The **Bomb** will explode when it's touched or when its timer runs out. It would be very unwise to be near it when it goes off.
> By throwing my Shurikins and kicking at seemingly empty locations, I may find many other hidden weapons.

The most powerful "weapon" of all is Ninjitsu, the Ninja magic. There are four jitsus I can use.

> **Ikazuchi** will call Thunder out of the sky to protect me. I will not be injured, and my Life Bar will not lower. After several hits from the Neo Zeed, Ikazuchi will fade out.

> **Kariu** will call Fire from the sky to surround me with a fire column, which will then split and fly across the screen, destroying every enemy in its path.
> **Fushin** will add strength and ability to my jumping. My jumps and somersaults will attain maximum distance and height.
> **Mijin** is an act of last resort; I call upon my inner spirit to release itself, causing my body to explode. The explosion will destroy anything nearby. I will obviously lose a life when using this jitsu.

I am allowed to use one jitsu during each area.

SPECIAL ITEMS

The crates also contain items that assist me on my mission.
> A **Small Heart** will add two segments to my Life Bar.
> A **Large Heart** fully replenishes my Life Bar.
> The **Musashi** gives me an extra life. There are 1-Up Musashis and 2-Up Musashis.
> The **Ninjitsu** gives me the power to use Ninjitsu. Normally, I can only use one jitsu in each area. The Ninjitsu symbol allows me to use another jitsu.

FRIENDS

Naoko is my friend as well as my love, and I will do anything for her—as will you if you join me on my quest.

ENEMIES

The Neo Zeed is a huge clan; however, evil draws to itself the weakest minds, which in turn leads to weak bodies. The only people of the clan worth mentioning in detail are the Power Villains. Even my sensei would gasp at the thought of the Boss.
> **Blue Lobster** is a huge samurai warrior armed with a sword that can swipe away Shurikins with ease.
> **Shadow Dancer** spins and twirls around in the air, throwing Shurikin at any time.
> The **Computer** is invulnerable except for its brain, which it keeps concealed most of the time.
> **Master Attacker** is so strong, he throws cars at you!
> The **Armored Car** is a massive vehicle that must be disabled by shooting its controller domes.

Spider-Man is a heinous robot that will turn into another, even more dangerous form.

The **Brontosaurus** is a huge animal with more than a passing resemblance to Godzilla.

The **Boss** is the leader of Neo Zeed, and the embodiment of all evil. When I destroy him my mission will be complete, the world saved, and I will be reunited with Naoko.

STRATEGY SESSION
General Strategies

Here I repeat the guiding words of my sensei, as he told me long ago during my training.

"When you take part in combat for the first time, make it as easy upon yourself as possible. Use all the Options at your disposal. Take all the Shurikin you can hold. Also, each Power Villain has a weakness that you can exploit—but you must look not with the eye, but with the mind."

"When you break open a crate, get close enough so that you use your sword or kick instead of wasting a Shurikin."

"See The Secrets for a way to obtain your goals without risk—and without honor."

On the night before he was killed, my sensei awoke me to tell of a vision he had during his after-dinner meditation. At the time, I did not know its significance. Only after my mission against the Neo Zeed had begun did I realize it was a warning of the incredible dangers I would face. Here is the vision, edited slightly by myself to make the Control Pad user's task easier.

Round One: The Bamboo Garden.

"When you enter the Garden, run to the right. Several of the Neo Zeed's Ninja will materialize in front of you. Use the Shurikin or get close enough to kick them. Then a sword-armed Samurai appears. You must get close enough to hit him, without him blocking your Shurikin. He will not present much challenge."

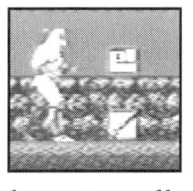

Revenge of Shinobi

"Open the two crates for a Power Pack and some Shurikins. Now you can block the enemy Shurikin with the Cross Guard. You can jump up and walk along the top wall or stay on the ground; the Ninja will jump up to attack if you are on the top."

"You will have to walk along the ground a short while, but do not let down your guard; a dog will attack you. Then you'll find two crates; open the second one for Shurikin. Continue until you reach another ledge. Open the first two crates you find for Shurikin. At the end of this ledge, two Ninja will appear; watch out for them. Open the next crates you find and walk out of the Garden."

The House of Confusion. 
"Kill the guard and walk onto the stone with the triangle. The door will open. The crate above the door and the crate to the right of it both contain precious Shurikin. Continue until you reach the bamboo grills. These are very sharp and very dangerous indeed."

"Walk atop the elevator grill. You must use this to get to the crate on the far right of the top ledge—a 1-Up. Then go down and to the right."

"The next crate you find will contain the Power Pack. Take it and continue right. Open the crate. An arrow will appear directing you to the left—this is because you have opened a secret path inside the House. So return to it. Before you enter, position yourself just outside the door. Face right and do a somersault throw of Shurikin. A Large Heart will be revealed. You must do another somersault to grab it."

The secret path.

"Just past the moving grill will now be a pit. Fall down and pass the door, but watch out for the Ninja that will emerge from it. Crouch to walk past the grill. Then jump over the next few."

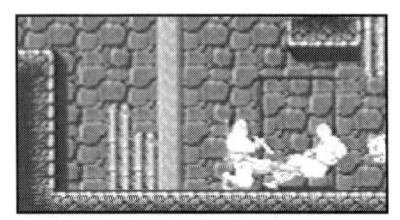

"You will have to pass several doors and grills, but it will not be too difficult—use the sword when they are in close range. You will soon reach the end of the pit. Now you will have to use a somersault jump to escape. You will need to jump slightly to the left to avoid hitting the platform."

"The upper ledge of this House contains two crates—a Small Heart and Shurikin. Collect them and leave the House. Find one final crate—and then you will face a Power Villain!"

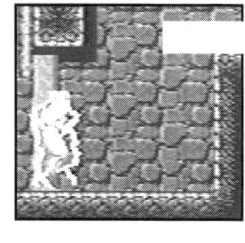

JITSU OF

IKAZUCHI

Escape!

"This Villain is named Blue Lobster. He is grossly huge, and wields his sword as only the masters do. Destroying him will take patience and skill."

"Jump onto the top ledge and stay there. Face to the right. Now Blue Lobster cannot harm you with his sword. Do a series of somersault jumps. During each one, fire the Shurikin to hit him while his sword is lowered. If you do this correctly, the Blue Lobster will fall to defeat within a few hits."

Round Two: The Waterfall.

"Using the jitsu of Fushin is something you should carefully consider. There will be many treacherous jumps, difficult in the extreme."

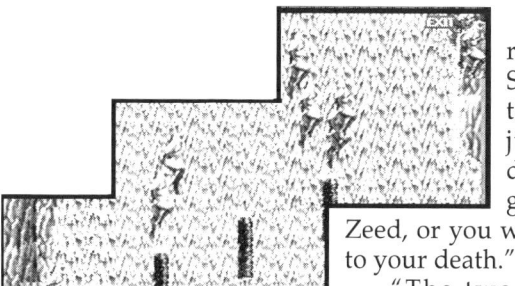

"Walk to the right. Open the Shurikin crate. Continue right. The jumps are indeed difficult—do not get hit by a Neo Zeed, or you will surely plummet to your death."

"The two crates contain a Small Heart and Power Pack. Then, next to the Go arrow pointing upwards, will be a Shurikin crate. Open it, take them, and prepare for the next jump."

"You will need to leap onto the log, and then to the ledge. If you have used Fushin, this will be easier. Without it, you will need to use the somersault jump. Either technique will still not guarantee success. Complete the jump and run to the right. The crates can be passed. Continue until you reach the next arrow."

"You must leap to the right, stopping on the ends of the logs only briefly before your next jump. Three jumps will take you to the end of the Waterfall."

The Backstreet. 
"At the start, leap upwards until you reach the roof. Avoid the two stacked crates—they are Bombs. Go right. The single crate has Shurikin, the stacked crates a Bomb and Shurikin. The next crate you reach contains the precious Power Pack."

"Keep going right, grabbing crates. Try to stay at the top of the buildings; below are false nuns and pits that are quite fatal. Before long you will reach the end of these dark, evil streets."

The Bistro

"The strobes in this building will make it difficult to see your enemy, the Shadow Dancer. Use the mind's eye to concentrate."

"This Villain will spin around, with several afterimages following him. Stay close to him, and kick him when he's on the ground. One by one, the images will fly off of him until you reveal his true self—a mere shadow! The strobes will now help you to see him. If you have a jitsu remaining, use Kariu."

Round Three: The Airport Compound.

"Open the two crates at the beginning. You'll need the Power Pack and Shurikin inside. You will be on one side of the fence; if you wish to go over, do a somersault jump."

"Your enemies will be very well armed—flame-throwers, grenades and other dishonorable weapons. Flip over the fence as needed to avoid the Neo Zeed and to collect crates. The somersault Shurikin throw will be of much help here, if you have the Shurikin to waste—which is doubtful."

Over the fence.

"If you ever get weak, use the jitsu of Ikazuchi to protect yourself. If you are as unfortunate as to die, you'll be able to use another jitsu in your next life, so do not worry about waste."

The Cargo Jet.
"I have never been happy with the airplane—if the gods had wished us to fly, we would be given wings. But you are going to have to ride the wind aboard this monstrosity to succeed."

"Jump over the door and ride the elevator up. Kill the Neo Zeed and gather the crate. The reason you must avoid the doors is that when they open, they will suck anything out that is near them—including yourself."

Revenge of Shinobi

Stay away from doors.

"Use the elevators to go up and down, checking every section of the plane for crates. The jitsu of Ikazuchi can be useful here."

"The exit of the plane will thankfully appear soon, at the top level of the plane. Go through."

The Computer Vault.
"Walk forward immediately to the round Vault. Avoid the laser at the top of the room. Once the Vault is visible, walk to the left again until you can't see it. Then walk right again; now the brain of the Vault can be seen. This confusing technique is not a result of your actions; the Vault periodically opens and closes. You are trying to catch it during its open period. At the same time, you must avoid the lasers in the ceiling."

"When the vault is open, do a jump and throw the Shurikin to hit it. Then do a somersault jump and hit it again. Repeat the back-and-forth walk until the brain is again visible, then repeat the jumps. If you run out of Shurikin, use the jitsu of Kariu."

Round Four: The Junkyard.

"The Neo Zeed will use the cars in this junkyard for defense, but they don't work well. You will easily kill the Zeed fools and collect the crates."

"A crate at the bottom of a pile of cars will contain the Power Pack; this will make your journey even easier. If you are very cautious, you could use the jitsu of Ikazuchi, but it should not be necessary."

The Motor Mill.

"There is a challenging jump at the very beginning of the level. Use a somersault jump to reach the conveyor belt, and then use normal jumps to prevent a tragic fall. Jump onto the platform with the crate. Wait until a lifting hook slides at you from the right. Jump onto it and ride it. If you miss the jump, you'll fall into a blowtorch, but you won't be killed."

"You must walk off the hook as soon as it begins to slide left again. Fail, and you'll plummet into liquid metal hot enough to dissolve you. Remember not to concentrate on this horrible possibility. Horrible. What a disgusting fate that would be."

"Walk to the right until your progress is blocked by a wall. At this point, using the jitsu of Fushin will help you immensely. Jump up and walk to the left. You must make it to the top of this Mill."

A horrible fate.

"At one point, you will need to do a somersault jump—with the power of Fushin. Start going right after you complete this jump. Jump onto the hook and ride it again. Leap past the blowtorches. You will need to fall down the final hole so that you land on a platform; do this and run out the door for your next confrontation with the Power Villain."

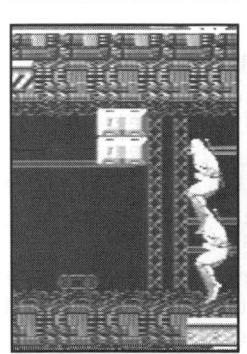

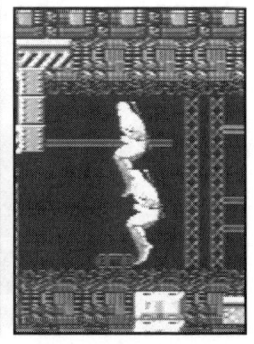

The Side Yard
"There is something about the Master Attacker that is not quite right—as you soon discover."
 "Use the jitsu of Ikazuchi. Wait until he lifts a piece of metal into the air. Then run towards him and slash him. After he throws the metal, he will try to charge at you. Stay next to him and keep slashing. He'll keep turning darker and darker colors. Eventually, he will explode to reveal his true self—an android! Hit him once by doing a somersault jump throw. He will explode again—this time for good."

Round Five: The Laser 'Scraper.
"Use Fushin before you even start to move—its jumping power is very much necessary here. You will need to leap upwards from platform to platform. There are lasers on certain platforms, and plenty of dishonorable Neo Zeed. Do not be conservative with the Shurikin—you will need to use many to reach the top. Once at the top, move to the right."

It's a trap!

The Freeway.
"The somersault jump will take you from the platforms to the freeway. You will need to jump back and forth to collect crates and avoid or destroy your enemies."
 "There will be many false nuns on the freeway, and gunners on the platforms. You might find it safer on the freeway, but you won't be able to stay on it for too long. Most cars will miss you, but the Red Cars must be driven by

the Zeed. They'll hit you every time. Find the end of the freeway quickly."

High-Speed Chase.
"This huge Armored Car must be stopped! You must destroy the red domes that emerge at intervals. At the start, stand still and wait for the first dome to come out. Shoot it with the Shurikin. Avoid the sparks by jumping over them. When the first dome is gone, walk to the right. Try to jump onto the platform so that you are in front of the dome, but not on it. Now kick the dome as it emerges. When it is gone, walk to the right again until you are standing in a gap. Here, you must leap the sparks and shoot the final dome as it comes out. If you have a jitsu, use the Kariu now."

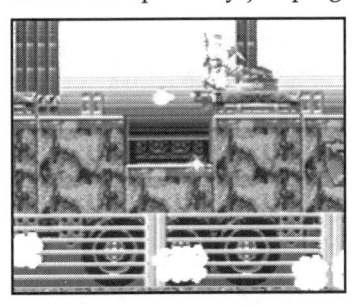

Round Six: The Kung Fu Gang.

"Use Fushin at the start. Jump up to the platforms and fight the Zeed members. There will be crates scattered amongst all the levels."

"*One enemy will be armed with a twirling object that will make it very difficult for Shurikins to hit. Get close and use your kick.*"

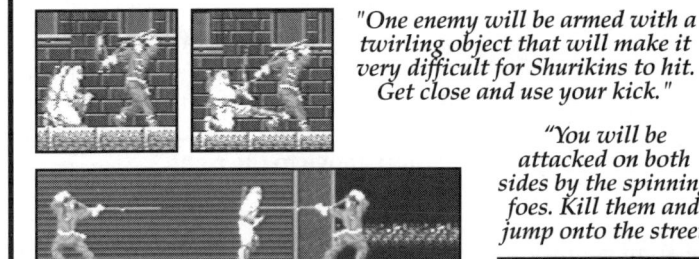

"*You will be attacked on both sides by the spinning foes. Kill them and jump onto the street lamp just past them. Jump left and use a somersault jump throw to reveal a Power Pack and 1-Up. Collect them, jump up, and then jump right.*"

"Get the 1-Up. Then the next building will have the same opponents as the last one, but none of them will be overwhelming. Finish them off and enter the subway."

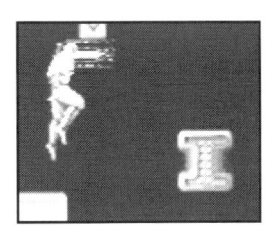

The Train.
"Move to the right, collecting the crates. Platforms will fly onto the screen from the right; you must dodge them or you will suffer damage. You will eventually have to deal with Ninjas as well as the platforms; move slowly and nothing will surprise you."

"Eventually the train will leave the tunnel. Now your attackers will include machine gunners as well as Ninja. Take it slowly. When you reach a row of crates, the fourth one from the left contains a Small Heart. When you reach a Zeed armed with a flame-thrower, you are almost ready to depart the train."

Spider-Man.
"This is not the 'comic-book' character from that magazine I once found in your room. He is an evil creation of the Neo Zeed. He crawls along the ledges above you, firing three webs downward. Then he drops on his own web, trying to kill you with a glowing radiation."

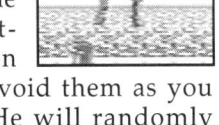

"Use your jitsu of Ikazuchi. Jump between the webs and avoid him as he drops down. Shoot him when he's crawling around on the roof. Eventually, he will turn into a Bat-Man! He will summon bats to his defense; avoid them as you shoot the Bat-Man. He will randomly swoop down at you; avoid these attacks. If you hit him enough, he will finally explode."

Round Seven: The Breakwater.

"The ocean passage is guarded by Ninja and machine gunners. Walk slowly, for some Ninja will hide in the waves below. This is especially true when you have to cross the gaps on the rafts."

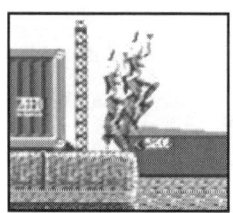

Get a good take-off.

"There is not much else to say about this section. You will need your best jumping ability. Also, use the cunning you have learned. Do not charge straight ahead, but find a way to attack your enemies from safety."

The Machine Room.

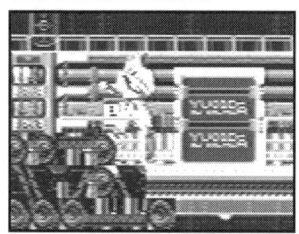

"Walk to the right. Sliding hunks of machinery will head at you; jump over them or outrun them. Continue until you reach the wall; then jump down and start going left."

"There will be machine gunners in addition to the machinery; neither should be of major concern. You will soon reach another wall; jump down and you will be at the bottom of this room."

"The glowing pools are harmful. You will need to jump from platform to platform, killing the gunners to stand safely on the platforms. Using Ikazuchi can be very helpful if you happen to fall into the pools. At the end of this level is the exit."

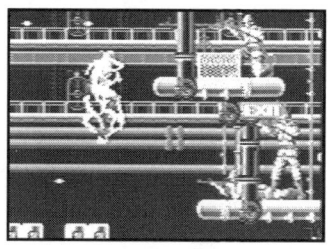

The Cargo Hold.

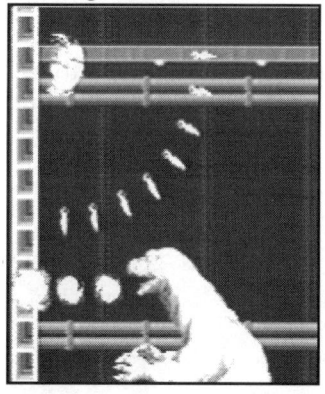

"This huge Brontosaurus will walk right up to the platform and start exhaling deadly flame—you will know when his belly glows. You must jump upwards, using the somersault jump throw to do damage. When you have been weakened by his flame, use the jitsu of Mijin—it will be the only way. Repeat your jumping with your next life, and use Mijin again. The Brontosaurus should die, or be very near death."

Revenge of Shinobi

Round Eight: The Searchlight.

"Practically all of the foes you have faced will be here—gunners, grenade throwers, spinners and more. There will be deadly guns that raise and lower, firing huge fireballs."

"There will be a ledge where the spinner will knock you off if you try to leap to it. Use Shurikin to drive him back, and then leap. Shortly after that, you will find the entrance to the Cellar Maze."

The Cellar Maze.
"There are many doors within this chamber; the way is both difficult and simple. The doors with white rings upon them are doors that lead further into the Maze. To succeed, you must pass some doors and go through others."

"By the way, if you want, you can search for the secret basement storehouse of the Neo Zeed. However, here is how to find the Boss and your beloved Naoko."

"Walk to the right, past the first two doors with rings. Continue until you reach a pit."

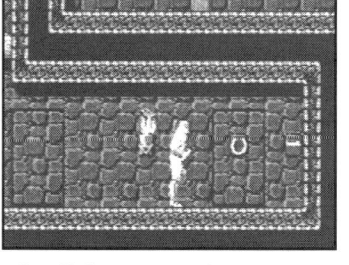

" Fall down to the bottom and enter the door with the ring at the end of the corridor."

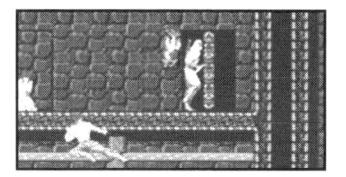

"Again walk right and enter the ringed door. Walk right once more, jump over the half wall, and fall down the pit."

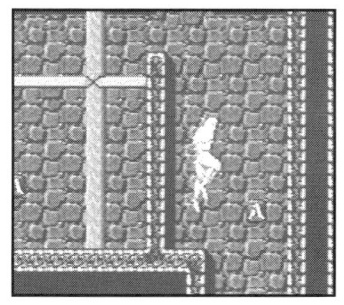

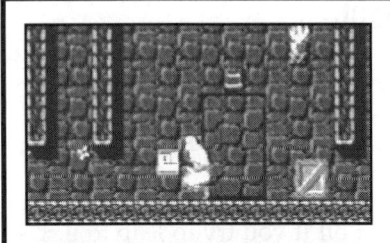

*"Walk left along the ground. Using Ikazuchi may help because there are many Neo Zeed. Enter the bottom ringed door at the far left.
Now walk right and on to your final confrontation. Before you enter the last door, find the secret Power Pack, then prepare for battle. You must remember all your training to defeat The Boss."*

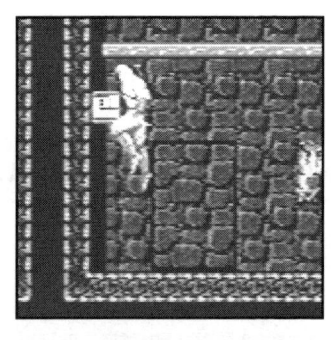

The Inner Sanctum.
"The Boss is both evil and sadistic. He has taken Naoko and put her in a room with a huge stone above. Unless you stop it, the stone will crush Naoko—and your heart with her. And a Ninja without heart is better off as a spirit."

"The Boss will twirl his hair around; it is sharp and deadly. You must... you must..."

My sensei could not recall anything after this point. However, when I found him after the Neo Zeed's attack, he told me—with his dying breath—how to defeat The Boss.

I have kept this information secret—but you will need to know it. See The Secrets and it will be revealed.

SHH... THE SECRETS

Here are the final words of my sensei:
"The holes on the walls, both left and right, will stop the lowering of the stone, but only briefly. Walk toward The Boss,

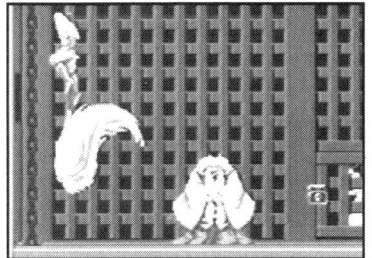

Revenge of Shinobi

crouching and shooting until you hit him. When you do, jump up quickly and shoot the slot. You must avoid being hit by his hair."

"When you are feeling weak, wait until he lashes at you with his hair. He is open to attack then, so use the jitsu of Mijin. Defeat him! Do not let my training be for nothing..."

Hit The Boss, then jump and hit the hole in the wall.

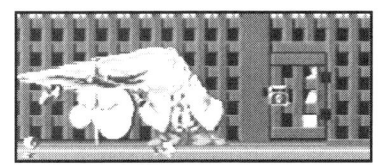

Use Mijin when you feel weak.

My Sensei actually told me something else, but I've just remembered it. It was when he was describing the Motor Mill area and the jump at the beginning of that part of my mission. He said, "Now is a time for your spiritual training to move to a new level. You will need practice in this place, but the reward will help you attain your goal. Shoot at the base of the first conveyor belt. There will be revealed a special symbol of Musashi. Jump to it and let the conveyor carry you back. You'll lose a life, but gain two! Continue this practice to the limit of your patience, and you will have learned the trick of nearly endless life. Use your new skills to help you to your goal."

Spiritual Practice.

I later found out that there are other places to gain nearly eternal life. For instance, I found the secret on the airplane, too. Perhaps airplanes aren't as bad as Sensei thought.

There is another technique that the Control Pad user may benefit from, as dishonorable as it is. Go to the Options screen and select 00 Shurikin. Now wait a while, or press some buttons, and the two zeros should merge into an infinity symbol! I will now have an infinite supply of Shurikin.

CHAPTER 15

Space Harrier II

Distributor: Sega of America
Game Type: Arcade Action

WHAT'S GOING ON?

The Space Harrier has been recuperating for the last ten years. His victory over the evil forces of Dragon Land had taken a heavy physical toll. But the familiar call for help is heard again—this time from Fantasy Land. And once again, Space Harrier must do all in his power to destroy the evil forces that have taken over Fantasy Land—and their leader, Dark Harrier!

WHO ARE YOU?

You control the Space Harrier, once again. You're armed with an autolock launcher and a will to win.

PLAYERS

Space Harrier II allows only 1 player. Sorry!

SCORING

Spacey gains points by destroying Dark Harrier's forces. He also gains points in two bonus rounds where he rides a destructive jet-sled!

LIVES AND HOW TO LOSE THEM

You start out with five lives. Being hit by a bullet, running into an enemy, or hitting something on the ground reduces your count by one.

Gain extra lives for every 1,000,000 points. Yes, that's right. This is a very high-scoring game! In fact, since you score points as you advance forward, you should gain extra lives pretty fast. The best place to gain lives, though, is in the bonus stages which occur after each five areas you complete.

CONTINUES

None. Space Harrier has to do or die. However, you can select the level you start on at the beginning of the game—you may start at any level except Level Thirteen. You have to earn your way to that one.

CONTROLS

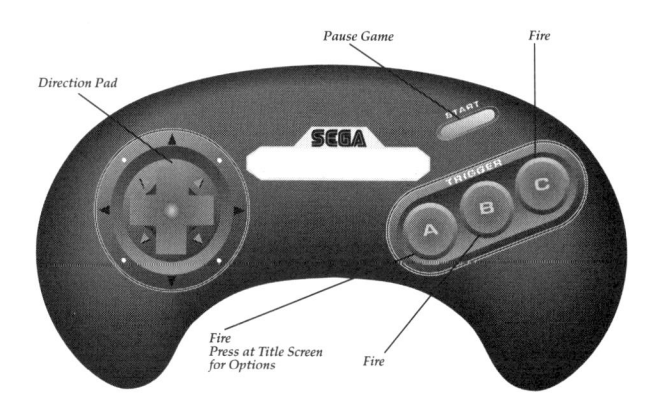

Pause Game
Fire
Direction Pad
Fire
Press at Title Screen for Options
Fire

WEAPONS

Spacey has but one autolock launcher to use—but he uses it well, doesn't he?

SPECIAL ITEMS

'Fraid not. Who wants to waste time with those when there are aliens to zap?

FRIENDS

None. Space Harrier likes to fight alone.

ENEMIES

The Dark Harrier has gathered an impressive lineup of bad guys for Space Harrier to fight. There are some familiar enemies and unfamiliar ones. Here's a roundup of your foes.

The Trimuller is a three-headed turtle that doesn't move at a turtle's pace at all!

Paranoia might scare you, but will it instill paranoia? As long as your trigger finger is fast, probably not.

Brizard is a cool-headed dragon.

Neo Doms are larger, more deadly Doms than you've ever fought before.

The Mantichora is a huge flying tiger! Shoot his wings and he'll attack you from the ground!

The Wizard is an evil ghost that can split into several versions of himself.

Medusa has looks that could turn most guys to stone!

Neo Tomos, like the Doms, are bigger and better than the original spherical Tomos.

Cragon is a huge mushroom being with a see-through brain!

Bins Been is a huge angled ball that will bowl you over!

Love Face obviously hasn't been in love for some time—he's not very happy-looking.

Cthugha is almost the brother of Brizard—except Cthugha's hot stuff.

The Dark Harrier is very powerful and very sturdy. You'll need all your skill—and a lot of lives—to beat him!

STRATEGY SESSION
General Strategies

Space Harrier II, like the original Space Harrier, is a fairly simple game. The Options Screen will let you make the game easier at first, and then make it tougher as you progress. Other than that, the descriptions of each level below will help you prepare for the heady task that awaits you. Shall we dance?

Level One—Stuna Area

The attackers in this Level are Jets. They attack from both sides and from the front as well. If you position yourself correctly, you can shoot all the Jets before they get a chance to get close to you. After

Space Harrier II

their attack a Dragon appears! Watch out for his fireballs as he heads toward you; when he turns around, let him have it.

The Boss on this Level is the Trimuller! (You can tell a Boss is approaching when there's thunder and lightning; now you know!) Dodge his fireballs as he approaches; when the heads pop out, shoot them! Get rid of all three heads and you've saved the Stuna Area.

Level Two—Fors Yard

Pillars make their appearance here. They're not too tough to dodge—yet. Your attackers will come in waves from the distance—once again, you can shoot most of them before they get close. After a brief intermission with some Jets, the pillars will return.

A ring of the nasties will zoom at you; fly carefully as you shoot them. Beat them and the next Boss shows up—Paranoia. Shoot the energy balls revolving around the 'Noid while circling to dodge his fire. Get rid of all the balls and Paranoia will just float there; fire away!

Level Three—Yees Land

This level is walled in from the top and the bottom. Your attackers vary; first some Jellyfish, then Doms, then Frogs that will hop at you while they fire. Later on, they'll jump from behind you. Turn them into frog's legs and Brizard will make his appearance. Use the same technique as you did with the Dragon, and Brizard will be bruised quickly.

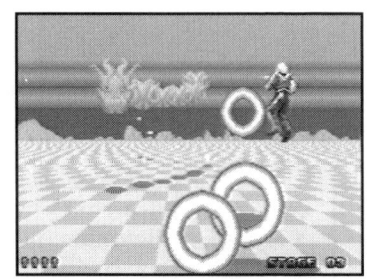

Circle around and over his shots.

Level Four—Zero Polis

The name of this level should be "Dom Polis", because that's what you'll be fighting on this level. Doms will attack from all directions; you've got to dodge carefully thanks to the Pillars. They won't be too tough, but the Boss Doms will be! They spin around in a circle, firing lasers like they're going out of style. They'll fire no matter where they are on the screen, so circling and shooting is the way to go here.

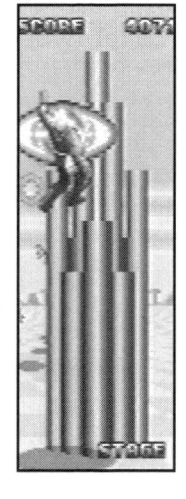

Bonus Stage

You'll only get the Bonus Stage if you've completed four levels; so if you started on Level Two, you wouldn't get this until the end of Level Five. But no matter when you get it, the strategy is basically the same: shoot everything in sight! Slight movements left and right work better than big ones, but even then you should still shoot like crazy. Each object you hit is 50,000 points!

Level Five—Copper Hill

The Pillars will be more difficult to get through—they come at you faster and in groups. Each group will have a hole that you can run through—but it will be tight, to say the least.

Your enemies will be pretty easy, although the Jets can give you fits. Before you know it, you're at the latest Boss; the Mantichora! It will fire at you and fly towards you until it covers almost the whole screen! Keep pumping energy into it and it will lose its wings—but not its drive to get you!

Its attack pattern will change. Now it will run left and right, left again, and then towards you. When you do damage and

Weird stuff!

it starts to turn colors, it will fire at you as it runs back and forth. If you're patient, the Mantichora will fall without problems.

Level Six—Fallpyram

Gargoyles and circling attackers lead off the level; then the Pillars arrive. After them come some Doms from behind you. Beat the Doms and the Boss will arrive. The Wizard is a pretty scary-looking apparition! He'll back up and then split into three! Fire at any of them; they'll all take damage. Circle-and-shoot until the Wizard's spell on life fizzles out.

Level Seven—Craddha

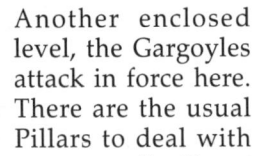

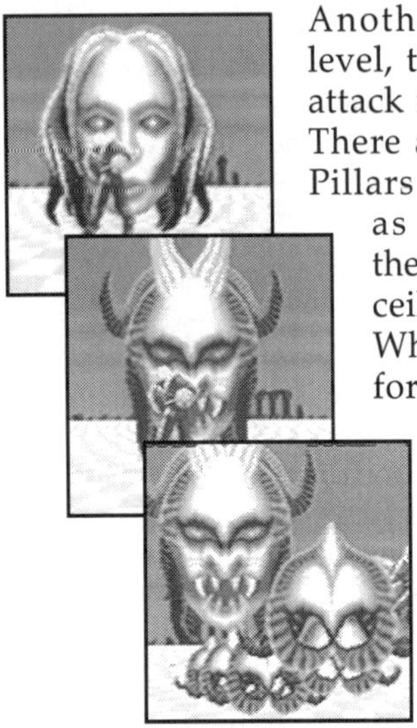

Another enclosed level, the Gargoyles attack in force here. There are the usual Pillars to deal with as well. Shoot the Rocks on the ceiling for lots of handy-dandy points. When the ceiling peels back, get ready for an attack; Medusa! She'll fly up to you, open her eyes, and reveal her true self! Yuck!

Luckily, she's much like the Dragon; use the circle technique and she shouldn't even come close to hitting you with a bullet. She won't turn to stone when you finish her off; she'll explode!

Level Eight—Monark

Attack of the killer Tomos; they'll lead off the level and make return visits. Jets, Frogs and other flying beings make your job tough as well. And when you've finished the level, the Neo Tomos attack again! Spin in a circle or you're toast.

If you started from Level One, you'll get another Bonus Stage. It's much the same as the first, so you should use the same strategy and make your fire button go into meltdown.

Level Nine—Felcold

Jets and Clams never made a Space Harrier so miserable before! The Jets will attack in the usual patterns; the Clams will be on the roof. The Boss is the gross Cragon. It will circle around, firing huge spores at you. Circle in kind. When it flies toward the screen, feed it some laser beam. Not good for the Cragon's health, but good for yours!

Level Ten—Hope City

The first half of the city is Doms; the second half is Jets. Both of them will attack the way they did in previous levels; use the same ways of killing them that have gotten you this far! The Boss is the Bins Been; watch out as it comes from the left side of the screen. Wait until it opens, and then fire at it to blow it up!

Level Eleven—Hell Peak

From hope to hell? Hmmm. But don't spend your time thinking about the weird level names; go into action against the Gargoyles and Rocks that attack. Tomos appear halfway through the level. Fight your way to the Love Face. Hope to hell to love? It's getting really weird now!

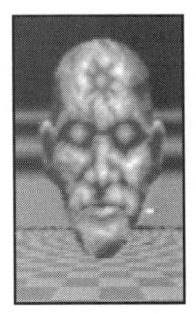

When the face comes at you, fire at it until it splits into four. But it's not gone yet! It will reconnect and start firing at you. Return the fire until it flies back up to you. Repeat until the Love Face is a Lost Face.

Level Twelve—Hot Palace

This is the last Level you can select at the start of the game, but it's not always wise to start from here, mainly because you need to build up your points (and consequently build up your men) on the lower levels.

Your enemies, mainly Gargoyles, are secondary compared to getting through the Pillars. You'll learn their patterns with experience, but they're still very difficult to run through without losing several lives. Get past them and you're up against Cthugha. Treat this Boss like you did Brizard, and you're off to the final battle!

Level Thirteen—The Dark Harrier

The Dark Harrier has arranged a little reunion for you. He's brought all the Bosses that you already fought! Here's the order of the reunion: Trimuller, Paranoia, Brizard, Neo Doms, Mantichora, Wizard,

Medusa, Neo Tomos, Cragon, Bins Been, Love Face, and Cthugha. If you mastered them the first time, do it again!

After you've greeted all the Bosses with your laser, Dark Harrier intervenes. At this point, you should know how to take care of him. See The Secrets if you just want to get it over with—but what kind of attitude is that?

SHH... THE SECRETS

How do I defeat the Dark Harrier? Dark Harrier will appear and disappear, firing all the time. He'll occasionally drop back and turn into a huge swirling fireball! If you circle-and-shoot, he should be kept off guard and on the defensive. He'll take a lot of hits—but you can beat him!

CHAPTER 16

Target Earth

Distributor: DreamWorks
Game Type: Arcade Action

WHAT'S GOING ON?

Everybody knows that space is the final frontier. Did you know that Earth is the final target? Find out in Target Earth.

You see, a large invading force is attacking Earth and all its galactic outposts. You must defeat them and learn about Earth's forgotten legacy, the secret of the Chron.

WHO ARE YOU?

Your name is Rex. You command an Earth Defense Force Assault Suit Wing at Ganymede Base. Assault Suits are awesome twelve-foot tall, armored battle machines with radical fighting capabilities. You are a master at Assault Suit combat, and it's up to you to defend the human colonies from Chron.

SCORING

Score points for each enemy you defeat, as well as a time bonus at the end of each round if you complete it quickly. At two different points in the game you can earn bonus points for defeating your enemies in quantity.

LIVES AND HOW TO LOSE THEM

Start out with three lives, each with a full life meter. When the meter reaches zero, that's it. Your Assault Suit explodes and you die. Standing still for a short time lets your life meter recover. You can recover all your strength if you stand still long enough—even though it costs you bonus points. Lose your three lives and the game ends. Then you have the option of continuing or beginning a new game.

CONTINUES

Target Earth has three continues. You can get more continues—sometimes—when in the Option menu. If Sergeant Leana appears with the legend "Continue Up" you may begin the game with 9 continues! Each continue will put you at the beginning of the last round you played.

CONTROLS

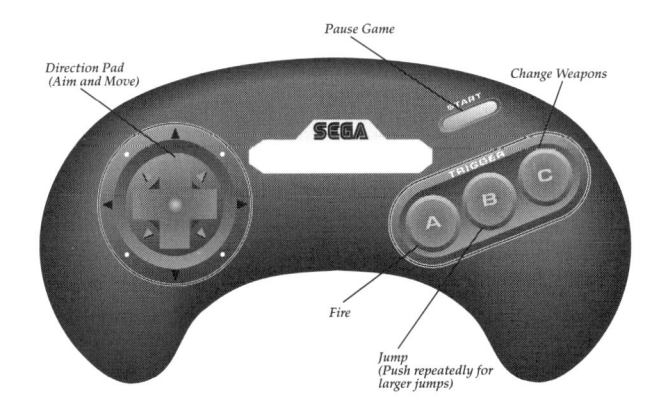

- Direction Pad (Aim and Move)
- Pause Game
- Change Weapons
- Fire
- Jump (Push repeatedly for larger jumps)

WEAPONS

The Assault Suit carries the most powerful array of weapons known to man. As the game progresses you will be able to select from a growing field of weapons. Add weapons to your arsenal, or drop them in the "select weapons" segment at the beginning of each round.

LG Gun: A single gun. The least powerful weapon. It almost never runs out of ammo.

HG Gun: A larger, higher-powered version of the LG Gun, it can fire only a limited number of bullets.

25 SC: Fires three shots with every burst. A good general weapon.

40 SC: A more powerful version of the 25 SC.

GL: A pistol-shaped grenade launcher. Grenades explode on contact with the enemy or the ground.

MGL: A more powerful version of the GL. Has a larger blast radius.

DD: A variable direction launching grenade that explodes in the air, releasing a small cloud of explosive projectiles.

150 BZ: A bazooka type weapon. Fires high-explosive shells.

203 BZ: A more powerful version of the 150 BZ. Can destroy larger targets with relatively few shots.

Missile: Guided missiles that strike the closest enemy target.

M Pod: Each Pod holds 50 rockets, but they are not as strong as missiles.

EAS: A laser weapon that fires a piercing beam. Can only be fired horizontally. Each weapon holds 70 bursts. Effective against large numbers of weaker enemies.

Burst Attacker: A bouncing weapon which explodes on contact with the enemy... or after a certain amount of time.

SPECIAL ITEMS

Armor: Armor gives you added protection against enemy fire and contact. It grows stronger with each round.

B Pack: The Back Pack will give you the ability to fly—for short periods of time—in gravity environments. It can get you out of many a tight squeeze by putting you above the line of fire.

Shield: When worn, it will cut your damage in half. It's hard to get—but worth it.

FRIENDS

You can identify your friends by their colors. Friendly troopers of the Assault Suit Wing wear brown armor, and fly in brown or white spacecraft. Their laser fire is blue and cannot hurt you.

There is also Sergeant Leana. Sometimes she will give you extra continues in the Option menu. In any case, she is your girlfriend and will be on your mind if you make it to the end of the game!

ENEMIES

Your Chron enemies wear green or blue armor. There are more than a hundred varieties. They will fire at you as soon as they spot you! Chron attackers range in size from micro-robots to full-scale, deep space flag ships! In addition, expect to battle against machine-gun nests, computer-operated Gatling cannons and a wide range of attack aircraft.

Your main enemy in the game is Rance Culzus, your counterpart in Chron. You must face Rance four times in the course of the game. Only by defeating him can you move on. Listen carefully to what Rance says. He gives you clues as to what Chron really is.

STRATEGY SESSION
General Strategies

Target Earth is a game of eight stages. Each stage is a mission in itself. The missions take place in outer space, on land, in the air, and below ground in the enemy fortresses.

Maneuvering in the air and on land are slightly different. In the air, you will move in whatever direction the firing arm is pointed. On the ground your movement choices are restricted to left or right, and to jumping. Whatever you do, don't rush! If you move too fast the enemy will blast you faster than your life meter can recover. It's best to move, fire and rest. You may lose some bonus points, but you will get farther in the game.

When fighting, save your most powerful weapons for the largest enemies. And look for weak spots. When you shoot and see the enemy "flash," you've scored a telling blow. Here are the missions and what, briefly, you must accomplish in each.

Stage 1—Raid on Ganymede

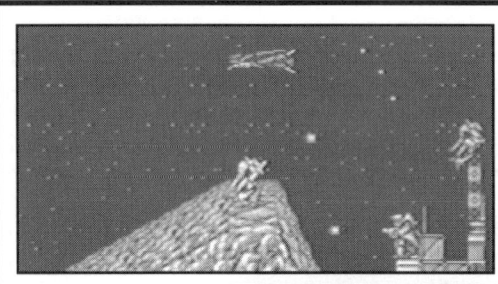

O.K. Here are your orders. Start out from the Ganymede Base.

Destroy the enemy war ship before it crosses the D Line.

Try running past it and attacking from behind. Get the guns first!

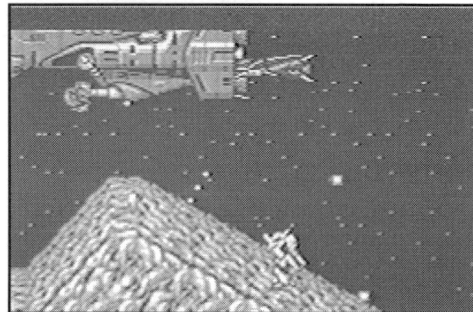

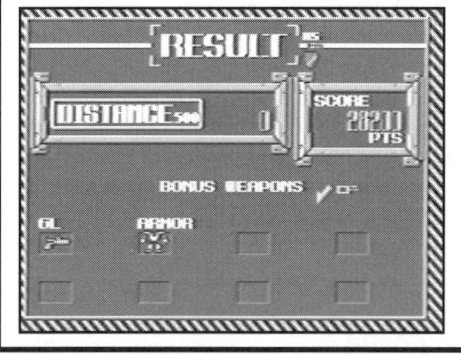

Finally, collect some bonus weapons and points for a good performance. Get ready for the next stage of the mission.

Stage 2—Escape

Protect the base inhabitants as evacuation procedures are carried out. Use the shuttle's cover fire as long as possible to preserve your life meter. Remember to jump on the shuttle just in front of the yellow arrow.

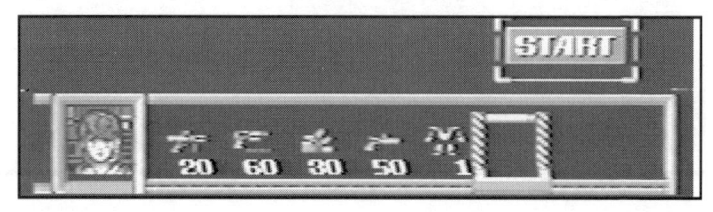

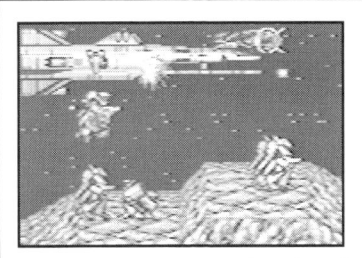

When you come to the edge of a cliff, jump out, away from the edge. There's an enemy waiting directly below. Get ready for some fast action at the bottom.

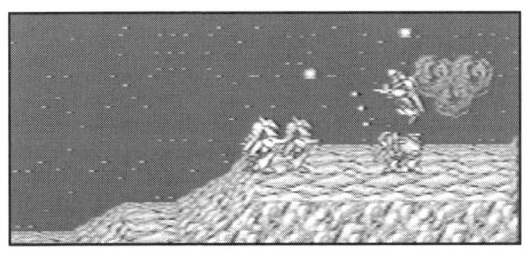

Advance at a medium pace, letting your companion ship blast some of your enemies. Their aim isn't all that good, though, so be ready.

Stage 3—Orbital Attack

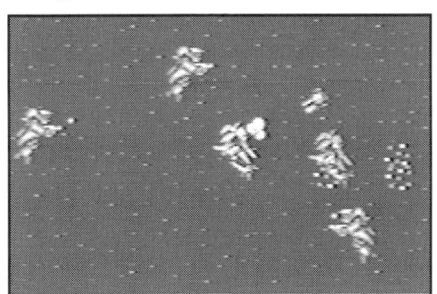

The action starts to heat up now. Guard the space shuttles before atmosphere re-entry. Stay below the shuttle, so it is just off screen. The enemy will not attack it and you will benefit some from its cannon fire.

These guys are tough. Be sure to shoot them as fast as possible.

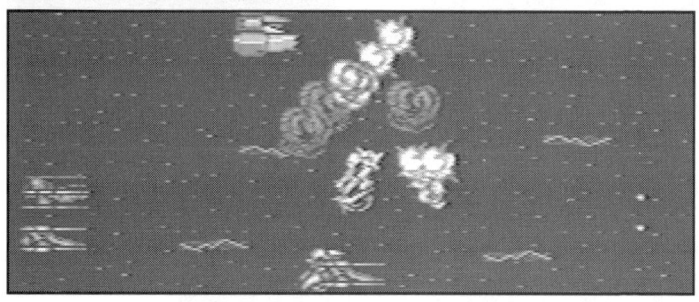

You aren't alone. You'll get some help from time to time.

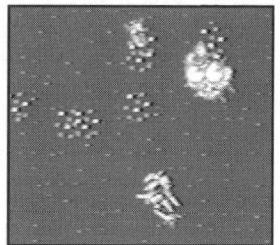

Circle around the big ship and blast it into space dust.

Stage 4—Front Line Assault

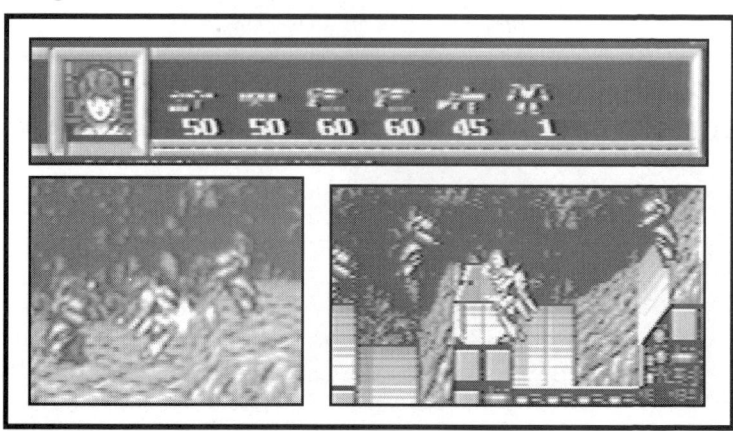

Target Earth

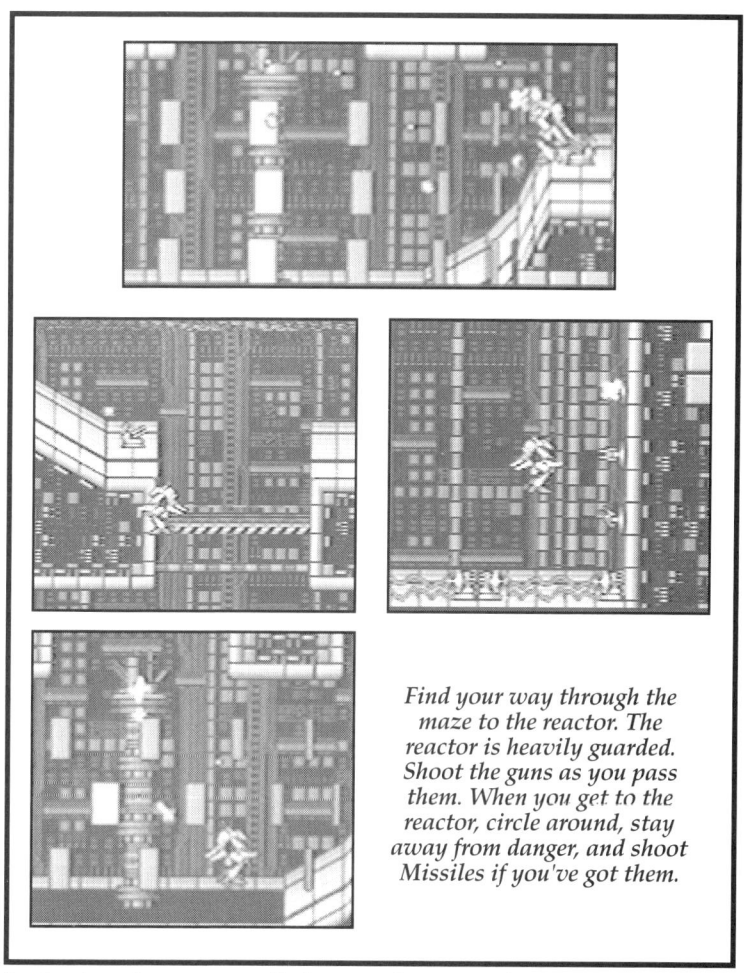

Find your way through the maze to the reactor. The reactor is heavily guarded. Shoot the guns as you pass them. When you get to the reactor, circle around, stay away from danger, and shoot Missiles if you've got them.

In the fourth stage, you'll destroy the enemy's power reactor. It's guarded, so shoot out the guns first. Watch out for the pit trap on the far left of the maze. There's no way out!

Stage 5—Surprise Attack

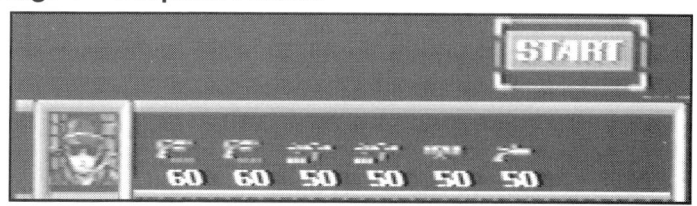

Defend the base against an enemy surprise attack. Here you meet Rance Culzus. Try fighting back with the more powerful single shot weapons! You will get bonus points for each enemy you destroy!

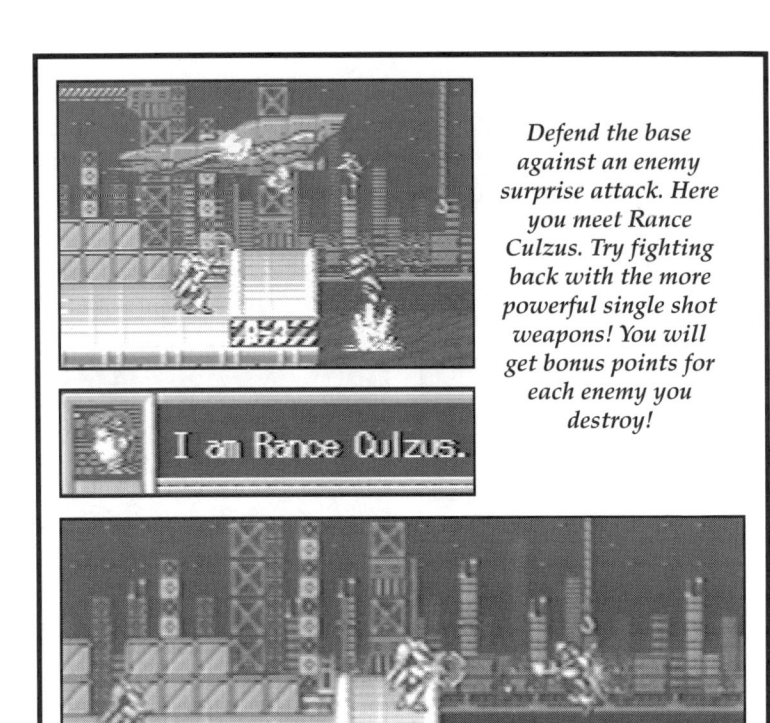

Stage 6—Headquarters Blitz

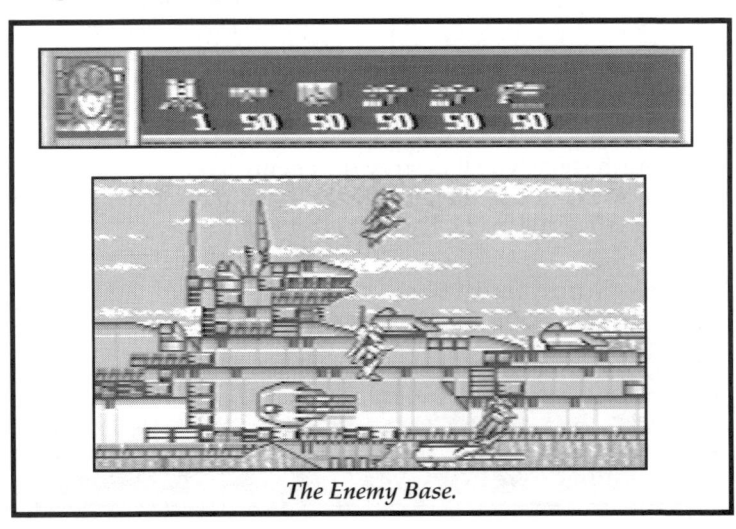

The Enemy Base.

Target Earth

Infiltrate the enemy headquarters. There's no welcome mat, so blast your way in.

When you get inside, nobody looks happy to see you. Oh well... You're not so happy to see them, either.

This time Rance is waiting in cyborg battle armor.

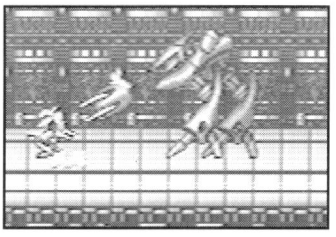

Use Missiles against Rance and avoid his claw.

Stage 7—Space Colony Smash

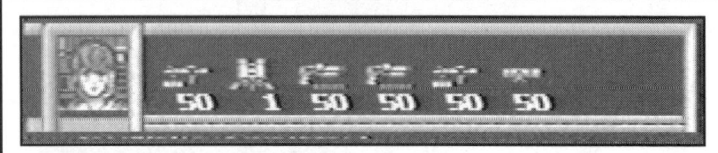

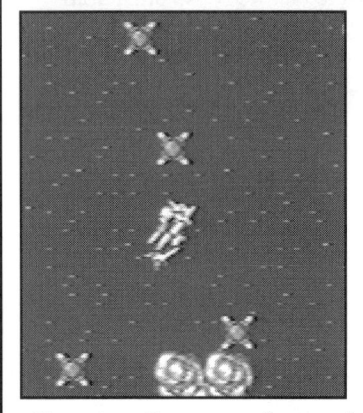

Recapture the space colony and destroy the enemy war ship. This time get bonus points by destroying ammo containers. Watch out for the enemy ship's jet flames. They can fry you from a distance!

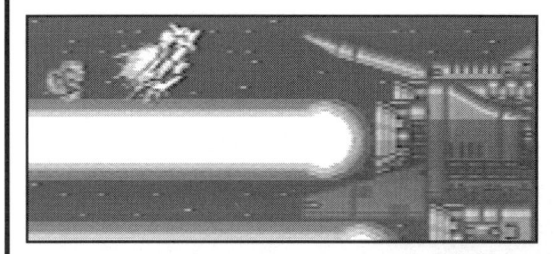

Look out for sneaky blasts from parts of the warship.

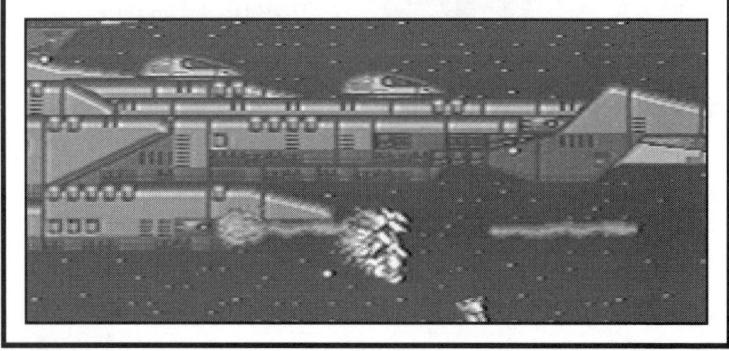

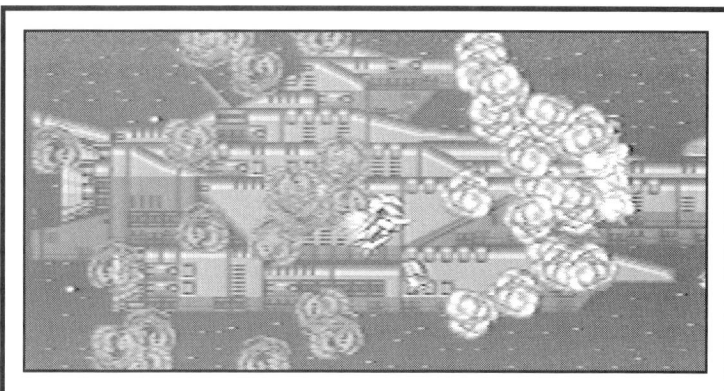

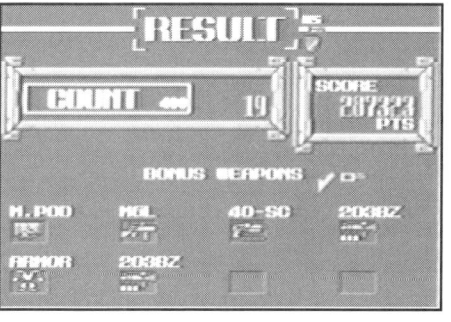

Blast the ship to space waste and collect a suitable reward for your efforts. Now you're beginning to collect the big guns. Think you'll need 'em? You bet you will!

Stage 8—The Final Conflict

You should start out this mission with a big assortment of weapons. Choose them carefully. You don't want to get there without the right hardware.

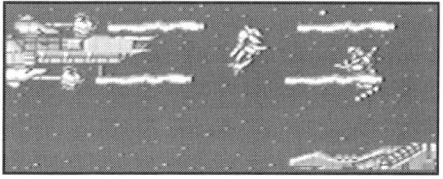

Save bullets: Let your friendly battleship's blast help you out.

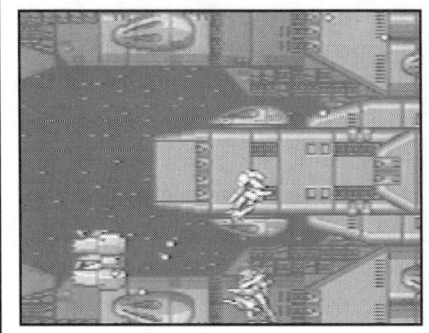

Battle your way through the enemy fleet.

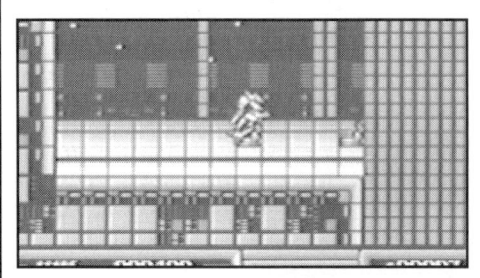

Head mostly down and to the left, then you'll go right at the bottom to find the entrance to the ship's Command Room.

Rance is back again, but this time he really doesn't fight fair.

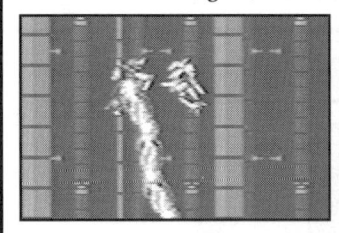

Meanwhile, the real Commander sits protected by an energy shield.

While the real Commander sits safe behind his shield, hordes of his weapons attack you.

Use the heavy stuff on the Commander.

Once the energy shield is down, the Commander is yours.

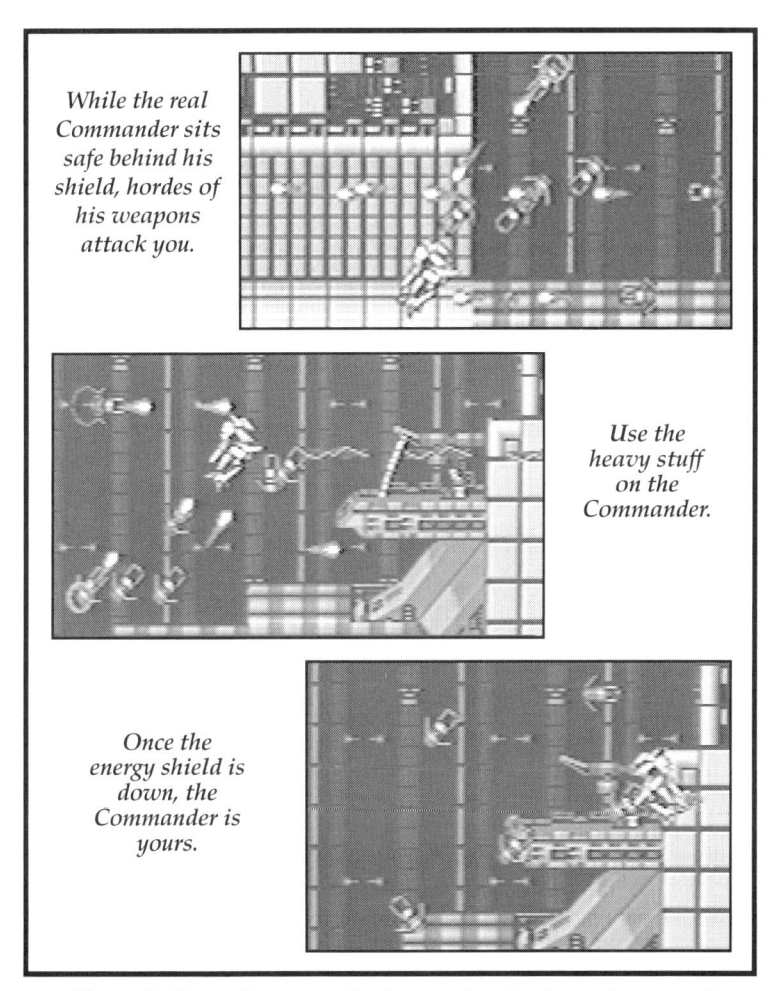

The evil Chron Commander is very hard to beat. Your weakest weapons are effective against the Commander's torpedoes. Save the heavy stuff for him. Good Luck... and pray for help!

If you actually beat the Chron Commander, sit back and enjoy the final scenes in this drama. You've earned it!

SHH... THE SECRETS

Having a hard time? Try playing with invincibility: Press the Start button on Control Pad 2 when the game begins. That was simple!

CHAPTER 17

Truxton

Distributor: Sega of America
Game Type: Arcade Action

WHAT'S GOING ON?

Gidans. They're ugly, they're mean, and they've attacked the Belery, a transport ship carrying valuable secret weapons to Borogo. Borogo needs those weapons! But no one knows how to fight the Gidans! That's where you come in. Tom the Bomb, ace fighter pilot and savior of Borogo. You've been given the Super Fighter—a ship equipped with weapons that haven't even been tested! Can you destroy the Gidans?

WHO ARE YOU?

Tom the Bomb. Nothing makes you feel more alive than being strapped into the cockpit of a souped-up space vehicle.

PLAYERS

Truxton is a one-player game.

SCORING

You get points for destroying the cretinous Gidans. The bigger the enemy, the more points he's worth. The Monster Powers (the end-of-level craft) are worth the most points of all.

LIVES AND HOW TO LOSE THEM

You start out with three Super Fighters. You'll get an additional Super Fighter at 70,000 points, 270,000 points, and at every 200,000 points after that. (That's a lot of Gidans!) You can also gain more Super Fighters by finding and flying over 1Up and 2Up symbols.

CONTINUES

The number of continues you're allowed depends on the difficulty level that you've chosen. If the level is Easy, you can continue as many times as you like. At Normal, you're given 6 continues. And at the Hard level, you'll only get 3 continues. There are five levels of Gidans for the blasting; you continue from the level where you lost your final Super Fighter.

CONTROLS

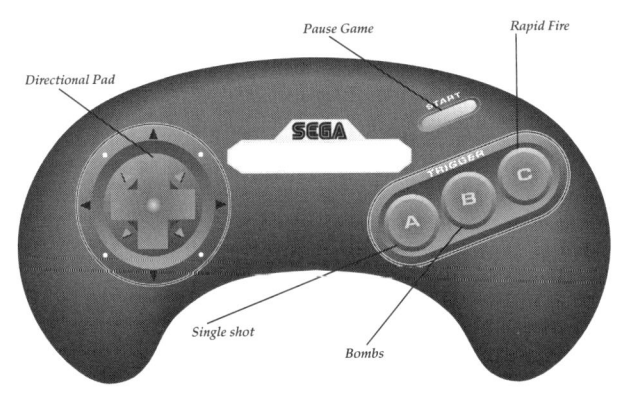

Pause Game — START
Rapid Fire — C
Directional Pad
Single shot — A
Bombs — B
TRIGGER

WEAPONS

As you're flying your deadly mission, you'll see Skulls on the screen. Shoot them and they'll leave a symbol behind. Grab it to equip your Super Fighter with a Weapon or Booster (see Special Items). The color of a Weapon represents its type.

Power Shots (Red) fire a spread of bullets.

The **Truxton Beam** (Green) fires a swath of beams in front of you that hit everything in their path.

The **Thunder Laser** (Blue) fires a beam that not only covers a huge area in front of you, but will track targets that you lock onto!

The **Destroyer Bomb** is a special weapon that covers the screen with a huge skull-faced explosion! It destroys smaller foes, and will weaken the larger ones (like Monster Powers) greatly.

SPECIAL ITEMS

There are two items that power up your Super Fighter.

The **Power Booster** boosts the strength of your weapon. There are three levels of Power for each weapon. You start out at Power 1. Collect five Boosters and you're up to Power 2. Collect ten and you've reached Power 3.

You can hold as many Power Boosters as you can grab, which is good because when you're destroyed you lose Power Boosters. If you're at Power 2, you lose five Boosters. At Power 3, you're penalized 10 Boosters.

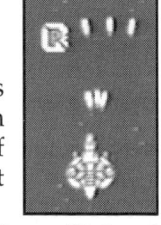

The **Speed Booster** boosts the speed of the Super Fighter! There are five levels of speed to your Fighter. You start out at the lowest speed. Each Booster you collect adds a level of speed until you're flying at five times your original speed. If you're already at your maximum speed, each Booster is 5,000 points.

FRIENDS

In space, no one can hear you trying to be friendly. So once you've left Borogo, you don't have any friends.

ENEMIES

These are a lot easier to find in space! There's a plethora of names for your opponents, and the manual covers them all. The only Gidans that are worth naming are the five Monster Powers: **J Tank** (25,000 points), **Badron** (30,000 points), **Gurus** (40,000 points), **Dosvam** (35,000 points), and **Dogurava** (50,000 points), the leader of the Gidans!

STRATEGY SESSION
General Strategies

You'll ignore Button A in this game. There are so many enemies on the screen that single shots just won't clear them out fast enough. Using rapid-fire isn't being a poor game player; it's being a smart one!

Truxton

The Difficulty Levels are very helpful. Use the Easy level until you learn the various attack patterns of the enemy. Then, when you feel ready, start using Normal. Don't even try Hard until you can cruise through the Normal mode with ease!

The different weapons are all extremely powerful when Boosted; so much so that the differences are minor, with the exception of the Power Shots. When at Power 3, the Power Shots create a ring called the Rainbow Circle Shot around the Super Fighter. This lovely device will deflect almost all of the enemy's bullets!

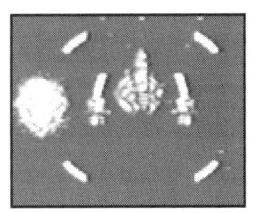

Rainbow Circle.

Stage One.

You take off from a Borogo ship and into the action! The first Gidans attack before the ship is even off the screen. Swing left and right to shoot the incoming fighters. Pretty soon, your first symbol should appear on the screen; a Speed Booster. Take it. Now you'll be swaying a little faster.

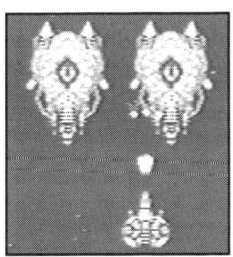

The next symbol comes up shortly afterwards; the Power Booster. Nothing happens when you first take it, but that's expected. You'll need four more to see any effect. Some rather big ships come onto the screen soon after the Booster. Move in close to them, but not directly in front of them. Then fire away. They're history.

Stay at an angle.

You'll arrive at the first of eight Asteroids in the game—the Blue Asteroid. The Asteroids and the Stages have nothing to do with each other; the Asteroids are more a change of scenery than anything else, although your enemies get a bit harder on each.

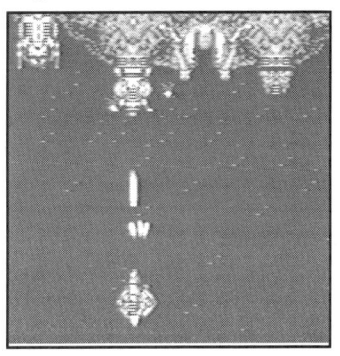

Take out the cannons on the front of the Asteroid. There will be a lot more cannons rooted in the Asteroid; the more you hit, the safer your journey over it.

By the time you reach diagonally-driving cannons and

Blast onto the Blue Asteroid.

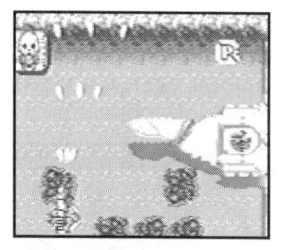

roads, you should be starting a nice collection of goodies. You'll come to two Skulls with the other two Weapons in them; take your pick.

Back in space, more big Gidans attack; let them fly to the bottom of the screen, and pump 'em full of laser! A few attack waves later, you've reached the Yellow Asteroid. There are more cannons on the front; in fact, this Asteroid is covered with them! Fortunately for you, a Power Booster should appear very soon. You should be up to Power 2 now; notice the difference?

Waves of scorpion-looking aliens will attack, but they're not very hard to beat. You should be finished with this Asteroid in no time.

The ships that appear between Asteroids just seem to get bigger and bigger, don't they? You can't get in front of these guys, or they'll plug you with their front-mounted lasers. Stay to one side and let the angle of your laser work for you.

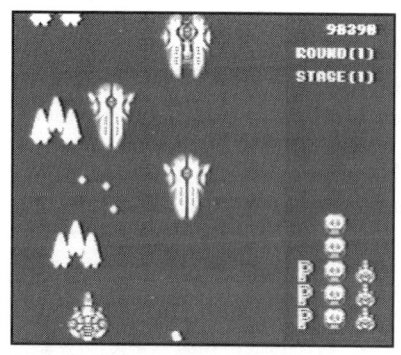

The Yellow Asteroid.

Four ships will arrive in a straight line and start to move around. They're only vulnerable to your weapon when they open up to fire at you! Stay in the lower-left of the screen, avoiding their fire as you give them your own.

The Red Asteroid! You're moving fast, aren't you? Once again, there are lots of cannons to see and destroy. Move back and forth to get all the cannons. Look for a Power Shots symbol. Remember that Power 3 Power Shots give you the Rainbow Circle.

You'll arrive at your first Monster Power—the J-Tank! Now's the time to use what you've been hoarding until now—the Destroyer Bombs! One of them should take out the cannons on the front of J; this will give you breathing room as you shoot the cannons in the back.

Truxton

Finish off J and there's still some flying to do before you leave the Red Asteroid and the Stage as well. Get the cannons on both sides of the ship and the cannons on the end of the asteroid, and the Stage counter increases by one!

Stage Two.

You'll get a couple of Skulls to start the Stage. It's smooth sailing from there until five round ships fly onto the screen.

The J-Tank.

Stay at the bottom and shoot them quickly; their shots tend to fan out right in your direction. Beat them and you'll soon come to the Orchid Asteroid. At this point, the aliens will start soaring from the bottom of the screen; stay towards the middle to compensate.

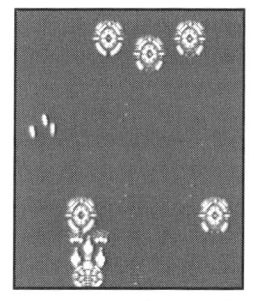

Here come the round ships.

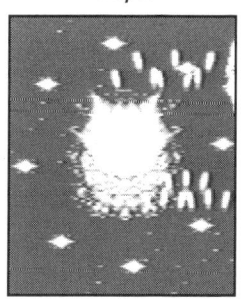

The lightbulb objects are very dangerous. When hit, they first crack and stop firing; then they explode into three bullets. Be aware of this as you shoot them. There will be the occasional Skull in the middle of the ship for you to shoot.

Towards the end of the Asteroid, the attackers come at you hot and heavy. Stay to one side of the screen so that you're not hitting all the lightbulbs. Reach space and you'll meet two long ships. They're easy to destroy, but blow up into eight bullets!

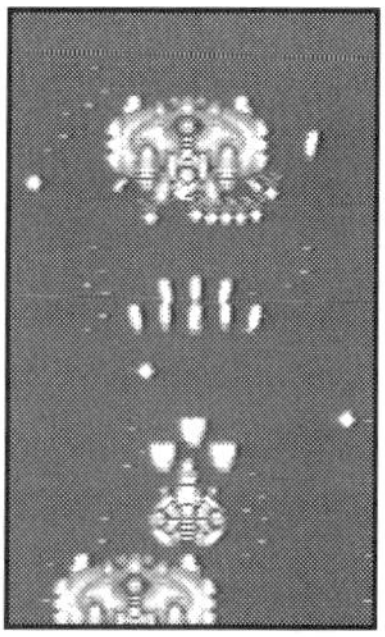

Waves of ships will come from the upper-left and upper-right; line up below them to make quick work of them. Everything is beautiful until a large, fat ship flies onto the screen. It fires eight bullets at once while moving around the screen. Watch out for the second one that comes from the bottom of the screen.

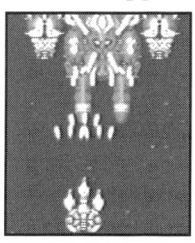

Here's the Purple Asteroid. There are lots of cannons, but more importantly, lots of Power-Ups. There are four for the taking. After them, you'll be over some tracks; ships will be sliding along them, firing all the way. Watch out!

There's nothing very tough until the Gidans bring in the heavy artillery; Badron! The weakness of this huge craft is its middle. It'll take a lot of shots and Destroyer Bombs to bring down. Try to get rid of the cannons on its wings before you concentrate on the middle.

You'll go back into space, but you'll have to beat quite a few waves of fighters before you reach the next Stage. Be patient.

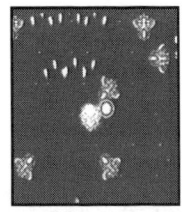

Stage Three.

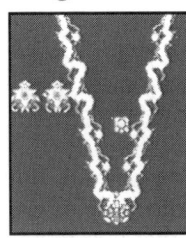

When the green Gidans appear, you're here. There's nothing you haven't seen before until the hopping ships. Luckily, they're very easy to kill.

Waves of green ships and scorpions pour onto the screen, mainly from the top; stay at the bottom and swing to the left and right as needed. Keep going and you'll reach the Poison Asteroid.

The cannons sliding back and forth on the diagonal bars are full of Weapons and Power-Ups. Unfortunately, they won't be easy to collect. The greenies will be coming from all directions on the screen. You may even want to use a Destroyer Bomb or two just to take a momentary breather.

Care to continue?

The Poison Asteroid comes to a welcome end shortly afterwards; but there's no time to rest. Three Gidans come from the top of the screen; they'll shoot five

Truxton

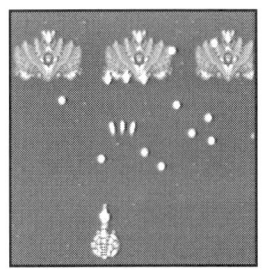

Get ready to move.

bullets downward. Use a Destroyer Bomb or two as you scorch them.

There'll be a few more waves of Gidans; mainly from the sides of the screen and nothing you can't handle. You'll reach the Galaxy Pool Asteroid. You won't see any water, though. The lightbulbs are back; stay alert.

A few cannons later, you've reached yet another Monster Power; Gurus. You'll need several Destroyer Bombs to weaken him; if you have the Thunder Laser, you'll be able to finish him off more quickly. His bullets will be extremely hard to dodge, but you can (and have to) do it!

There are a lot of cannons on the edge of the screen shortly after Gurus; then a green-tiled ground with lots of cannons and power-ups. Past another Stage!

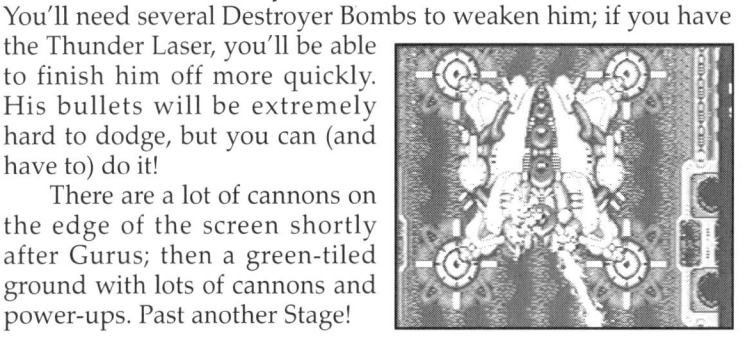

Stage Four.

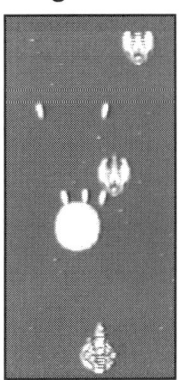

Into space, you'll tussle with more green Gidans (watch your back); then over more tiles. In the next space, the Gidan waves will be coming from the sides of the screen again. Back over the tiles again!

After these tiles, some extremely speedy Gidans attack from the top of the screen. If you have a Power 3 weapon, you won't have to dodge them; if you don't, you'll need to shoot the Gidans on one side of the screen while dodging the ones on the other. To do this, shoot on one side, but keep moving oh-so-carefully back and forth to keep the Gidans on the other side from flying at you.

You'll come to a long line of Skulls on the right; it's a Power-Up and Weapon feast! Large waves of Gidan scorpions attack from the sides, but they're no trouble.

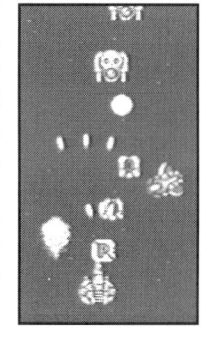

227

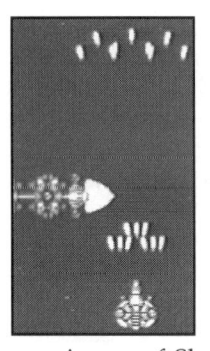

When two tough Gidans come onto the screen, you've reached the Space Spikes. These things will shoot onto the screen without warning. There are four green segments and a pointed tip; the tip contains a Weapon or Power-Up. Stay at the very bottom of the screen so that the Spikes won't get you; when one comes onto the screen, blast it from tip to end.

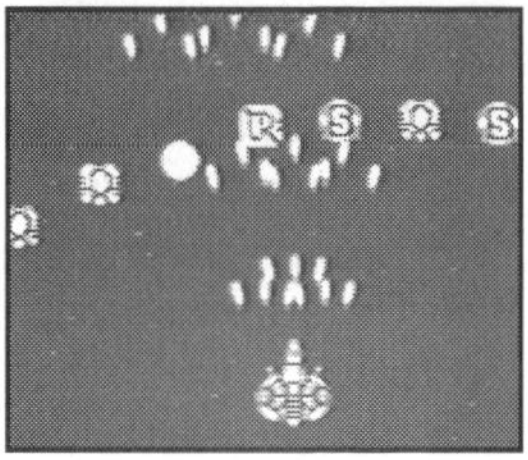

A row of Skulls follows, then large waves of green Gidans. Finally, you'll reach the toughest Monster Power yet; Dosvam! Its weakness is the very middle of its frame. Use your Destroyer Bombs!

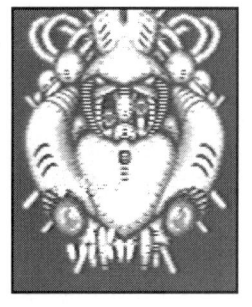

You'll need to pass several very difficult waves of Gidans (a Power 3 Rainbow Circle helps a lot) before you reach the final Stage.

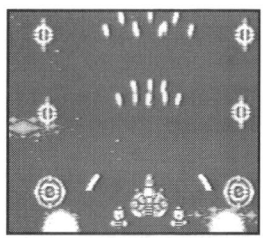

Stage Five.

The attackers on the right will be mostly Skulls; there'll be lots of goodies to collect. The next waves of Gidans will be coming from all sides; stay in the middle of the screen. Soon, you'll reach the final rock; the Magman Asteroid.

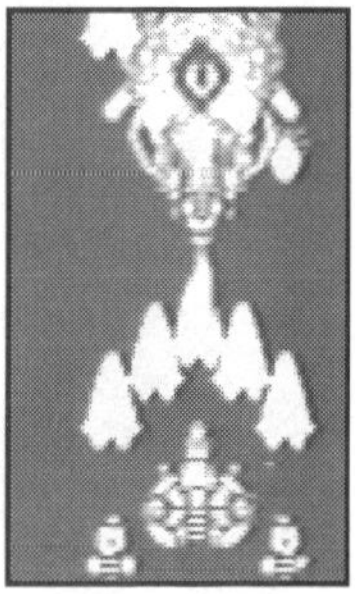

Speaking of Asteroids, they'll start pouring from the top of the screen. Keep firing as you get all the cannons. The Gidans get even thicker; a wide weapon is the only way you'll make any progress past this point.

Some of these ships are hard to beat.

The three metallic Gidans won't be easy to eliminate. You may even want to use a Destroyer Bomb. A few more of these waves and you've left the Asteroid.

Truxton

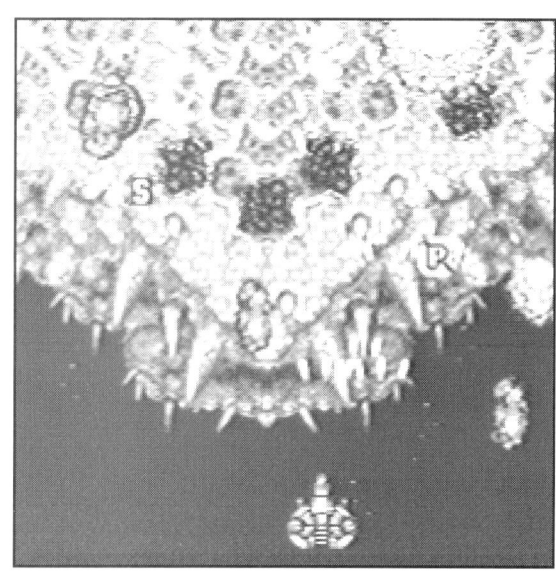

It looks like an asteroid. It acts like one, too. But it's the Dogurava ship, and it isn't here to have a picnic with you!

The next background you come to isn't an Asteroid; it's the Dogurava's ship! You'll need to take out even more cannons. Nothing's tough until you come to the two large Gidans. Use Destroyer Bombs! The next waves of Gidans are the toughest you'll face; huge formations that will cover the screen. More Destroyer Bombs will be needed.

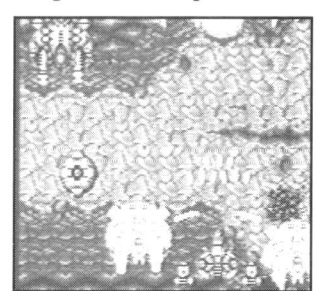

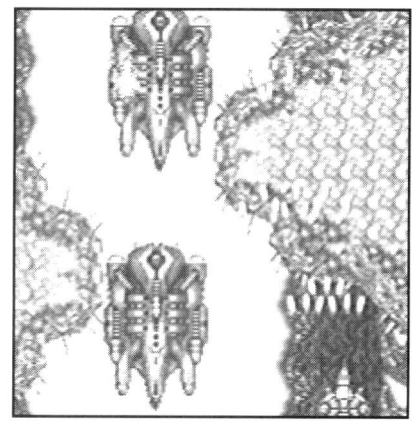

Use the Rainbow to help you survive.

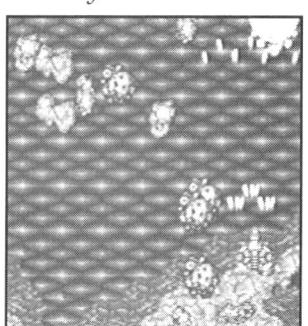

They just keep getting meaner.

Now you're surrounded. Better think fast!

Finally, after all the work you've done, the final Monster Power: Dogurava! Use every Destroyer Bomb you have. You need to shoot its face when the armor is open; unfortunately, that means it's firing a spiral of bullets onto the screen. Good luck!

SHH... THE SECRETS

Is there a trick to using the Destroyer Bombs? They don't seem to do as much damage as you might like when used against the boss tanks. Funny you should ask! There's a quirk that makes the Destroyer Bombs a LOT more useful. When you use one, pause the game. Leave it paused for about 20 seconds. Some people like to pause and unpause very quickly. Either way, the effect will be much greater than it would have been with an ordinary bomb blast. Many of your stronger enemies will succumb to one such *pause bomb* (as we like to call it).

CHAPTER 18

Whip Rush

Distributor: Renovation Products
Game Type: Arcade Action

WHAT'S GOING ON?

Everyone said it was going to happen, but no one believed it—until now, in the year 2222. The Earth was, to put it bluntly, tapped out. Its resources were gone. In desperation, three Alpha-Type spaceships were sent to a neighboring solar system to find more materials for Earth. The ships disappeared around the planet Voltegeus, and were presumed lost. For five years, all was quiet.

But the five years have passed. Now a huge alien spaceship—with the Alphas at its core—is headed for Earth! And it seems quite hostile. The planetary defense forces have put all the energy and resources left into a super-spaceship: Whip Rush. Whip Rush will have the power to destroy the alien vessel. And guess who gets to pilot it?

WHO ARE YOU?

Yes, you're the pilot of Whip Rush. Names aren't important—saving the world is!

PLAYERS

Whip Rush is a one-player game.

SCORING

Accumulate points by blasting the mysterious invaders. The big guys are worth more than the small fry, of course. You'll also get bonus points for completing each Stage; you get 5,000 points multiplied by the number of the Stage. So for example, you'll get 15,000 points for completing Stage Three.

LIVES AND HOW TO LOSE THEM

Depending on what you select on the Options Screen, you will start the game with three lives (Hard), four lives (Normal), or six (Easy).

If you are hit by an enemy or a bullet, or steer yourself into the alien framework of the various levels, you'll either lose a power-up (if you have one) or lose one life (if you have no power-up). You can win an extra ship when you reach 50,000 points, and at every 100,000 points thereafter.

CONTINUES

You get a total of seven continues. If you use one, you'll start from the beginning of the last Round you reached.

CONTROLS

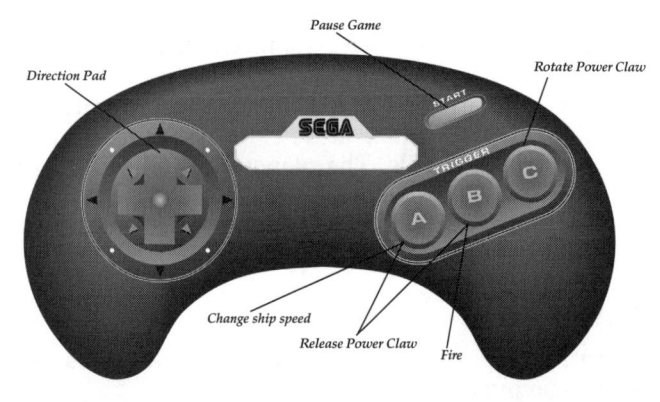

Pause Game
Direction Pad
Rotate Power Claw
Change ship speed
Release Power Claw
Fire

You can also change the functions of Buttons A, B and C on the Options Screen.

Whip Rush

WEAPONS

Whip Rush starts out with the generic cannon. You gain weapons by shooting the Power Capsules that appear on the screen at various points during the Stages. When shot, the Capsule will start to cycle between four letters; these letters indicate the power-ups available.

The **Laser** (L) is a powerful beam that will only shoot forward (to the right, actually, since that's where Whip Rush faces for the entire game).

The **Missiles** (M) will shoot left and right. Missiles shot from the Power Claw will track your enemies!

Fireballs (F) shoot opposite to your direction of movement. They're large blobs of flame.

The **Power Claw** (P) is a small pod that will float around Whip Rush, firing the current weapon available. You can rotate the Claw to cover any side of Whip Rush. The Claw can't be damaged by hitting enemies, so you can use it as a battering ram to destroy any enemy it touches. You can also send the Claw away from the ship to get to enemies you can't otherwise reach.

Each of these power-ups has three levels of power; if you collect three Missiles, for example, you've reached its power-up limit. The exception (there had to be one) is the Power Claw; you can only have two of these. Note that the Claw is the only power-up that can combine with another one.

SPECIAL ITEMS

Just the Power Capsules.

FRIENDS

There are none; just you against the alien horde.

ENEMIES

The enemy forces have a variety of names. We'll just describe what they look like as we go through the game.

STRATEGY SESSION
General Strategies

The most important step is determining the speed level that you feel gives you the best control of Whip Rush. Most players find a level of four or five bars to be excellent. Of course, there are spots where adjusting the speed is necessary for easier movement.

Take advantage of the Options Screen. Make the game easier for yourself the first few times you play. Don't mess with the controls, however; the Buttons are fine the way they are.

Stage One—Drive Out The Intruders!

The round starts out with a wave of Voltegians (how about Volts for short?), and then a Power Capsule. Blast it and wait for it to cycle to the weapon you want. For this Round, take Missiles.

A second wave of Volts and a second Capsule will appear; collect another Missile and now you're firing left and right! This will help a lot in just a while. Destroy the next few waves of Volts. Then watch the bottom of the screen. When you see what looks like a splash, get ready for the Helicopters!

These guys deliver three bullets at once while firing lasers at you too! Take out the bottom one; once he's gone, quickly get the second one before more Volts arrive on the screen. Otherwise, you'll have to shoot and dodge at the same time—not very easy!

Very shortly, you'll be hemmed in by two huge platforms. This Volt will fire his lasers at you, and they're not easy to dodge! You'll have to be very careful not to hit the platforms as you dodge the missiles. You'll have to pump quite a lot of laser into this ship before it explodes.

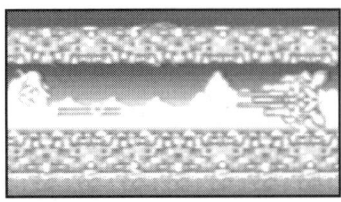

Right after it, you'll get a Power Capsule. If you lost your power-up, you can rebuild it. If you've still got two-way Missiles, grab a Power Claw. This is one of the best weaponry setups in the game.

Dodge to avoid laser blasts.

Now you're going down. Rotate the Claw (if you have it) so that it's shooting to the left. This will cover your rear. Watch out for the yellow structures; these are fatal to the ship.

Whip Rush

Another Helicopter will appear at the bottom of the first yellow structure; rotate the Claw around to help you zap it. Yet another Capsule appears after it; another Claw or another Missile is what you want. Get ready to fly between a group of the yellow structures while round ships attack from both sides. Luckily they don't shoot.

Get by two Helicopters, and you'll start moving right again. There's a Capsule, and then three ring-laser Volts attack you. These guys are tough. Work your way from top to bottom.

After a few more Volts, the Boss will arrive. This huge spaceship looks like a plane, but it's a lot more dangerous! Adjust your speed to five or six bars, get right up to the ship, and start shooting at its nose. It will fire a volley of missiles that circle a short distance in front. Stay within the ring and you'll be safe.

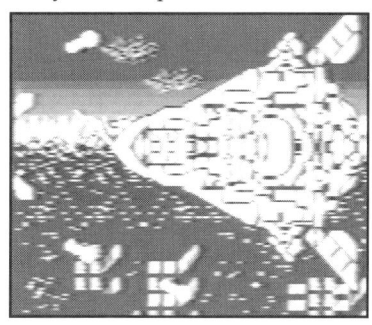

After this Boss ship fires a second volley, it will get so close to you that you'll have to dodge. Fly upwards and around it. It can fire volleys from behind, so watch out! Let it fire a volley, and get close to you. Then zoom back around it and fire at its nose again. It should explode in a huge ball of flame!

Stage Two—Seek Out The Enemy Base!

A Capsule leads off the level. Now stick to the top of the screen and shoot the bomb-dropping aliens. Pillars of water will shoot out from the pool below, so watch out!

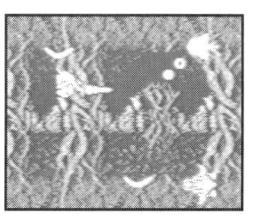

A Volt will appear and shoot a boomerang device from its nose! It'll fly outward a short way and then return to the ship. Fire at the ship when its boomerang is doing its thing, and then avoid the boomerang on its return trip. Notice the cannons that are now on the pipes in the water; shoot them before they fill the sky with ammo.

After a wave of Volts, you'll find yourself lowering into the Water. Whip Rush will slow down in this environment; the Speed Gauge will lower to two bars, and you can't change this. So maneuvering will be important.

The Volts underneath here will fire three torpedoes at you; dodge between two of them. There's a Capsule soon after you start moving right again.

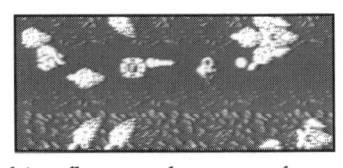

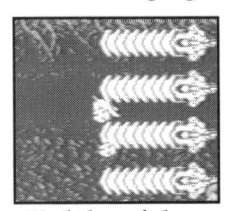

Find the safe lane.

When two ships fly onto the screen from the right, start moving toward them—but don't get too close. Huge blue spikes will pop out from them. Fly between the ships quickly, or the spikes will crush the Rush. A solitary Spiker will appear after these two, and then more Torps. Stay to the right side of the screen. Four Spikers will appear. If you find the right position on the screen, you won't be surprised by these four. The safety zone is narrow.

You're out of the cold water and into hot water! Adjust your speed back up; this is important! A huge wave of Volts will attack; with a Claw and Missiles, you can take out most of them. There will be two Capsules; one before the wave and one afterwards. The pipes will get a lot closer together now, making your piloting job a lot harder.

More cannons will also be on the pipes; two of the cannons will be larger and harder to shoot. After the second one of these, you'll reach the Boss.

This Boss will send out guns above and below you; they'll roll down their support, firing beams between them with tight spaces for Whip Rush to fly through. A cannon will periodically emerge from the center of this Boss; it will fire a stream of bullets aiming at the top of the screen and then working its way down.

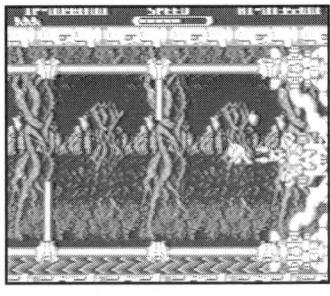

Fly up to the cannon; shoot it until it starts to shoot. Get ready to dodge to the left, flying through the beams. Then fly back up to the cannon and wait for it to come back out again. Repeat until the Volt is shorted out.

Stage Three—Destroy The Base!

The Volts at the start are tough; you'll need to dodge them more than shoot them. A Capsule will appear after the first wave of them; go for the Claw.

Whip Rush

The spider-like Volts will split apart and attack from above and below; the Claw will get one while you get the other. There will also be robotic Volts on the ground that will shoot volleys of Missiles up at you; shoot them before they fire the Missiles, which are very hard to dodge or shoot.

Just before you start going up, a Capsule appears. Go for another Claw or Missiles. The robotic Volts will march back and forth, firing when they see you; the laser pillars are easy to blast. There will be one point where the robots leap through the hole you need to fly through; use the Claw to get rid of them as you fly through and grab the Capsule they're guarding.

Use the Claw to clear the way.

Now you're going left; adjust the Claw accordingly. Ships will attack from the right, shooting corkscrew lasers; spiders will attack from the left. Concentrate on the corkscrew ships, since they're more immediately deadly.

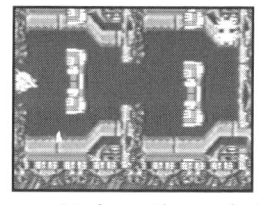

You're going up again, and a few robots will appear. Then you'll head right. The trick to flying through these platforms is to hang out on the left side of the screen, sliding through openings as they appear. There's a Capsule halfway through these, but don't lose a life for it.

Make it through those and the Boss shows up. It will scroll onto the screen from the left, shooting pods from its body. These pods will attack you as well. You must shoot the green center of the ship via the opening left by the pod that's currently shooting at you. The pods can't be harmed. Get in close to do maximum damage. You'll do it (with a little luck).

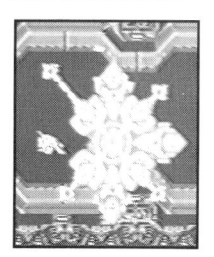

Stage Four—Engage Incoming Aliens!

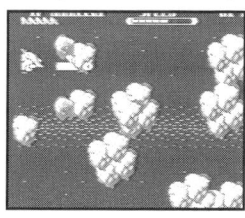

Grab that first Capsule! Then negotiate your way through a huge belt of asteroids. The larger ones will blow up into smaller ones, which will thankfully blow up when shot. You'll want to dodge most of the asteroids, shooting only the ones that get directly in your path.

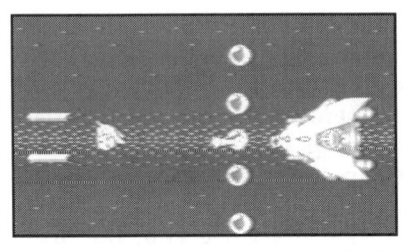

After the belt, you're attacked by a huge yellow Volt. It alternates between shooting two lasers from its nose and shooting a spread of five bullets. The bullets can be shot; the lasers cannot. You should move up to the top of the screen; half of the ship will follow you! Then fly back towards the middle of the screen, blasting the unprotected innards of the ship. Keep doing this and the innards will blow up; the halves of the ship will soar at you!

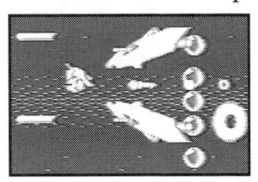

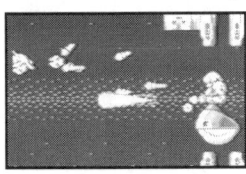

Two Capsules appear right after this ship; get a Claw and Missiles. Your next encounter is with the Floating Volt. This guy shoots huge fireballs out of his arms! Dodge the fireballs and fire away with the Claw.

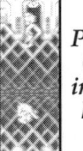

Now the Volts will start popping out of the holes at the top and bottom of the screen, firing at you. Use the A and B buttons to make the Claw shoot away from you for a moment. Do this in the holes as the Volts get ready to come out and they'll be wasted.

Pop the Claw into the holes.

There's a Capsule coming up, just before some framework. Volts scurry back and forth on this framework; shoot them before they get too close to you.

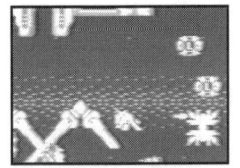

After the framework are three Capsules to grab; try for a Claw. Three Volts emerge from the right; fly behind them and use the Claw. Beat them and the Boss will arrive shortly.

This round Boss will fire five huge bullets in a spread; it will also shoot a quarter of itself off to reveal two cannons! Shoot it in the quarter that's unprotected when the first part flies off; otherwise, just dodge its fire!

Eventually, all the quarters will fly off and the Boss will reveal its true self! Avoid its tail,

238

Whip Rush

and shoot the heads that emerge from the sides. Stay as far away as possible from the tail! Blow up the heads and you've beaten the Boss!

Stage Five—Push Back The Alien Fleet!

There are two Capsules at the start; a good time to get a Claw and Missiles. This ship will be armed very nicely with cannons; rotate the Claw below you to get them. One of the weapons up here traces you with an energy trail; don't hit the trail or you'll be one unhappy camper.

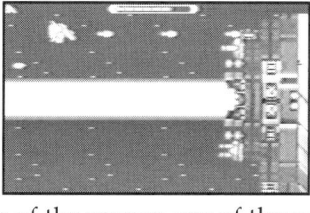

The screen will scroll down now; keep concentrating fire on the cannons, because the longer they're on the screen the more of a problem they become. The screen will scroll right for a while, and then start down again. Stay towards the top of the screen; one of these cannons shoots a very large laser beam that won't disappear until the beam is near the top of the screen.

Find power-ups, but avoid the energy trail.

A Capsule will appear at the bottom of this scroll; grab it and the screen will head right again, taking you with it! There will be a few Capsules to get, but the intensity of the enemy fire might make taking them too risky.

More of the energy trails will chase you upwards; remember to shoot their tips. Hope and pray you have a Claw to shoot to the left; otherwise, you're certain to lose a life.

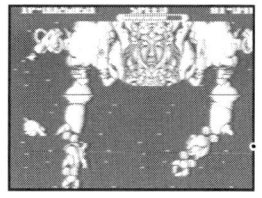

A few scrolls later, you've reached empty space; and that means the Boss. It shoots two fireballs from the cannons mounted near its top, it arms will sway around trying to swat you out of the picture, and a cannon appears from its middle. This weapon shoots lasers down, left and right!

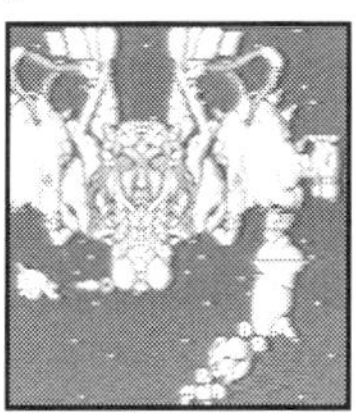

Shoot at the upper portion of the left arm; this is its weakness. If you have the Claw, you can try to shoot from below, but it's safer to get rid of the arm first, anyway. Once the arm is history, stay at the left side of the screen and

239

shoot the cannon when it emerges. Move down when it's about to shoot! Be patient. It could take a while!

Stage Six—Destroy The Mothership!

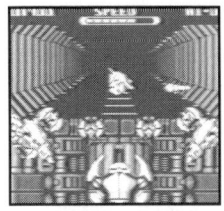

Stay in the middle to avoid being hit.

There are a few Capsules as you move upwards; but there are also huge Volts! These spidery ships shoot a bunch of pods upward until they reach the halfway point on the screen. Then they stop firing until just before they leave the screen, when they give you a few volleys of fire to remember them by. You'll need to dodge cannonfire from the sides as well.

Watch out for the weights that will try to drop down on you. Next you'll find circular Volts with gaps at two points. Fly between the gaps, through the Volt itself! Keep your speed at five or six bars to make this radical maneuvering possible.

There will be a few more weights (with two Capsules to grab), and then you'll meet more Circle Volts. This time, they're staying still, but you'll still have to fly through them!

You'll start to move down; these passages will zig and zag from left to right, and Volts will be floating around each. With the Claw and Missiles, they won't be a problem; otherwise, you'll need to be fast and lucky.

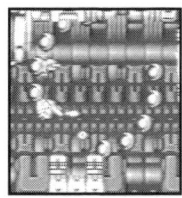

Fly through the Circle Volts.

After you come out of the maze of corridors, you'll move down a bit more before the screen stops. Here comes the Boss!

It will fire circular Volts at you, which you'll once again have to fly through to dodge. It will also shoot spores that explode in eight directions!

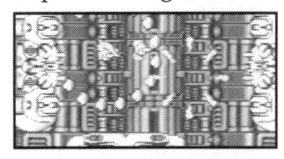

Shoot at the right half of the Boss; aim for its middle. Fly through the Circle Volts, and dodge the blue spores. This Boss is actually easier than some of the others.

Stage Seven—Seek Out And Terminate The Enemy Leader!

You Whip-ped the fleet. You're heady with the Rush of victory. It's time to find the being behind this whole affair and introduce it to a laser beam fired at close range!

Whip Rush

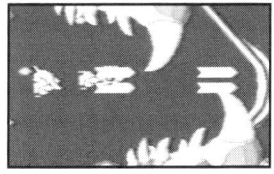

You'd better be powered up; go for Lasers when the Capsule appears. The opening wave of Volts will be big, but they're easily passed. When the teeth appear, things get tough. Huge probes will pop out from the red pods on the walls; with Lasers, you can get them before they extend into your path.

Pass the red pods, and jellyfish (or something closely related) will swim out from the bottom of the screen. Watch out! Now you'll be flying through some exceptionally narrow tunnels. The jellyfish and some other type of swimming Volt will pester you at first; then Volts will start zooming at you from the right side of the screen. Stay towards the left side of the screen and you'll get all of these.

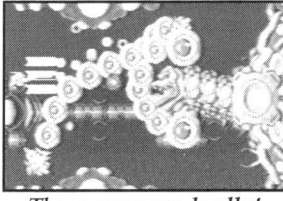

These arms are deadly!

Here it is! Whatever it is, it's pretty ugly! At this point, your superior skill should let you beat this monstrosity easily—but see The Secrets if battle fatigue has set in.

SHH... THE SECRETS

How do I beat the final Boss? Stay at the far left side of the screen; this way those huge arms won't get you. Keep plugging away at its head; when it shoots a crisscrossing beam, dodge upwards and let it pass underneath. Then move back down and start shooting again.

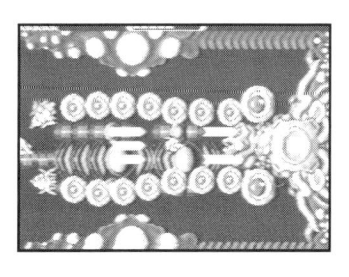

Pretty soon, it'll get ticked off and start extending at you! Now you'll have to scoot right up against the walls of the cavern to avoid being smashed. Keep at it and you're bound to win!

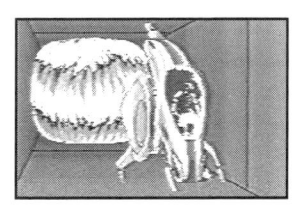

By the way, in case you didn't notice it, at the end of Stage 4, just before you meet the Boss, there are three ships. Each is worth 100,000 points. Put it another way: There are three free men waiting at the end of that stage.

CHAPTER 19

Zany Golf

Distributor: Electronic Arts
Game Type: Sports (Arcade Action)

WHAT'S GOING ON?

Ah, yes. There's nothing like a nice summer day out on the miniature golf course. But the course you're playing today isn't your average Putt-Putt course. It's downright Zany!

WHO ARE YOU?

No alter egos in this game. You are yourself for a change!

PLAYERS

Anywhere from one to four players can participate. Each player has a different-colored ball; White, Black, Red or Blue.

SCORING

In all forms of golf (even the Zany kind), the object isn't to score the most points; it's to score the fewest. Each hole has a Par. The Par is the number of strokes it should take the average player to finish the hole.

Each player starts out with five strokes. Every time you hit the ball, you use a stroke. Run out of strokes and you're out of the game!

Every time you start a hole, you get the Par for that hole added to the strokes you have left. For example, if you use two strokes on the first hole, you'd have three left. The second hole is Par three, so you'd now have six strokes.

LIVES AND HOW TO LOSE THEM

As we said above, running out of strokes is bad. You can win extra strokes by doing one of three things; completing a bonus on a hole, touching a fairy with the ball (see Friends), or by getting a Bonus Timer and finishing the hole with time to spare (see Special Items).

CONTINUES

Once all the players have lost, that's it. Back to Hole One.

CONTROLS

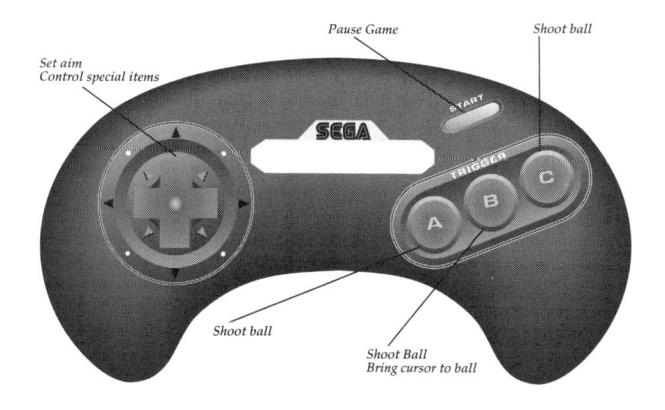

Set aim / Control special items
Pause Game
Shoot ball
Shoot ball
Shoot Ball / Bring cursor to ball

WEAPONS

No, no, no! This is Zany Golf—not "Rambo IV: Rambo Blows Up Pinewood Country Club."

SPECIAL ITEMS

Sometimes during play, the game will inform you that the next hole will have a Bonus Timer. The Timer is a clock that starts out with four Balls, representing Strokes, next to it. Whenever it's your turn, the Timer starts counting down. If you finish a hole before the Timer runs out of Balls, you'll win extra strokes equal to the number of Balls left on the Timer.

FRIENDS

The Fairy will sometimes appear on a hole you're playing. If you touch her with the ball, you'll win five strokes!

ENEMIES

The various obstacles and your aim are the only enemies in this game. It's even beneficial for the players to cooperate to pass certain holes where tasks must be performed.

STRATEGY SESSION
General Strategies

Aiming the ball isn't just letting rip with a monster shot; you have to consider both your aim and the length of the aiming line very carefully. Generally, medium-strength shots are the best.

This is so obvious that you can forget it, so don't forget it: the aiming line should be pointed directly opposite to the direction you want the ball to go in.

To practice, start a four-player game—and be every player! This gives you the ability to try a lot of ways to approach each hole. Also, sometimes there's an advantage to being the first player. Other times there's an advantage to being one of the later players. By playing all the players, you get all the advantages.

Hole One: Windmill

Bonuses: One stroke for entering the windmill.
Best Score on Record: 1
On this first hole, you'll learn about a technique that works for all the holes: aiming for a landmark on the hole. For the first shot, move the aiming cross to the left until you can see the roof of the house. You should aim your shot to hit the wall right at the top of the house. See the picture to get a better understanding of this. The shot should be at full power.

If you get it into the windmill, you'll get a free stroke and a very good lie for your putt. If you don't, it will roll down the ramp and come out at the bottom of the lighthouse—and may or may not roll past the wall. If it does get past the wall, you'll have a good putt. If it doesn't, you'll have to waste a stroke.

Your putt should be very soft; possibly even less than medium strength. This way, even a miss will leave you very close to the hole. And don't worry about the flag—it will automatically drop down into the hole whenever the ball gets close.

Hole Two: Hamburger

Bonuses: None
Best Score on Record: 1
Before you even take your first shot, get that burger bouncing by pressing a Button (except D) rapidly. Keep pressing until the burger's bouncing so high that the bottom bun is clearing the arrow. This will give you the most time to get the ball past the burger.

Your first shot should be aimed to follow the arrows. Be sure to aim more to the left of the catsup than to the right, or else you'll rebound right back to where you started! Use medium power, or you'll overshoot the hole and roll into the dirt.

Getting onto the green if you've rolled off can be tricky. You can try to aim right for the hole, or aim behind it. Either way, try to get as close as possible to the hole. Be sure to adjust your power for the slope.

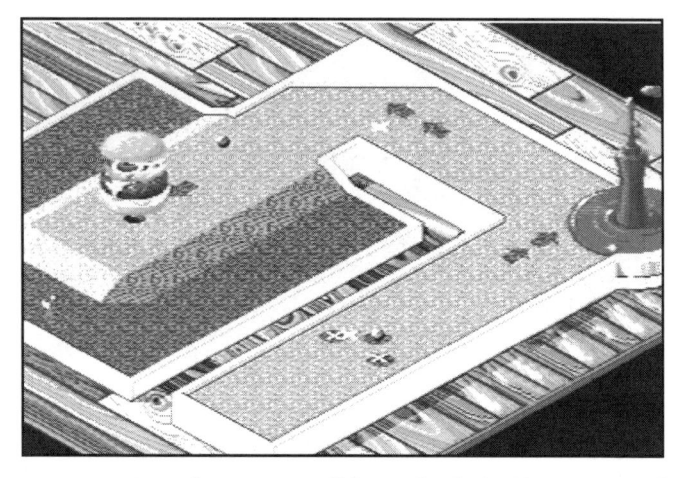

Your putt has to be timed to get past the flubbery food, but as long as it's bouncing high you'll have plenty of time.

Hole Three: Walls

Bonuses: None
Best Score on Record: 1

Use the aiming cross to move the screen around until you can see the first two walls. Now aim your shot (at full power) and wait until the first wall is down, and the second one just starts to drop. Let fly and the ball should hit the third wall and roll down towards the hole. If it doesn't make the hole, it will bounce back a ways, but not too far.

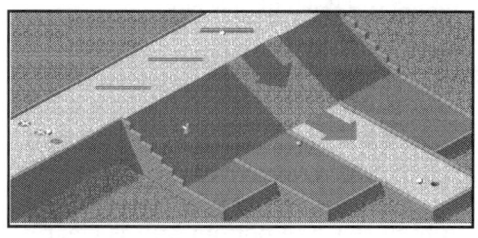

If you get stuck in one of the side traps, your shot to get to the hole should be straight up. The hill will then curve your shot to the hole. If a Fairy is present on the level, it will almost always be in one of these traps.

Your putt could be quite long; just remember it's better to make two soft putts than one hard one that misses and rebounds even farther than it was before.

Hole Four: Pinball

Bonuses: One stroke for hitting the targets and entering the top-left hole.
Best Score on Record: 1
For the "plunger" shot, move the aiming cross all the way back to the third arrow; then release. This should get you onto the table.

Once you're pin-balling, the object is to hit the two side targets. This makes the hole at the top-left of the table start to glow, and getting the ball into it will either roll you right into the hole or put you very close.

Use a Button (except D) to work the flippers and the bumper at the top of the table. Hold the Button down when the ball is at the top of the machine to keep the bumper up—and hopefully knock the ball into the hole.

There's also a hole at the lower-left of the table. If you lose three balls, you'll automatically fall through that lower hole. You should concentrate on getting the targets. You're also supposed to be able to tilt, but this is both very difficult to do and unnecessary.

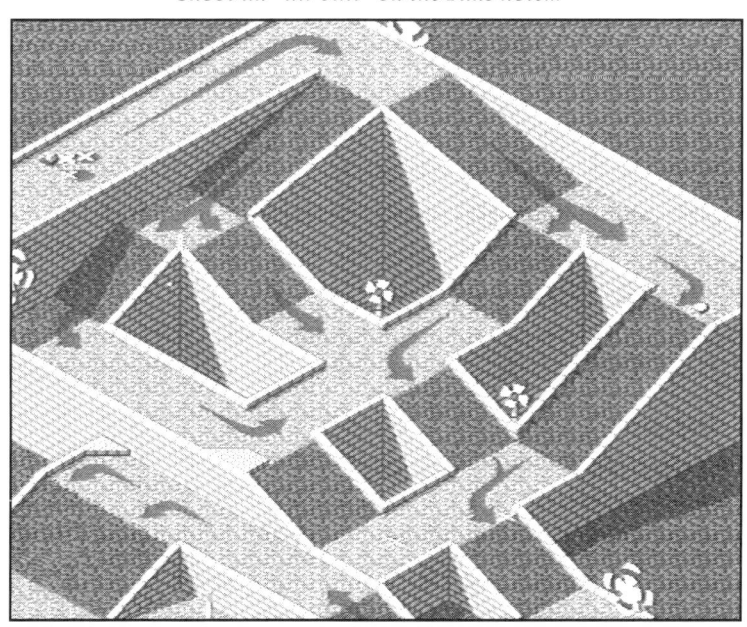

Shoot an "air ball" on the Fans hole...

Hole Five: Fans

Bonuses: None
Best Score on Record: 2 (a 1 is possible)
This is a very intimidating hole—but it's quite easy. Your first shot should be at full power. Hit the corner and then start spinning Button D counterclockwise or clockwise. This will get the fans going.

Follow the arrows to get to the hole. If you know when to let the ball roll on its own and when to blow it toward the hole, you can get a hole-in-one.

If the ball doesn't make it to the green, use a soft shot to get it in the path of a fan again.

Hole Six: Castle

Bonuses: One stroke for entering the castle gate.
Best Score on Record: 2 (a 1 is possible, but not likely)

The bonus on this hole just isn't worth the trouble—you could spend two or three strokes going for one! Your main concern should be to get onto the green.

A full-power shot should send you right up to the castle and into one of the side holes. This will leave you at the other side of the green. From here, use a bounce stroke to get the ball past the walls.

If you're really going for the castle gate (and of course you'll want to try it), wait until you hear the trumpet fanfare. That signals that the gate is open.

Hole Seven: Ant Hill

Bonuses: None
Best Score on Record: 1
The hole on this round moves whenever your ball is on the slopes. To get a hole in one, find where the hole is before your Tee shot, then fire a shot a little to the right of that position. The

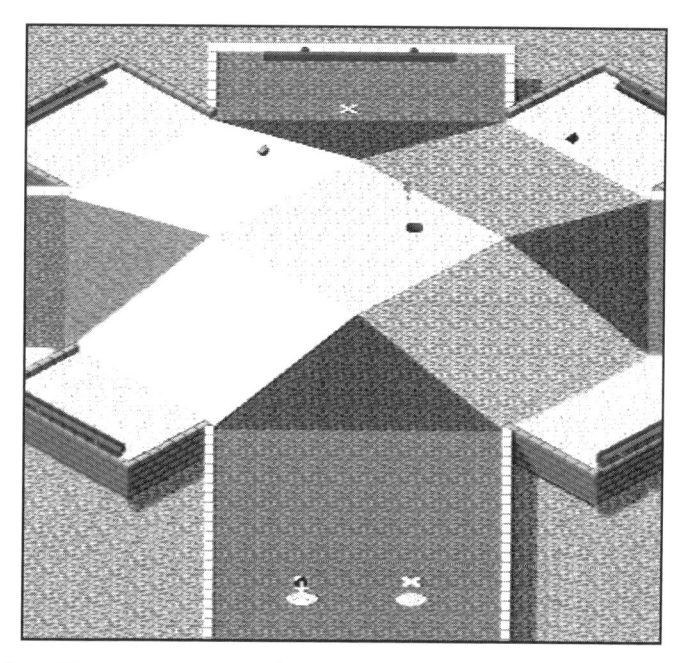

hole will move to the right when your ball is on the slope. If your aim is good, you get it in the little round circle. After the first player, you'll have to hope for a little luck.

The other way to play the hole is to use a full-power shot to get the ball going. From here, you should be able to keep the ball in play continuously until you make the hole, or until you blow the timing of the bumpers. If the ball comes to rest on the green itself, make sure you putt on a horizontal line with the hole. This way, if it moves, it will move right into the ball!

Hole Eight: Knock-out

Bonuses: None
Best Score on Record: 2
This hole is tough! Get the ball in play with a full-power shot. Once the ball is moving, Button D controls the paddle. What you want to do is hit all the blocks, causing the holes to light up. If the ball enters either hole, and there are still blocks left, all the blocks come back up.

Try to get the blocks on the left first, then work your way right until you've got them all. The holes light up to show that it's safe.

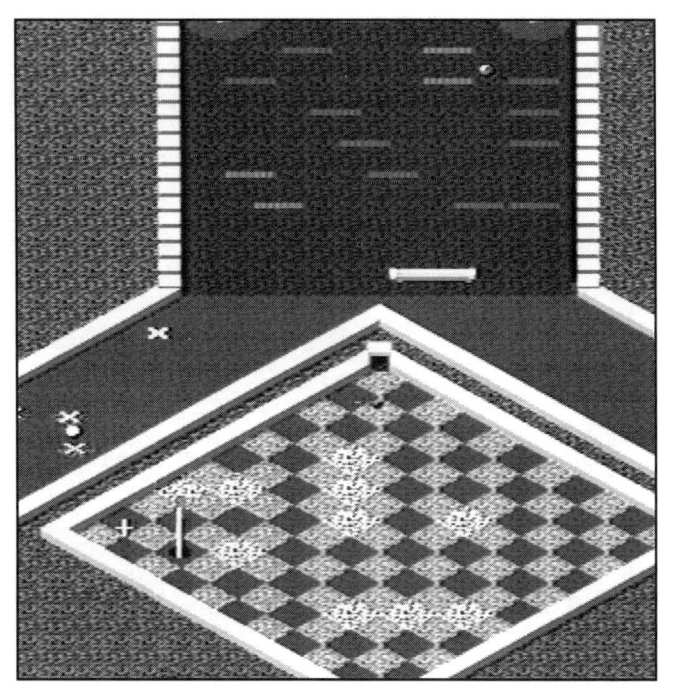

The lighted areas are the trap squares.

On the checkerboard green, things get even tougher. See the blinking squares? You must avoid them whether they're blinking or not—something the game doesn't tell you. See the picture we've given you—it shows all the squares lit up. This way, you can plot a path to the hole.

By the way, on computer versions of Zany Golf, this was the secret 10th hole. The Genesis version doesn't have a secret hole. Sorry.

Hole Nine: Energy

Bonuses: None
Best Score on Record: 3 (a 2 is possible—in your wildest dreams!)
No instructions? Oh man! But that's no problem—that's what we're here for. To get anywhere on this hole, you have to hit the two buttons on the computer and turn them white. Once you've done that, there are two routes you can take upwards. The circle will teleport you up to the circle next to the ramp. The vacuum will take you up to the hole.

From there, you have to take it very slowly. Putt very carefully past the false holes to the real one. If you happen to go into one of these holes, you'll be ejected on the right side of the vacuum. Good luck!

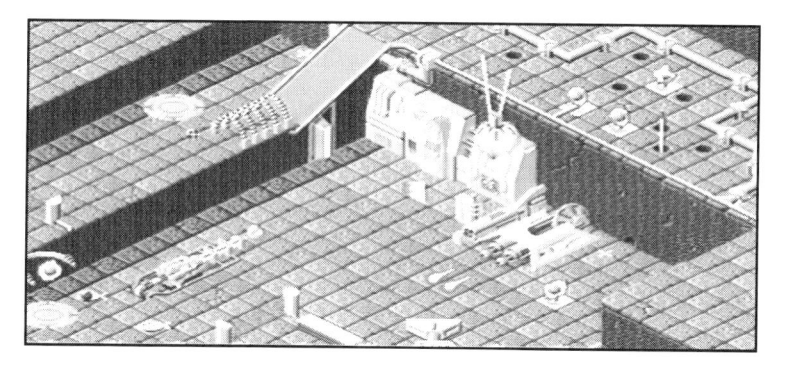

SHH... THE SECRETS

Practice makes perfect! That's the main secret there is to this game. However we do have one hint for Hole Nine. There is an angle you can take that will hit both buttons and, if you're really lucky, go up the vacuum to the upper level. It takes perfect timing, placement, and lots of luck, but it can be done. At the top, if you're lucky, you can use the glowing orbs to avoid the trap holes. These orbs will attract or repel the ball, so it is possible to use them to curve the ball's path. But it isn't easy.

By the way, those "Best score on record" numbers we've printed with the hole descriptions are really from ONE GAME! Total score for the nine holes—14!!!!!!!!!!

Just so you know, though, the only holes on which you can't get a hole-in-one are Eight and Nine. However, getting a hole-in-one on Six is very rare. It's a matter of luck. Speaking of luck, the best possible score for one round of Zany Golf is, theoretically, an 11! Good Luck. We thought a 14 was pretty unbelievable!

CHAPTER 20

More Mega Drive Tips

Here are a few more secrets. Look for more in future editions of Sega Mega Drive Secrets:

ALEX KIDD

The goal of this game is to reach the Sky Castle. Concentrate on that. Near the middle of the last level, use the Pedicopter to get to the castle.

In the Paper, Rock, Scissors game, you'll win most of the time if you use this technique. First choose Rock. Now wait until the countdown or push the button to speed things up. When the count reaches "Shan," quickly switch to Scissors. You'll fool your opponent and win most of the time.

ARNOLD PALMER GOLF

Putt 100 times on a hole to see a screen from Fantasy Zone when the game is over.

HERZOG ZWEI

In Herzog Zwei, you can beat the computer, at least on some difficulty levels, by making tanks and taking them to the unprotected part of the computer's base. Then let the tank blast away while you stay around to protect it. The computer will keep building killer stuff, but it isn't very smart about protecting its base. You can win. At the higher levels, though, you're on your own!

TOMMY LASORDA BASEBALL

An invisible team? Try this password:

Zb6jpqrnmGnYWQXaHuFFAB

CHAPTER 21

A PARENTS' GUIDE TO VIDEO GAMES

I am a game player. I've played computer and video games actively since the mid-70s. Obviously, I enjoy games.

I am also a parent. At the time I write this my stepson, Shan, is 17 and my son, Max, is four and a half years old. Max has played video games since he was two and a half.

What I want to offer in this chapter is a little reassurance for worried parents. People who don't play video games often don't understand what the attraction is or whether the games will encourage negative social behaviors. They also don't know whether their children are addicted to games. It sure seems like it sometimes. Let's address the addiction issue first.

ADDICTION OR WHAT?

The good news is that experts in child behavior and learning have been studying video game playing. The ones who have been most public with their findings to date do not call video game obsession an addictive behavior. Some studies show that what appears to be addiction is really a quest for mastery, and my own experience coincides with that opinion. Once a game is mastered, it is no longer of much interest. In some cases, mastery is beyond the reach of the child. Often this is because they lack some basic knowledge of the strategy necessary for success. That's why a book like this can help. If they've tried everything, they can find some hints and solutions in this book that may allow them to accomplish more than ever before.

But I'm digressing. The point is that the temporary obsession that kids feel about their games is not an addiction. In fact, in most households children begin their association with video games by playing for hours every day. They do seem quite obsessed. Some parents feel considerable alarm at that point.

However, my experience is that these same kids will start to taper off. They'll go back to other activities that give them pleasure if left to their own devices. They'll watch television or read books. They'll participate in sports or other social activities, and they'll generally live a healthy life.

"But," you ask, "what if they keep going and getting new games to the point that they never stop the obsessive behavior?" My answer is to draw from my own experience. My own children (and some of my young game testers) have been able to choose from literally hundreds of games on just about every computer and video game system made. They do like to play the new games when they arrive, and they have certain favorites that they return to from time to time. However, they have cooled off on video games somewhat. They like to do lots of other activities. My 17-year-old plays much less than before, though he sometimes encounters a game that absorbs his attention for a few days. (Since I'm paying him to play games for me to write about in my books, he now sees many of the games as business opportunities.)

We have never restricted my younger son's playing. We never tell him he can play only a certain number of hours a day, or anything like that. You might think he'd be glued to the screen every waking moment, but it isn't true. He does play often—usually for short periods. But he still prefers free play with friends or drawing or just running around outside. There are those days when he seems to want to play video games a lot, but usually he's pretty moderate.

Two of my other good players are very motivated to master the games they play, but one plays in a local championship soccer team and the other plays baseball and other sports at his school. These are kids who really love video games and spend the time necessary to master them. But they are also normal, bright, active, healthy children.

While researching this chapter, I spoke with Patricia Greenfield, author of *Mind and Media: The Effects of Television, Video Games, and Computers,* and one of the people currently researching the effects of these games on people. She told me her opinion: "Kids will play to master the game. When they finish mastering the game, they will quit. They will be quite intense while mastering the game. If your child couldn't put down a book, would you say he was addicted? No. In fact, my personal experience shows that kids are in much better shape mentally after playing video games than after watching TV. Certain brainwave studies confirm this. "

I also spoke with Peggy Charren, president of Action for Children's Television in Boston. She said, "Our position is that video games are fine if that's not the only thing the child does. They are actually interactive at a time when much of a child's experience is too passive. TV is a passive exercise. Too often parents aren't able to provide interaction—single working parents, for instance. We generally tell parents to relax."

These examples and opinions are not definitive. Each child is an individual, and each family must set its own rules and expectations. However, I think my experience with games and children would indicate that there is nothing inherently dangerous or addicting about video games.

Later in this chapter, I'll offer some ideas about constructive play.

THE ISSUE OF VIOLENCE AND SEXISM

Again, I don't have a lot of research and facts to offer, but my experience would indicate that children who play a lot of video games are not particularly violent. My game players are, in fact, quite non-violent. They have never been involved in fighting at school or any other kind of violent behavior.

Does this mean that children are never affected by the violent content of many games? I don't know. I think the very young children may exhibit some violent behavior since they have a harder time distinguishing between fantasy and reality. For a while, when he was around three years old, my son acted out some of the ninja moves he learned from the games. That was all right until he kicked a few kids at school. However, all it took to stop that behavior was to talk with him about it. As he has grown older, he seems to see the difference between the fantasy world on the screen and the world he lives in.

Another problem in deciding whether violent games are bad for kids is in isolating the influences on them. Many of them see violence on TV (both in the news and on their own programming), and some see violence in their own homes or school yards. In contrast, the violent content of games is almost always so steeped in fantasy that participating in these games might even discourage violence in real life by offering an outlet in which the child has a measure of control over his or her environment. Most violence in this world is completely beyond our control. It's nice to know that when you've had enough of it, you can simply press a button and turn it off.

I've heard of studies that showed a reduction in body tension among gang members who play video games, indicating that the games may serve as a release. I've found this to be true around my own household. There is often some frustration involved in mastering a game, but that frustration can be channeled into the game and not into the family environment.

There are many games where violence is not a part of the game, but most games do involve some kind of conflict. Even chess is a modified war game, but I've never heard anyone say it promotes violence. Does Monopoly encourage everyone to become a Donald Trump? Not one game player I've met wants to go into the armed services and be a soldier, but every one of them has enjoyed simulated war games of one kind or another. There may be subtler effects, and, once again, each child is different, but I don't see that much correlation between violence in video games and violence in real life.

Perhaps my biggest concern with regard to younger players is that they have an appreciation for life. Since many games involve the wholesale destruction of enemy monsters and other characters, it is important that they recognize this destruction as a challenge in a game, but that they don't think destroying real creatures is OK. Again, I haven't seen that to be true, but it wouldn't hurt to discuss the issue with very young players.

There is concern that girls don't play video games as much as boys. There are some new games coming out that will appeal more to female players, and at least one game developer has asked me to consider developing games that women would enjoy. In my own experience, I've found that women prefer puzzle games over shoot-'em-up action games. However, the problem of the gender gap has not yet been solved, and I don't have any easy answers. On the other hand, the situation hasn't been entirely ignored. I expect lots of research will be done and lots of new approaches tried. Perhaps some will succeed.

FRUSTRATION

Many games are very hard to master. One thing you'll notice (and this varies from player to player) is a certain level of frustration. Some players are very mild about their frustration. As an example, one of the best-known video game players in the country, Donn Nauert, rarely gets flustered. If he encounters a situation where he has a lot of problems, his usual response is to mutter a mild "OK," and then he tries again. Perhaps that's why he's one of the best.

In contrast, you may see your own kids yelling, crying, or even throwing the controller on the floor. Remind them that it's only a game. They won't appear to listen, but if you keep telling them, they'll hear you. If the frustration gets too acute, tell them to take a break and come back to it.

I don't tolerate any kind of violence. When my young son threw the controller across the room once, he was barred from the games for several days. He learned very quickly that such action wasn't tolerated, and he stopped acting out that way. He still gets frustrated, but he controls his violence. I also get frustrated when I play some games, so I understand his feelings and can sympathize with him. On the other hand, I don't let him keep playing if the frustration appears to get too acute. It is clear that my son is learning to control his emotions by dealing with these frustrations. It's early to tell if that control will carry over to his "real" life, but I think it will.

In time, most players will give up on a game that's too hard and move on to something easier. However, they may return to the hard games a month or more later and suddenly find success where there was only frustration before.

WHAT DO CHILDREN LEARN FROM VIDEO GAMES?

It is clear to me that children learn a lot from video games. Obviously they learn a certain kind of motor skill. Their eye-hand coordination is often very well developed, and anyone who has watched their split-second reactions and carefully timed leaps must appreciate this skill.

Game players develop other skills that aren't so obvious. For one thing, there's a great amount of visual information being displayed in a typical video game. Processing all this information stimulates a different kind of thinking. In her book, Ms. Greenfield calls it "parallel processing" (not to be confused with computer technology of the same name). In contrast to serial processing, parallel processing allows one to track and understand several elements at the same time. In the case of video games, players may typically be aware of two, three, or even twenty different objects on the screen at once. They learn from experience and practice how to deal with this diversity.

Many games appear to be impossible at first. Part of the reward of such games is figuring out how to beat them. It's a challenge just like a crossword puzzle or landing a big business deal. However, the process of learning itself is a skill. As Greenfield states, "Part of the excitement of the games surely must lie in this process of transforming randomness into order through induction."

People who play games are learning to use their minds as well as their eyes and fingers. There's a lot of strategy and cleverness needed to be successful. Even the very young players exhibit this inductive reasoning without being consciously aware of it. At two and a half years old, my son was showing me his strategies for playing certain games, and now, at four and a half, he can play sophisticated logic puzzle games (like the Adventure of Lolo on the Nintendo Entertainment System) in which hand-eye coordination is not a prerequisite. Instead, he needs to plan and then execute a series of puzzle moves.

While players of action games must develop strategies to play successfully, they often do so quite unconsciously unless required to explain what they are doing to someone else. As a suggestion, instead of staying completely away from the games, ask your kids to tell you how they "pass" these games. They might surprise you (and even themselves) with the depth of their thinking in some cases.

Fantasy and adventure games are becoming more and more popular all the time. These games are more obviously thinking games. Although the action is implied in the game, there is little hand-eye coordination in them. Instead, players must solve puzzles to succeed. In addition, in the role-playing games, they must maintain their characters. That means making sure they have food and other necessities as well as proper attire (armor and weapons usually, though sometimes there are special items they must use in special circumstances). In addition, these characters must grow, becoming more competent in their world and more powerful. Role-playing games are very popular in Japan, and are beginning to catch on here in the U.S., where they have enjoyed a small but dedicated following for years.

In my opinion, these games teach not only puzzle solving and logic, but a certain level of responsibility. Role-playing games can take many hours to play all the way through. If gamers are careless or irresponsible with their characters, they can lose the results of many hours' work. Role-players learn quickly to show some responsibility for their characters (who are, after all, extensions of the players themselves).

In an expert opinion written for the Tel Aviv Supreme Court in Israel, Ms. Greenfield cites some additional studies. These studies indicate that the same skills learned and used by video game players have a high correlation to the skills needed by such professionals as engineers, architects, air traffic controllers, pilots, and many more. Other studies show that the kinds of visual/spatial skills developed in video games also helps in all other areas of computer work.

A corollary benefit of video games is that children who grow up with them tend to be much less intimidated by computers. In fact, they think of computers as more sophisticated video game machines and have no fear or apprehension of them. When they need to use computers, they will do so with little or no resistance. These same video game players also find themselves right at home with modern gadgets. Most kids can program the VCR or set up the stereo better than their parents can. How important these skills are in the world of the future remains to be seen, but many people believe that today's video game players will be tomorrow's explorers and space travelers and that the skills they learn today will make them uniquely suited for the world of the future.

Ms. Greenfield recommends that we view literacy in new terms. In addition to the literacy of reading and writing, we should recognize the new language of visual cognition that has become so much a part of our fast-paced world. She recommends a multi-media approach to education in which more than one kind of teaching is used. She also recommends that reading be taught early, before school, so children can grow up seeing reading as a pleasurable experience. Her suggestions make sense to me, and as much as I like electronic gaming, I would be sad to see reading become a lost skill.

HOW TO LIVE WITH VIDEO GAMES

Here are some home-grown guidelines and suggestions on how to coexist with your video game machine.

Communicate. Tell your children just what is expected of them. Make it clear that the homework must be done, the grades kept up, and the lawn mowed (or whatever they do around the house). Make sure they know that playing games is OK, but it is a privilege that can be revoked if they don't keep a sense of responsibility about their lives.

Encourage Other Activities—Especially Exercise. You want your kids to engage in physical activity and not sit with their eyeballs glassily staring at the screen for hours on end. That goes without saying. But how do you motivate them to abandon the quest and do something else?

In most cases, you won't have to do anything. Kids naturally need to expend their physical energy and they're great at finding ways to do it. On the other hand, if you can encourage your children to participate in sports activities, or provide them with situations in which they'll get healthy exercise, it will help. You might also remind these kids that the healthier they are physically, the better they'll play video games. Bad health makes bad players. If they want to rack up their highest scores ever, have them get in really good shape. Their hands will move faster and their eyes will see better.

Greenfield also cites studies that show a reduced usage of drugs among kids who play games. The studies show that kids can't do well when they are "high." My own thought is that they also don't need the escape of drugs since the games can serve a similar purpose without the obvious health, legal, and social tragedies associated with drug use.

Use the Desire for Games as a Motivator. Most kids who play games are never satisfied. They'll master one game, but already be wanting to buy another. But, as I'm sure you know already, games cost money. The kids know that these video cartridges are expensive. Use their desire for more games to motivate them to earn money or at least to do extra chores around the house. However you organize it, you can use the desire for games as a motivating force for better behavior.

Get Involved. Green-eyed monsters or machine gun-toting muscle-bound soldiers are probably not your idea of entertainment, but you can share a lot with your kids if you ask some questions. Try to see beyond the subject matter. Realize that those same monsters and soldiers could be cubes and triangles and the game play would be essentially the same. It's the challenge and the action that attracts the kids. So ask them how they play the games and how they succeed. The kids will think you're cool for being interested, and, who knows, you might even learn something.

THE FUTURE

There is more research to be done, and, like anything else, it is clear that video games can be abused or over-used. At the same time, it seems equally clear that today's games offer special preparation for the future. I hope the suggestions and insights in this chapter will help you be more at ease with what is obviously a new kind of entertainment medium. Since electronic gaming doesn't appear to be just a fad, we may as well get the most out of it, use common sense in dealing with it, and find what positive effects we can.

A lot of work is being done on what is called *virtual reality*. Virtual reality simulators seem to place the participant inside the simulation. Current VR technology has people wearing special helmets in which they move through a fully rendered three-dimensional world created entirely electronically. Using special gloves and treadmills, they seem to be walking through the world and manipulating objects in it.

Although current VR research is at its early stages, the future may bring us very compelling VR simulations ranging from your driver's test to aircraft simulation, from a fully realistic mock surgery lesson to a walk through your prospective home. Future games will be as real as technology can make them, and there's no telling what powerful learning and growing they will let us do.

One of the most encouraging aspects of games is the emergence of truly educational games that contain the same attractions as ordinary games. These games will teach children about financial planning, ecology and conservation, city planning, music, reading, math, logic, and much more. We're only at the beginning of the information age, and many believe that games will be one of the most powerful and positive forces to influence future generations. Some people have even postulated that future wars would simply be played on video screens instead of battlefields. Whatever the far future holds, the near future will certainly produce new ideas and new opportunities.

Mind and Media: The Effects of Television, Video Games, and Computers by Patricia Greenfield *is available from Harvard University Press, 79 Garden Street, Cambridge, MA 02138. Telephone (617) 495-2480 or (617) 495-2577. $14.50 in cloth or $5.95 in paperback.*